Completed 7/23/12

FATAL COLOURS

FATAL COLOURS

Towton 1461—
England's Most Brutal Battle

GEORGE GOODWIN

W. W. NORTON & COMPANY

NEW YORK • LONDON

For information about permission to reproduce selections from this book,
write to Permissions, W. W. Norton & Company, Inc.,
500 Fifth Avenue, New York, NY 10110

For information about special discounts for bulk purchases, please contact
W. W. Norton Special Sales at specialsales@wwnorton.com or 800-233-4830

Manufacturing by Courier Westford
Book design by Akasha Archer
Production manager: Devon Zahn

Library of Congress Cataloging-in-Publication Data

Goodwin, George, 1956–
Fatal colours : Towton 1461 : England's most brutal battle / George Goodwin. — 1st Ameri-
can ed.
p. cm.
"First published in Great Britain in 2011 by Weidenfeld & Nicolson, a division of The Orion
Publishing Group Ltd, London, under the title Fatal colours: the Battle of Towton, 1461"—
T.p. verso.
Includes bibliographical references and index.
ISBN 978-0-393-08084-1 (hardcover)
1. Towton, Battle of, Towton, England, 1461. 2. Great Britain—History—Wars of the Roses,
1455–1485. I. Title. II. Title: Fatal colors. III. Title: Towton 1461.
DA250.G675 2012
942.04'3—dc23
                          2011050958

W. W. Norton & Company, Inc.
500 Fifth Avenue, New York, N.Y. 10110
www.wwnorton.com

W. W. Norton & Company Ltd.
Castle House, 75/76 Wells Street, London W1T 3QT

1 2 3 4 5 6 7 8 9 0

For Frances, Cecily and Arthur

CONTENTS

LIST OF ILLUSTRATIONS

INTRODUCTION

David Starkey

This is a book about a battle. But it is also a book about kingship—or rather, as the King in question was Henry VI, its very present absence.

> To be short the prince is the life, the head and the authority of all things that be done in the realm of England. And to no prince is done more honour and reverence than to the King and Queen of England; no man speaketh to the prince nor serveth at table but in adoration and kneeling; all persons of the realm be bareheaded before him; insomuch as in the chamber of presence where the cloth of estate is set, no man dare walk, yea though the prince be not there, no man dare tarry there but bareheaded.[1]

Sir Thomas Smith wrote these words of his own sovereign, that most kingly of queens, Elizabeth I. But they apply equally to all her predecessors, including that least kingly of kings, Henry VI. His court, contrary to what most historians have supposed, was magnificent. The rituals of his chapel royal were held up for emulation in Portugal. His badge was worn with pride in Italy. And at home, for almost forty years, he was treated with all the solemn, quasi-religious respect and ceremony that Smith describes.[2] Thus it is kneeling and bareheaded that the Lords and Commons appear before their young master in the illuminated foundation charter of King's College, Cambridge, the second of Henry VI's two great works of piety—just as they did in real life.[3]

Now contemporaries were not fools and most of them were as well able to gauge Henry VI's inadequacies as we are. But they were able to discount them because of a difference between their thought patterns and ours.

Nowadays we distinguish between the office (abstract) and the incumbent (person). They thought instead of two different royal persons or kings: there was the actual King (the *rex nunc* or 'King for the time being', as the records of the Exchequer, the principal department of finance, put it with wonderful coolness) and there was the permanent King. The latter never died, as the herald's cry at a royal death made clear: 'the King is dead; long live the King!' And he embodied the essence of kingship. But he was absorbed in whoever was *rex nunc*.

Moreover, this other King was not only eternal, he was also ubiquitous. The actual King, like other human beings, could only be in one place at a time. He was at Westminster. Or Woodstock. Or Windsor. Or even—God forbid—in prison. But his *alter ego* had no such limitations. He could, at one and the same time, be in every law court and every county. His person travelled with his seal and his most potent symbol—as Smith makes clear—was an empty throne.

In short, this King was a royal god. And, like God himself, he was self-created. For these emanations of royal power were the creation of a long line of earlier kings. They went back to the Conquest and beyond. And the best of what they built survived. The French have a word for it: *acquis*. That is, a power which is accumulated and added to and hardly ever diminished. Such was the nature of English government.[4]

Oldest, most important and the foundation of everything else was the unity of England. This was the achievement of the Anglo-Saxon kings of Wessex: Aethelstan, the great Alfred's grandson, who was the first king to rule over all England, and Edgar, whose 'imperial' consecration at Bath some fifty years later in 973 set a precedent of magnificence and liturgical coherence whose effects were still felt six centuries later in the two coronations of Henry VI.

This hard-won unity was built on natural advantages. England was comparatively small; as the larger part of an island it had clear natural frontiers and its stock was relatively homogenous. But royal initiative was more important still. The key was the characteristic unit of local government: the shire (in Anglo-Saxon) or county (in French). These were established first in Wessex and then spread, with the power of Wessex, over the whole country. The shire had a double face: it was both an area of royal administration, headed by a powerful royal official, the *ealdorman*, and a unit of local self-government. But what it was *not* was just as important. The *ealdorman*, who became known as the *earl* under the Danish occupation of Canute, might be the predominant landowner in the shire. But he did not own it outright. This meant that the shires did not become semi-independent territorial principalities, as in France or, still more, in Germany.

There were still important regional differences of course: between North and South and the Celtic west and the rest. These differences emerge very clearly in the composition of the rival armies at Towton: the Lancastrian troops came largely from the North; the Yorkist, from the South and Wales. Moreover, Yorkist propaganda went out of its way to play on the fear of the Northern men as 'the other'. It painted them as violent predators, intent on destroying the peace and prosperity of the South. And it worked. It led, it is argued, to the extraordinary savagery of the battle, in which the defeated and defenceless Northerners were treated as an alien horde and slaughtered in droves. And it left a legacy, in 'the problem of the North', which is still with us today.

But, for all the differences and demonization, North and South did *not* go their own ways. Instead, Towton, too, was a back-handed compliment to the unity of England, in which the parts struggled, not for separation, but for control of the whole kingdom.

The unity, as well as the wealth, of Anglo-Saxon England had made it very appealing to would-be conquerors; it also made it vulnerable to conquest. This is shown most strikingly in the aftermath of William, Duke of Normandy's victory at Hastings. At that point, England was not conquered. But the death of King Harold II in the battle *had* decapitated royal government. Thereafter, without royal leadership, Anglo-Saxon resistance collapsed and delivered England to William with scarcely a fight.

Thanks to the brevity of the struggle, England was also delivered as a going concern. William was determined to keep it that way—and to keep it different from Normandy. His Norman followers were, of course, rewarded with vast estates confiscated from the dispossessed Anglo-Saxon aristocracy. But he made sure that the estates were widely scattered to avoid the sort of regional satrapies which bedevilled French—and Norman—politics.

His sons and successors went much further and in the course of the

twelfth century built a royal administration of unusual reach and ambition. It had two main departments. The Exchequer was the ministry of
finance. Twice a year, the sheriffs, the new royal administrators of each
county, were summoned to Westminster to have their accounts audited at
the Exchequer board or table. The table was covered with the chequered
cloth that gave it its name and turned it into a giant calculating machine.
The machine—and hence the Exchequer itself—was accurate to the last
penny and fractions of a penny, and it was inescapable.

The other principal department was the Chancery or secretariat. This
issued royal instructions known as writs. They were written on slips of
parchment and authenticated by a wax impression of the King's massive,
double-sided seal. One side showed him mounted and armed as warrior-
defender of his people; the other crowned and enthroned as their judge.
And it was royal justice which was the particular concern of the Conquer-
or's great-grandson, Henry II. He created both a machinery of royal justice
and a system of law, known as Common Law, which brought the King's justice to all his subjects, whoever and wherever they were. It was a two-way
traffic. Judges on tour took the King's law to the localities; writs, bearing
the King's image, summoned his subjects to his law courts in Westminster.

Anglo-Saxon England was an usually unified state; the bureaucratic and
legal reforms of the Anglo-Norman kings also turned it into one of the
most densely and effectively administered as well. But kings did not have
it all their own way. Starting with the Conqueror himself at his fateful
coronation on Christmas Day 1066, each king was first acclaimed by the
people in token of their consent to his rule. Next he swore to respect
the laws of Edward the Confessor, the last king of Anglo-Saxon England.
Then, and only then, was he anointed, crowned and invested with the rest
of the regalia.

As this sequence of rituals makes clear, even at the height of Norman
autocracy the kingdom was envisaged as having an existence apart from
the King. For otherwise, who or what was giving consent and to whom
were the royal oaths sworn? Moreover, and paradoxically, the unifying
drive of the Conqueror and his heirs only intensified this feeling of collective identity. The result was that the growth and consolidation of royal

power in the twelfth century was followed by its limitation and control in the thirteenth and fourteenth.

Unsurprisingly, the process began under incompetent and unsuccessful kings, like John and Henry III. But, strikingly, it also continued under some of the greatest rulers of the Middle Ages, like Edward I and Edward III. John contrived to have the worst of both worlds. He was oppressive at home and a failure abroad, losing all the vast Continental lands of his ancestors. By 1215, disenchantment was universal and he was faced with an ultimatum: concede a general charter of liberties, or face deposition. With bad grace and in worse faith he agreed. But he immediately obtained absolution from the Pope on the grounds that the charter had been extorted by force.

Exasperated, the English now invited the French Prince Louis to be their king. Fortunately at this point John died. The guardians of his nine-year-old son, Henry, reissued the charter, though shorn of its most offensive clause which authorized the use of force to compel the King to adhere to its terms. With the charter conceded, support for Louis collapsed and Henry III was acknowledged as King.

There followed decades of political strife as the implications of Magna Carta, as it became known, were worked out. One side was led by Henry's brother-in-law, Simon de Montfort, Earl of Leicester; the other by his eldest son, Edward. De Montfort wanted to reduce the King to a cipher, with executive power transferred to a noble council. Edward, on the other hand, was determined to preserve the reality of royal power which by rights would one day be his. Eventually Edward won and de Montfort was defeated, killed and posthumously dismembered as a traitor.

But Edward's victory came at the price of conceding de Montfort's most daring innovation. Once again, it went back to Magna Carta. The charter's guarantees of the inviolability of property, the impartiality and availability of justice and the rule of law were not only ringing declarations of right; they also transformed the practice of politics. They did so above all by establishing that taxation required consent. But by whom? At first, enlarged sessions of the King's Council were used. The bishops, the greater nobles, who were now dignified by the hereditary title of *earl*, and some other leading landowners were summoned, in addition to the King's regular advisers. The meetings were known by a variety of names, like 'great council'. But the term 'parliament' came into increasingly general use.

De Montfort spotted his opportunity. Hitherto membership of parliament had been *individual*. He broadened it dramatically by summoning *representatives* of two important groups: the wealthy citizens of the greater towns and the middling landowners of the shires. Individually, such men could not compare with the bishops and earls. But collectively they at least matched them in wealth.

De Montfort's actions were self-interested and opportunistic. He aimed to score a propaganda coup and broaden the base of his political support. But a precedent had been set. And it was followed by de Montfort's great opponent when he succeeded as Edward I. Almost all of Edward's parliaments included burgesses and knights of the shires, as the representatives of the towns and counties became known. And their writs of summons defined the nature of representation itself. 'What touches all', the King declared, 'should be approved of all, and it is also clear that common dangers should be met by measures agreed upon in common.' The result was that by the middle of the fourteenth century a recognizably 'modern', bicameral parliament had emerged, with two 'Houses', the Lords (the bishops and the landed nobility) and the Commons (the burgesses and knights of the shire), which were summoned together but met and deliberated separately.

Edward I and his successors were no more altruistic than de Montfort. They accepted parliament, increased and broadened its personnel and developed its powers, not out of principle, but because it was *useful*.

And it was useful, above all, for the warfare that became the principal 'common danger' or business of king and kingdom. Parliament gave its consent to war, voted the taxes to pay for it and agreed the terms of truces and treaties that suspended or ended it.

Except that the war never really seemed to end.

First, Edward I fought the Welsh, won and occupied Wales. Then he fought the Scots and seemed to win there too. But, by the end of his reign, the Scottish campaign had turned to stalemate and, under his son, Edward II, to catastrophic defeat. Edward III, however, redeemed the reputation of English arms with conquests in France that seemed destined to re-create the Continental empire, lost under John, of the Norman and Plantagenet kings. But these conquests too were eroded in the great warrior's dotage and lost entirely in the reign of Richard II, who preferred to do his fighting against his own subjects at home rather than enemies abroad.

The greatest warrior king of all was Henry VI's father, Henry V. By a combination of diplomacy, dazzling generalship and driving single-mindedness he brought France to her knees and, at the Treaty of Troyes, was acknowledged as heir and regent of France. Two years later he was dead, leaving the nine-month-old Henry VI as heir of his vast conquests and still greater reputation.

The road to Towton field had begun.

There is, in short, a pattern. Militarily successful kings die, full of honours if not years, in their beds; military failures do not. Instead, they die very unpleasantly. Edward II was dethroned by his wife and her lover and murdered, the story goes, by having a red-hot poker rammed up his fundament; Richard II was dethroned by his cousin and starved to death at Pontefract Castle; Henry VI was dethroned—twice for good measure—and finally finished off by a heavy blow to the back of the head.

But these are more than 'sad stories of the death of kings'. They also point to a fundamental truth about the nature of later medieval English kingship. England was a war state and could only be ruled successfully by a warrior monarch.

Which brings us to the title of this book. The phrase 'Fatal Colours' is taken from Shakespeare's *Henry VI: Part 3*, act II scene v. The scene deals with the battle of Towton, and it does so in a fashion which shows that Shakespeare fully understood both the scale of the battle and its peculiar, intestine savagery. At the climax of the action, a man drags in a body, and, as he begins to pillage the corpse, he discovers that he has killed his own father; another, also intent on spoiling a body, finds out that he has slaughtered his only son. Henry VI, observing the pair, takes up the father's lament for his slain child:

O! pity, pity, gentle heaven, pity.
The red rose and the white are on his face;
The fatal colours of our striving houses

> *The one his purple blood right well resembles;*
> *The other his pale cheeks, methinks, presenteth:*
> *Wither one rose, and let the other flourish!*
> If you contend, a thousand lives must wither
> (*Henry VI: Part 3*, II.v.96–102)

The actual name, 'Wars of the Roses', goes back only to the early nineteenth century, when it seems to have been coined by the Romantic novelist, Sir Walter Scott, in *Anne of Geierstein* (1829). But the *idea* is much older. The principal root is of course Shakespeare himself. But Shakespeare in turn got it from Edward Hall, whose chronicle history of England from the death of Richard II to his own time has for its full title:

> The union of the two noble and illustr[ious] houses of Lancaster and York, being long in continual dissension for the crown of this noble realm, with all the acts done in both the times of the princes, both of the one lineage and of the other, beginning at the time of King Henry IV, the first author of this division, and so successively proceeding to the reign of the high and prudent prince, King Henry VIII, the undoubted flower and very heir of both the said lineages.

Moreover, as presented in Hall, the idea is as much visual as verbal. The title page of the second edition shows two family trees in the form of climbing roses. One springs from John of Gaunt, Duke of Lancaster; the other from Edmund, Duke of York. And they unite in the marriage of Henry VII of Lancaster with Elizabeth of York and its issue in Henry VIII. Henry appears at the top of the page, crowned and in majesty, with a rose of Lancaster on his right hand and one of York on his left.[5]

Hall's *Chronicle* was first published in 1548. But we can go back further still, to the fifteenth century itself. Or rather, we can half go back. The white rose of York *was* a frequently used emblem, both in peace and war. Under Edward IV of York, who defeated Henry VI at Towton, the white rose appears on banners, coats-of-arms, jewellery, stained glass, coins, seals and paintings. On the other hand, the red rose of Lancaster is conspicuous by its absence. The most thorough search has been made. But, for the sixty-odd-year rule of the house of Lancaster, from 1399 to 1461, not a single convincing contemporary use of the red rose as a royal dynastic emblem has been found.

Instead it appears, out of the blue, at the battle of Bosworth. 'In the year 1485 on the 22nd day of August', the Crowland Chronicler quotes from a contemporary poem, 'the tusks of the boar were blunted and the red rose, the avenger of the white, shines upon us'. The chronicler then explains the verses, 'taking into account the banners and badges of today's victor and vanquished'. The boar was Richard III, Edward IV's younger brother, who was defeated and killed in the battle. The red rose was the victorious Henry Tudor, Earl of Richmond, who claimed the throne as the descendant, through his mother, of the house of Lancaster. While the white rose, avenged by the red, stood for Edward IV's sons, Edward and Richard, who had been usurped and probably murdered by their uncle Richard III.

After his victory, Richmond, who reigned as Henry VII, made the red rose one of his principal badges. But he also, following his marriage with Edward IV's eldest daughter, Elizabeth, combined it with the white rose of York into the Tudor rose, red without and white within, as a powerful symbol of dynastic union.[6]

We are now, I think, in a position to understand not only *when* but *why* the badge of the red rose was invented. For there could be no dynastic union unless there were two royal houses. But by 1485 there was virtually no Lancastrian house or Lancastrian party left. Towton, followed by the even greater dynastic blood-letting of Tewkesbury, had killed off all Lancastrian claimants—apart from Henry Tudor. And twenty-five years of increasingly successful Yorkist rule had reduced the Lancastrian following to the merest handful.

So the invention of the badge of the red rose was a prelude to the larger invention of a continuous Lancastrian party. Such a double invention gave Henry equal dynastic weight with his wife-to-be, Elizabeth of York. It also provided a dignified and satisfying narrative for the previous century of English history. Its usurpations, occasional turmoil and moments of bloody savagery could be acknowledged or even exaggerated since they were about to be resolved by the marriage of Elizabeth of York and Henry of Lancaster.

Indeed, and strikingly, this historical narrative is first sketched in the papal bull confirming Henry VII's marriage and title to the throne. The bull, which is dated 27 March, declares that it was issued spontaneously and without any prompting by the King. Nevertheless its substance must have been drafted in England. Subsequently, because of its propaganda value, the text was also translated (pretty freely) into English and printed and published as a proclamation.

The Pope, it declared, was aware 'of the long and grievous variance, dissensions and debates that hath been in this realm of England between the house of the duchy of Lancaster on the one part and the house of the duchy of York on the other part'. It was the Holy Father's earnest desire and duty, as the promoter of universal peace, to knit up such quarrels. To this end, 'and willing all such divisions therefrom following to be put apart', he 'approveth, confirmeth and establisheth' the marriage between 'King Henry VII of the house of Lancaster of that one party and the noble Princess Elizabeth of the house of York of that other party'.[7]

The translator was John Russell, Bishop of Lincoln. Sir Thomas More thought him 'one of the best learned men undoubtedly that England had in his time'; he was also regarded as one of its best wordsmiths. And, as his very choice of words shows—'dissensions', 'house[s]', 'divisions', his translation is a sort of first draft of Hall. Hall develops, of course, and Shakespeare perfects. But Russell is the beginning of it all.[8]

Despite Shakespeare, therefore, and despite our title, there were no red roses at Towton. And only Edward IV's immediate following would have worn the white rose. But you only invent things because they are important. And badges *were* important; indeed they were the central emblem of the age and take us—as Shakespeare instinctively understood—to the heart of its life and politics.[9]

They do so because they symbolized a relationship: between superior and inferior, master and men. Fifteenth-century society consisted of a multitude of such interlocking hierarchies. Each centred on a landowner—either a nobleman, if he had broad acres, or a gentleman, if his estates were smaller—and his household. The household was made up of the lord's family, together with his servants, who could number scores or even hundreds. The servants were sworn to obey their lord in peace and war and, in token, wore his badge pinned or embroidered onto their clothing and 'livery' (or uniform) in his 'colours'. If the lord were rich and powerful, others, including neighbouring gentlemen and even noblemen together with their own household servants, would also be attracted into his orbit. These satellite lords likewise swore obedience but, in deference to their higher status, they wore their lord's badge on a gold chain round their necks. Finally, the ambitious could extend their reach still further by 'retaining' others with a money 'fee'. At its most developed, the transaction took the form of an indenture or contract. This specified in minute detail for how long, at what price, with how many men and against whom the retainer would serve. Normally, allegiance to the King was specifically 'saved' or excepted. But not always.

Historians call this structure 'bastard feudalism'. As the name alone indicates, it has enjoyed a bad press. In part this is deserved. Like any military machine, bastard feudalism existed to fight. It was developed to supply the troops for Edward III's wars and it was most effectively deployed by Henry V in his victorious campaigns in France. But, under his feeble son, it was another story. In the absence of war abroad, it turned inwards and made its own domestic conflicts. Retainer quarrelled with retainer; their lords were drawn in and small squabbles grew bigger, becoming—without effective royal intervention—first local, then regional and finally national disputes. The nadir was reached in 1461 when the nobility, the royal house, and England herself split into two more or less evenly matched parties. They came together at Towton, in the great and terrible battle which forms the subject of this book.

But Towton was more than a nadir; it was also a turning point. For bastard feudalism was not only about war, whether at home or abroad. It was also a force *in* peacetime, even, improbable though it may seem, a force *for* peace. It provided both the connective tissue that bound the centre to the localities and the muscle which enabled local gentlemen to fulfil their role as royal commissioners in the shires: raising taxes, administering justice and keeping order. It enabled a regional magnate to impose order on his sphere of influence; it might even enable a king to bring peace to the kingdom.

In short, bastard feudalism formed a parallel structure of power. It had the potential to remedy the defects of the English constitution and make England—which it had scarcely ever been before—governable in peace.

As usual, everything turned upon the King and how he chose to manage bastard feudalism. The great warrior kings, Edward III and Henry V, had done so *presidentially*, by uniting the lords and their followings in the common enterprise of war against France. But it was also possible for the King to deploy bastard feudalism *competitively*, by building up a royal 'affinity' or following of his own and making himself the biggest bastard feudal lord of all. This had already been tried by Richard II in the late fourteenth century. His band of Cheshire archers, all sporting his badge of the White Hart, had been the largest and most feared in the country. It had even been used to intimidate a meeting of parliament itself. But it could not protect him in the crisis of 1399 when the political elite deserted him en masse in favour of his more popular, shrewder rival, Henry IV.

Contemporaries considered the problem too, most notably Sir John Fortescue, the Lord Chief Justice and Lancastrian loyalist. Present at Towton, Fortescue fled the field; became a leading member of the Lancastrian government in exile and only surrendered to Edward IV after the final, irretrievable defeat of the Lancastrian cause at Tewkesbury. Fortescue, in short, had lived the failure of English government in his own career and in his last work, *The Governance of England*, he proposed the remedy. The existing parliamentary constitution, which, as a common lawyer, he valued profoundly, should remain. But it should be supplemented by the parallel structures of bastard feudalism. The crown lands should be increased and the revenues used to build up the King's affinity. The result would be a restoration of political stability and a 'refoundation of the crown'.

Circumstances did not allow Edward IV sufficient time to follow Fortescue's advice in full. But Henry VII was luckier. His leading councillor, John Morton, came from the same stable as Fortescue. He too had been present at Towton and was Fortescue's colleague in the Lancastrian government in exile, as Lord Privy Seal to Fortescue's Lord Chancellor. The result was the remarkable strategic thrust of Henry VII's government: the new royal badge of the red rose was invented; the royal affinity nurtured and developed and the crown lands extended beyond the dreams of avarice. The measures succeeded almost too well and, by the end of Henry VII's reign, the new structures were on the point of taking over from the old and making even parliament itself redundant.[10]

And it all began at Towton and its aftermath.

Fatal Colours is, therefore, more than a book about one battle, vivid, humane and superbly researched though it is. It is an account of a moment of profound crisis in English politics and a dreadful warning that the political process can fail—and of what happens when it does.

David Starkey

DRAMATIS PERSONAE: ENGLAND, 1422–1450

Henry V: victor of Agincourt. He reigned for only nine years, 1413–22, but is arguably England's greatest king.

Henry VI: Henry V's baby son and successor.

John, Duke of Bedford: Henry V's elder surviving brother, Regent of France in 1422. A highly capable commander. He dies in 1435.

Humphrey, Duke of Gloucester: Henry V's younger surviving brother, would-be Regent of England, who has the lesser title of Protector. His conflicts with the King's Council and, in particular, his attempts to destroy its pre-eminent member, his uncle, Cardinal Beaufort, poison the King's minority.

Henry Beaufort, Bishop of Winchester and then Cardinal: servant successively to Henry IV and Henry V, being ultimately trusted by neither. Beaufort is a brilliant administrator, banker and fundraiser for Henry V's wars. He is completely unscrupulous on behalf of himself and his Beaufort relations.

Charles VI, King of France: Henry VI's maternal grandfather, a sufferer from schizophrenia who dies in late 1422, making Henry VI the King of France.

Catherine de Valois, Queen of England: Henry VI's mother.

The Dauphin, later King Charles VII of France: Charles VI's legitimate heir, whom he disinherited in favour of his son-in-law, Henry V.

Joan of Arc: a teenage shepherdess and prophetess and the heroine of the siege of Orleans.

Richard Beauchamp, 13th Earl of Warwick: faithful servant to the House of Lancaster, tutor to the child King Henry VI.

William de la Pole, Earl, then Marquess, then Duke of Suffolk: from his position as Steward of the King's household, Suffolk progressively gains prominence and then dominance over the king's administration, from the onset of Henry VI's majority in 1437.

James Fiennes, Baron Saye and Sele; Adam Moleyns, Bishop of Chichester; William Ayscough, Bishop of Salisbury: members of Suffolk's governing clique, all killed by mobs in 1450.

Jack Cade: the leader of the uprising against London in 1450.

Edmund Beaufort, Duke of Somerset: the last Lieutenant-General of Normandy, before its loss in 1450. A nephew of Cardinal Beaufort and a close relation to Henry VI. After the death of Suffolk in 1450, he and Richard, Duke of York are the country's principal political figures.

Richard, Duke of York: following the death of Gloucester in 1447, the most senior royal Duke. York seeks to bring Somerset to account for what he regards as the latter's cowardly, negligent and dishonourable loss of Normandy.

DRAMATIS PERSONAE: ENGLAND, SPRING 1460

Henry VI: England's youngest ever king. At the age of seven, the youngest crowned King of England; and, aged only ten, crowned King of France in Notre Dame. His anointing at his coronations was a sign that his kingship was chosen by God and that he ruled with divine authority, making him king for all his natural life. But now, nearly thirty years later, with England's continental European empire lost for ever, he is mad, incapacitated and soon to disinherit his only child.

Margaret of Anjou: Henry's French consort, a warrior queen in defence of her son.

Richard, Duke of York: with a claim to the throne arguably stronger than the King's, but now in exile and nursing a deep sense of grievance. He is, by turns, distant and irresolute and then messianic and rash.

Richard Neville, Earl of Salisbury: for decades, the ultimate Lancastrian insider. Salisbury's father had been richly rewarded by Henry IV, had married Joan Beaufort, the King's half-sister and produced an enormous brood of children. Salisbury was to be, at one time or another, the brother-in-law or father-in-law of four dukes, one viscount and four earls. But in the 1450s there was a breach amongst the Beauforts and in 1460, as before, Salisbury stands behind his son and namesake.

Richard Neville, 16th Earl of Warwick 'The Kingmaker': Salisbury's eldest son. The son-in-law of Richard Beauchamp, 13th Earl of Warwick, and his eventual successor. It was this Richard Neville's vicious competition for the vast Beauchamp inheritance against Edmund Beaufort, Duke of Somerset, that had caused the Neville–Beaufort breach. Warwick is now York's staunchest ally and, like York, is exiled from his vast estates. He is poised to invade from Calais—the last redoubt of the Anglo-Norman Empire in Europe—which he has made his own fiefdom through piracy and propaganda.

William Neville, Lord Fauconberg: Salisbury's younger brother. Physically undistinguished and—a sign of Neville ambitions—married to a woman who had been insane from childhood so he could inherit wealth and title. He is an experienced and brilliant commander.

Humphrey, Duke of Buckingham: choleric commander of the Lancastrian armies. His Duchess, Anne, is the sister of York's Duchess Cecily and of the elder Richard Neville. Buckingham is now maintaining Duchess Cecily under effective house arrest and, in the words of *Gregory's Chronicle*, 'with many a great rebuke'.

Henry Holland, Duke of Exeter: the closest male relative to Henry VI, but through the female line, and thus not his expected heir. Violent, reckless and short of means, he is York's son-in-law and hates both York and his Neville allies.

Henry Beaufort, Duke of Somerset; John, Baron Clifford; Henry, Earl of Northumberland: the heirs to men cut down in battle five years before, on Yorkist orders and against all accepted codes of chivalry. These Lords are closely allied to the Queen. They seek revenge.

Andrew Trollope: Somerset's talented military adviser. A seasoned professional soldier and former second-in-command to Warwick at Calais. His eve of battle 'betrayal' of the Yorkists in 1459 led to their humiliation and to a desperate escape abroad.

Edward, Earl of March: eldest son of the Duke of York. As yet unproven in battle, this eighteen-year-old giant of a youth is with Warwick, his cousin, in Calais.

The Papal Legate—Francesco Coppini, Bishop of Terni: joins Warwick in Calais, Coppini is an unexpected but crucial ally of the Yorkists. But are he and England itself just minor pawns in the chess game of European politics? Are they being 'played' by Pius II, that most wily and most ruthless of Popes?

'O that my death would stay these ruthful deeds!
O pity, pity, gentle heaven, pity!
The red rose and the white are on his face,
The fatal colours of our striving houses:
The one his purple blood right well resembles;
The other his pale cheeks'.*

Henry VI—Part Three, *act ii, scene v by William Shakespeare*
Speech by King Henry VI to one of the dead at Towton

---

* This book owes its title to the world's greatest writer, but *not* its contents. Henry VI's Lancastrian army fought for him at Towton; Henry himself awaited the battle's outcome some miles away, inside the city of York.

FATAL COLOURS

PROLOGUE

On Palm Sunday 1461, in atrocious weather—howling wind, driving sleet and snow—the armies of two disputing Kings of England contested the fate of the crown. The fighting continued all day on a plateau of land a dozen or so miles south-west of the great medieval city of York, in the North of England. Chroniclers then and historians now dispute the numbers involved in the Battle of Towton, but it is most likely that up to seventy-five thousand fought and as many as twenty-eight thousand died in the battle itself[1] and in the rout and massacres that followed.

Towton was an event of the greatest importance for England. It was the bloody culmination of a campaign of seven military engagements over the preceding eighteen months and the final and decisive battle in the first of a series of English civil wars, collectively known as the Wars of the Roses, that took place between 1455 and 1487.[2] When the wars began, England was a medieval country, but after their conclusion, the victorious Tudor dynasty would make England a distinctly different nation-state.

The two rival Kings were Henry VI of the House of Lancaster and Edward IV of the House of York, and on that day the future of their dynasties would be decided. The magnitude of the battle was reflected by the proportion of the population involved: Professor Charles Ross, one of the most eminent historians of the period, estimated that of all Englishmen and Welshmen eligible to fight (those aged between sixteen and sixty) one-tenth were present on the battlefield.[3]

Towton may not have been an isolated event, but it was certainly unique. As well as its claims to be the biggest, longest and bloodiest battle on English soil, it was probably the most brutal. Such had been the length and exceptional uncertainty of the First War of the Roses that the size of the two forces had increased exponentially. So had their viciousness, which by the time of Towton had moved beyond victorious nobles taking swift revenge on defeated rivals and expanded to encompass retribution amongst the common soldiery. By Towton, the two armies had become regional in nature: the Lancastrians being stronger in the North, whilst the Yorkists had found it easier to recruit in the South, the West and Wales. They had one thing in common: the soldiers now demonised their opponents as alien, different, even sub-human. A struggle of factions had become a race war overlaying a civil war. Thus when one side, finally and after many hours of fighting, broke in flight and found itself trapped on the battlefield, there was little chance of escape and none of surrender. That, taken with the killing power of the medieval longbow at the onset of the battle, helps to explain such extraordinary casualty figures; it also explains the resonant names of places on the battlefield today—names such as Bloody Meadow and the Bridge of Bodies.

Singular in its excess, Towton was also singular in its import. The strength of the challenge to Henry VI by a minority of the peerage against the wishes of the majority was to undermine the model of late-medieval English monarchy itself. And it came just four decades after the untimely early death of Henry V, the Regent and de facto ruler of France as well as England's greatest medieval king.

At Agincourt in 1415, Henry V had won an extraordinary victory over the French in the face of seemingly overwhelming odds. It was at least on a par with the triumph of his great-grandfather, Edward III, at Crécy in 1346. Henry had revived Edward III's claim to the throne of France, but he also breathed fresh life into the model of governing that Edward had initiated. Edward III had taken power as a seventeen-year-old by mounting a coup against his own mother and the lover with whom she had dethroned the new king's father, Edward II. The younger Edward then created an approach to ruling that would later be held up as the apogee of medieval kingship. This may have grown organically, in reaction to circumstances and opportunities, but it had a strong coherent element at its core, which was that of a warrior nobility supporting Edward as its leader. It was reinforced by new and complex codes of chivalry, including the creation of the new Order of the Garter and the flowering of heraldry; it rekindled the mythical power of Arthurian legend; and it promoted Saint George as England's own heroic national saint. All these bound the nobility together to pursue Edward's aims of healing the wounds from his father's reign and defending England's interests in France.

When Edward died in 1377, after fifty years on the throne, the difficulties of the latter part of his reign, the years of his senility and of a stagnating and financially crippling campaign in France, were almost immediately forgotten and the earlier period cited as a golden age.[4] Thus when his successor, Richard II, gambled on crushing the established nobility, it was he who was seen as the destabilising force. Like Edward II before him, Richard was considered to have broken his coronation oath and was deposed.[5]

Henry IV, the man who replaced Richard, was unable to re-establish the bond between king and nobility: that was the achievement of Henry's son, Henry V. For the latter, like the young Edward III, was an exemplary king. A successful administrator and lawgiver, a man of great political dexterity mixed with firmness, Henry V harnessed a bellicose nobility to his will and might have ended the vast expense of the Hundred Years War with France by winning it. Only a strong but unifying king could properly utilise the military and financial potential of late-medieval England: Henry V was such a king and one able to exploit a crisis of factionalism and political incoherence afflicting England's French enemy.

But Henry died prematurely, leaving the question of what might happen without a strong king at a time of a future crisis, particularly if the lines between royalty and nobility had become blurred, as was the case with the descendants of Edward III's five surviving sons. For Edward III and his third son, John of Gaunt, father of Henry IV and thus of the Lancastrian dynasty, were the forbears of a new kind of elevated nobility. It was one that contained, for the first time, a number of royal dukes. That Gaunt was the third son is important: for with the death of Richard II, only son of Edward III's eldest son and previous heir, Edward the Black Prince, the senior line died. There was no claim at that time from the heirs of the second son, because that son had only a daughter, and direct line of male succession was in this instance taken as the norm. There were certainly other possibilities—after all, Edward III's claim to the throne of France was through his mother—but Henry V's success was sufficient to gain complete acceptance of the House of Lancaster's royal succession.

The Lancastrian settlement continued unquestioned in spite of the exceptional circumstances of Henry VI's long minority and the first dozen years of his personally inactive majority. Even the cataclysm of 1450—with the disastrous loss of France and popular revolt in South-East England causing the sack of London—was to bring no challenge to Henry's right to reign. The events of that year did, however, have a fundamental consequence, for the collective cohesion of the English nobility was smashed and so began an increasingly bitter division as Henry's leading subjects struggled to compensate for his inability to rule. Now in the new position of having neither a strong king nor a united nobility, England was set upon the course that led to the murderous First War of the Roses, with its highpoint of atrocity at Towton.

The bloody carnage of Towton showed that the system was broken, though the lesson was slow to be learned, as the Second War of the Roses between 1469 and 1471 and the Third between 1483 and 1487 were to demonstrate. The consequences of Towton were nonetheless deadly for the monarchy: between Towton and Henry Tudor's decisive victory at Bosworth in 1485, four successive English kings were dethroned, with three suffering violent deaths.

The smaller engagement of Bosworth may have ushered in a new dynasty, as Henry Tudor became Henry VII, but it was the cataclysm of Towton that was the game changer. The great Tudor monarchs learned the lesson neglected by their Plantagenet predecessors and thus survived: Henry VII through luck and guile; Henry VIII in his last years through tyranny and bile; and, not least, Elizabeth I through her extraordinary political dexterity. They adopted a more imperial style of monarchy,[6] but though they continued to make great claims for their personal inviolacy as rulers, they knew that the surer way to secure survival was not by expecting their nobility to respect 'God's anointed', but rather through their own personal control of raw, naked power.

One

A STEP TOO FAR

ST ALBANS
22 May 1455

They also serve who only stand and wait'.[1] Three thousand profession-ally trained men-at-arms and archers, with weapons ready and wearing the badges and livery of their masters, stood patiently in Key Field, a green space immediately to the east of the wealthy town of Saint Albans.[2] It was wealth that stemmed from its position on the main road north from Lon-don to the Midlands, sporadically the centre of royal government, which then went further to the distant lands of Yorkshire and even further to the border with the alien kingdom of Scotland.

These men had arrived three hours earlier, at 7 a.m. They had been brought together on this May day in 1455 to settle a matter of honour aris-ing from the loss of the ancient possession of Normandy, the source of Eng-land's own conquest four centuries before. The reason for their patience was that heralds had been dispatched to the King for a third time that morning, with a series of demands. These demands were couched in terms of the politest of requests, supplications even, to a 'most Christian King, a right high and mighty Prince' and to a 'most redoubted sovereign Lord'.[3] They were from 'true and humble liegemen'.[4] But they were demands all the same. The petitioners' stated purpose was to be admitted to the presence of King Henry VI to refute 'the sinister, malicious and fraudulent works and reports of our known enemies'. The spurning of these requests caused the 'liegemen' to conclude that the 'known enemies' were preventing even their heralds from seeing the King.

It was the only possible conclusion so far as the petitioners were concerned. As the troops stood easy over successive hours, the formal responses being returned in the name of the King could not have been clearer: 'I wish to know what traitor dares be so bold as to rise up in my own land' and 'I shall destroy them, every one of them, to hang them, draw them and quarter them, to make an example to all such traitors'.[5]

The leader of the petitioners, Richard, Duke of York, the foremost member of the nobility, a man of mature years and inflexible self-certainty and someone who had himself recently governed on behalf of King Henry, knew that these were not the personal words of the King. So did his illustrious allies: his brother-in-law Richard Neville, Earl of Salisbury, and Salisbury's son, another Richard Neville, who was Earl of Warwick in his own right. Not the words of the King but those of the 'known enemies'; and in particular those of York's and now Warwick's bitter rival Edmund, Duke of Somerset, and of the Neville family's traditional antagonists, the Earl of Northumberland and Lord Clifford.

There was an intermediary on the scene: another York brother-in-law, the irascible Humphrey, Duke of Buckingham, fanatically loyal to his unworldly King. It was he that was trying to mediate between the two parties, though, it has to be said, from his position beside the King in the town's market place, with his troops assembling alongside Somerset's and their allies. All were ready to fight together under the Royal Standard in the name of Henry VI of the House of Lancaster.

What happened next took Buckingham by surprise. With the 'parlaying' between the two sides having extended throughout the morning and set to continue, there seemed no reason for a sudden change of mood. The Yorkists thought differently. At 10 a.m., seeking 'to redresse the myscheff that now regneth', they moved forward.[6]

The nature of their physical position itself played a role. To launch an attack on the Royal Standard, raised in the King's presence, would indeed have been treason. From where they stood, however, they could not see it. With the justification that the King was not a free agent and that they sought merely to remove his 'Evil Counsellors', they told their archers to prepare.

The Royal Standard may have been out of sight, but so were the targets for the Yorkist arrows. Yet these were bowmen required by law to hone their technique through practice every Sunday and feast day; and to do so from childhood, through adulthood and into what was then most definitely considered as old age. These were extraordinarily skilled practitioners of war, whose rate of shot and accuracy was still to be envied 350 years later.[7] Now they assessed the wind, distance and the altitude required to take their arrows over walls, over houses, into the market place beyond and on to the unsuspecting and thus unprepared Lancastrians.

After the initial order to shoot, successive volleys involving thousands of arrows arced into the spring sky. These projectiles of around a yard in length and travelling at speeds approaching one hundred miles per hour,[8] reached the zenith of their flight in little more than a second. Then they began their descent, to arrive at maximum velocity and deliver their sharp steel arrow tips mounted on a projectile weighing a quarter of a pound. This swarm of wood and iron and steel created mayhem as it struck cobble, stone and armour; and sliced through flesh and bone. It was probably during the initial arrow storm that four of the King's bodyguard were killed. Buckingham was wounded in the face. The King himself, inadequately protected, was grazed in the neck and forced into the malodorous safety of a tanner's house.

As the salvoes continued, the Yorkist men-at-arms were poised to attack across the town ditch. The ditch was not problematic—generations of householders and innkeepers had filled it with their rubbish and in places it was a mere step rather than a trench.[9] Nor were town walls, thought unnecessary in a country with no expectation of siege and civil war.

Then a problem arose. Salisbury's and York's troops came up against well-constructed barricades at the ends of two principal thoroughfares which led to either end of the market place and the Lancastrian command. Frustratingly for the brothers-in-law, the troops met with stubborn resistance and the Yorkist attackers, forced in the constricted space to deploy with just a few abreast, began to be picked off by the Lancastrian archers.

Salisbury's son, the twenty-six-year-old Earl of Warwick, had been given command of the Yorkist centre. He faced similar barricades in his quest to break through to the market place. It was now that he made his military reputation. He did not try to attack these obstacles but went round them, straight through the houses and then into the gardens and orchards— known as 'the backsides'—beyond. This move, so sudden, swift and

unexpected, took him to the unprotected houses overlooking the Lancastrian positions almost before the defenders realized what was happening.
Whether Warwick's archers deployed the normal flesh-slicing broadhead
or the armour-piercing bodkin arrows, their longbows, supplemented by the
more manoeuvrable crossbows, were lethal when shot at near point-blank
range from the upper-storey windows of the houses and from the alleyways
to their sides.

It was at this point, if not before, that the Royal Standard bearer was
guilty of the heinous crime of deserting his post and leaving the Standard
propped against a wall. William Gregory, Mayor of London in 1451 and the
author of *Gregory's Chronicle*,[10] pinpoints James Butler, Earl of Wiltshire &
Ormond and the Lord Treasurer of England, as the culprit, adding that
Wiltshire 'fought mainly with his heels, for he was called the most hand-
some knight in the land and was afraid of losing his beauty'.[11] Wiltshire was
to prove a serial offender when it came to fleeing from battlefields, but the
safety of 'the flying earl' came at the vast expense of his having repeatedly
to replace his hastily discarded armour.[12] On this occasion he swapped it
for a monk's habit, purloined from the abbey, and slipped away in disguise.[13]

The clamour of Warwick's breakthrough to the centre caused the Lancastrian troops at the barricades to fall back. With the market place a
heaving mass of stabbing and chopping men, the Yorkists surged forward
and forced many of their opponents to retreat into the nearby houses.

Thus far, the entire action had taken under an hour and, fierce though
it was, had probably accounted for not many more than a hundred dead.[14]
Now the most momentous event of the battle took place. Whether it was
York or Warwick who gave the order is not known, but Warwick's future
record and position to the fore would indicate that it was him. Either way,
the Lancastrian leaders—the Duke of Somerset, the Earl of Northumberland and Lord Clifford—were, against any deference to the laws of chivalry, hunted down, cornered and killed. Somerset, realizing his fate, took
four of his reward-seeking attackers with him, before the remainder were
on him like dogs and he was finally dispatched with an axe.[15]

The King was taken into safekeeping in the abbey by the now dutiful
Duke of York, as was Buckingham. So great was York's hatred of the slain
lords that no one dared move their corpses. It was only when John Whethamstede, the Abbot of Saint Albans, demanded that proper provision be

made for the bodies that action was taken. It was Whethamstede, perhaps with an eye on future rewards from chantry chapels, who arranged that the lords should be buried in the abbey, their battered bodies to join the remains of his friend and fellow intellectual Humphrey, Duke of Gloucester, the famous younger brother of a far more famous man: England's greatest king, Henry V.

Thus, York hoped, would end a vicious five-year rivalry for pre-eminence between himself and Somerset which had its beginning in a dispute over honour, entwined with the permanent collapse of England's empire in France; a rivalry that had flared unimpeded when they each tried to fill the vacuum of authority left by a mentally enfeebled monarch.

In the event, Saint Albans served only to widen and deepen hostilities. There were two hugely important legacies of the battle. Hitherto, Henry's French queen, Margaret of Anjou, had largely been the very model of a traditional English queen consort—a dutiful, supplicatory force. Though Somerset had received a pension from her, this had not made Margaret the irretrievable and natural foe of York. Indeed, letters show Margaret to have been previously on good terms with York and with Cecily, his duchess, both up to and after the birth of her one and only son, Edward, Prince of Wales, in 1453.[16] But Saint Albans altered everything. With the forceful Somerset gone, Margaret stepped to the fore to protect her son's interests. This was not so much a change as a transformation, with Margaret becoming as aggressive as she had previously been mollifying. In York's eyes, she had stepped away from her true role, making her an aberrant opponent, as well as a fearsome one.

The second legacy resulted directly from the murder of the three Lancastrian leaders. Each of them had an heir. Henry Beaufort, the new Duke of Somerset, aged just nineteen at the time of the battle, and himself badly wounded, was placed in the ungentle custodial care and guardianship of Warwick. Revenge became the one aim of the three heirs and a vicious element of vendetta was introduced into the overall context of the quarrel.

The two legacies merged as the descendants of the butchered lords in time became the most loyal adherents of the warrior queen. It was not surprising that, as the vendetta spiralled during the course of successive battles between 1459 and 1461, all opportunity for compromise ebbed away. Less than six years later at Towton, it was the sons bereaved at Saint Albans, together with York's hated and hateful son-in-law, the Duke of Exeter, who commanded the Lancastrian forces.

In terms of numbers killed, the 1st Battle of Saint Albans was 'a short scuffle in a street',[17] 'an affray in the market place'.[18] But in its savagery towards a few it was highly significant. It proved an initiation into a new kind of warfare, one stripped of the chivalric concept which had prevailed amongst the knightly class and which, on the battlefield of Towton, would culminate in two tragically well-matched armies engaging in a day of unmatched bloodshed and brutality of Englishmen against Englishmen.

Two

A GREAT MAN'S LEGACY— MINORITY

On 28 September 1422, Thomas Langley, Bishop of Durham and Lord Chancellor of England, came into the presence of his new king. Witnessed by the assembled lords temporal and spiritual, the great nobles and clergy of the realm, he delivered the Great Seal of England into the hands of the new monarch. It was then taken from the royal palms and passed to its temporary keeper. This ceremony was ages-old; the same ritual was followed whenever a king died and his successor was recognized. What was unusual, in fact unique, about this occasion was the age of the monarch undertaking this ceremonial duty. The new King of England—and heir to the Kingdom of France—was a baby of just nine months old, and his country's youngest ever sovereign.

The infant, King Henry VI, was the third king in succession to bear that Christian name. His grandfather Henry of Bolingbroke, who seized the throne in 1399, had been crowned as Henry IV. Though he fought off successive challenges in order to retain the title, that initial act of usurpation had come at a terrible cost. In just a few years Henry IV had shrunk from a redoubtable military leader to a husk of a man, suffering either from leprosy or from an acute nervous psoriasis aggravated by his fear of eternal damnation. After all, he had first usurped an anointed king in Richard II, and then had him slowly and very secretly starved to death.

When Henry IV died in 1413, he was succeeded by an heir in his mid-twenties who was well qualified to wear the crown through previous experience both of war and of the exercise of power. One who, even as a teenage prince, had fought in battle and then won a campaign against the Welsh. Henry V came to the throne impatient to rule and wasted no time in still-ing the unquiet spirits of 1399 by having Richard II's body reburied in great style in the magnificent tomb in Westminster Abbey that Richard him-self had commissioned. (Henry IV, meanwhile, had chosen to be buried in Canterbury Cathedral close to Thomas Becket, England's premier medieval saint and worker of miracles.)

Any doubts about his right to rule were settled when Edmund Mortimer, Earl of March—the very man who, by descent through the female line (*see family tree pp. 190–91*) had the best hereditary claim to the throne—alerted Henry to a conspiracy to kill him and make March king. The plotters, including Richard, Earl of Cambridge (also close in the line of succession), were all found guilty and executed at Southampton in early August 1415. Within the week, Henry sailed to France with his invading army.

In order to secure the future of the new Lancastrian dynasty, Henry V sought to unite the quarrelling English nobility through preparation for battle and the promise of conquest and glory abroad. The Hundred Years War, begun by his great-grandfather Edward III in 1337, had settled into a truce under both Richard II and Henry's own father. Henry V soon set about rekindling the conflict with a vengeance.

At Agincourt on 25 October 1415, through his deployment of archers using the devastating longbow, he won a victory as great as that of Edward III at Crécy, and of the Black Prince at Poitiers over half a century before. But Henry was more than the tactical creator of victory; fighting bravely on the battlefield and saving the life of his youngest brother Humphrey of Gloucester, he was the epitome of the warrior king.[1]

In August 1417 Henry reinvaded France with a far larger military expe-dition, financed by a substantial parliamentary grant and loans, all orga-nized with exemplary flair and efficiency by his father's half-brother Henry Beaufort, Bishop of the rich see of Winchester.[2]

Over the next eighteen months, Henry successively and successfully besieged the great fortified towns of Normandy. Caen fell in September. By the following spring, Alençon, Falaise and Domfront had all been taken by forces under Henry's own command or that of his able lieutenant Richard Beauchamp, Earl of Warwick.[3] In September 1418, Cherbourg was captured by Humphrey of Gloucester after a five-month siege. Rouen, Normandy's capital and greatest prize, fell in January 1419, after holding out for five and a half months; this became Henry's administrative capital. In July, the strategic town of Pontoise was taken in a daring dawn raid and, from here, he was able to threaten Paris.[4]

Having succeeded militarily, Henry was to triumph diplomatically. Taking advantage of the weakness of the French King and a vendetta within the royal family, he advanced his own claim to the French throne. The long reign of Charles VI of France had been plagued by the King's prolonged bouts of insanity and a struggle for power amongst his kinsmen. On 10 September 1419 events took a fateful turn when Charles's cousin, John the Fearless, Duke of Burgundy, was assassinated in revenge for the murder of Charles's brother twelve years before. A hundred years later, a prior showing Duke John's traumatized skull to King Francis I had good reason to remark: 'It was through this hole that the English entered France'.[5] As a result of the murder, Burgundy formed an alliance with Henry that was to prove crucial for England's domination. Even more importantly, it led to the disinheriting of the assassination's prime instigator, the Dauphin: Charles's son and heir, another Charles, was obligingly declared a bastard by his own mother, Isabeau of Bavaria, Charles VI's long estranged and libidinous Queen.

Henry capitalized on this opportunity through months of patient negotiation backed by military force. On 21 May 1420, with the signing of the treaty of Troyes, he was formally recognized as heir to the Kingdom of France, while his rival the Dauphin was forced to set up a rival court at Poitiers, well south of the Loire.[6] The following month Henry married Charles's daughter Catherine. The newly-weds spent Christmas in Paris, the new centre of Henry's domain. In June 1421, after a brief return to England, he was back in France leaving behind a queen who was by this time pregnant.

Then, while besieging the great Loire fortress of Meaux over the winter and spring of 1421–22, Henry contracted dysentery—always a great threat to an encamped medieval force. The fortress fell in May, giving Henry control over the approaches to Paris, but at a terrible cost. Over the succeeding weeks and months, Henry became progressively weaker. Fearing the worst, he sought to put in place measures to consolidate all that he had gained for England and himself. On 31 August 1422, at the Château de Vincennes outside Paris, he died.

Had illness and death not intervened, he would have been King of France within just two months. One can speculate on what Henry might have achieved, had he enjoyed the fifty-three-year average life expectancy of his thirteen predecessors as King of England and his kingship had thus lasted three times as long.[7] He was already accepted as an effective ruler north of the Loire and if he had been crowned and anointed with the Oil of Clovis at Reims, the traditional place of enthronement of French kings, he could have established Lancastrian rule over the whole of France, just as he had made permanent the Lancastrian rule over England.

In a reign of only nine years, this greatest of rulers had demonstrated what an active king of England could accomplish. As well as being successful in war abroad, Henry had shown himself able to orchestrate the institutions of government for the proper administration of his kingdom and the taxation of his subjects. Scholarly, just and deeply religious—remembered after his death as Henry the Pious—he was perceived as his country's ultimate temporal authority and, in firm opposition to the challenges mounted by the Pope, its spiritual guide as well.[8]

Not all, of course, was brilliant sunlight; there were some shadows cast over Henry's achievement. The costs of his wars had been onerous. The ruthless execution of French prisoners on his orders at Agincourt, thought so necessary at the time to secure victory though against any concept of chivalry, was to reverberate bloodily on English soil forty years on, and even perhaps to blight Anglo-French relations to this day. And a final, perhaps ill-considered codicil to his will was to bring his chief counsellors—those expected to give good advice or 'counsel', rather than the more formal councillors of state—into immediate conflict upon his death. That said, it was a monumental inheritance to bequeath to his small, uncomprehending successor.

Henry V's reign had shown what might be achieved by a vigorous, ambitious, adult English monarch. But what if the king was a child? Or, uniquely, what if that child was a baby and there was to be a long period of interim government?

Certainly there were known, if not necessarily happy, precedents for the reign of a minor. This, however, was an entirely novel situation. On 21 October, Charles VI, the baby's maternal grandfather, died. Henry VI, still some way short of his first birthday, was now King of France as well as England. And the wishes of his father as to how the two countries were to be maintained for his infant heir were considered, by some at least, to be unclear.

Henry V had made some provisions before he died. A reassignment of responsibilities had been necessary anyway, following the death in a skirmish, the previous year, of his nearest brother and then heir, Thomas, Duke of Clarence. Henry declared verbally that John, Duke of Bedford, the eldest of his surviving brothers, should be Regent of France; and in a codicil to his will, made just five days before his death, that the younger brother, Humphrey of Gloucester, should be the infant Henry VI's 'custodian and protector', based in England. As John had previously been more involved in England while Humphrey served as a warrior in France, this was a change of roles.[9] Their previous incarnations gave them the interests and experience to challenge each other should they be unhappy with the new state of affairs. And neither brother was at all happy. Nor were their powerful, overtly ambitious uncles: the military commander Thomas Beaufort, Duke of Exeter, awarded governorship of the person of the young King by the codicil; and his brother Henry Beaufort, Bishop of Winchester, a councillor and former chancellor. All four men had in common the fact that they were, by birth and by inclination, entrenched supporters of the Lancastrian dynasty; but all four were strong personalities with a great sense of self-worth and entitlement. Each man individually felt he should have been given more personal power. In France such division around a king who could not rule had led to the internal power vacuum that had enabled Henry V to step in and occupy so much of the country.

There was to be no such situation in England, or at least not at first. In Henry VI's infancy the loyalty to the throne forged by the campaigns that Henry V had fought, both as prince and king, and the strengths of his great institutions of Church, Parliament and, above all, the King's Council, prevailed. The Council was to provide, in the 1420s and beyond, a cockpit for the hostilities between Henry Beaufort and his nephew Humphrey, Duke of Gloucester, but it also remained an arbiter recognized by all parties. Thus, some months after Henry V's death, a temporary accommodation, if in no way an understanding, was reached between the competing powers.

And the war in France went from strength to strength. Bedford was a highly capable and successful lieutenant governor there; his remarkable victory at Verneuil in 1424 fully secured Normandy and the approaches to Paris. By 1429 the land controlled by England and its allies had been extended to include all territory to the north and east of the River Loire. England was in control of the Île de France (including Paris), of Normandy, Maine and part of Anjou, as well as of Gascony and the great trading port of Calais.[10] The areas of France controlled were greater than those held by William the Conqueror. Henry II, through his marriage to Eleanor of Aquitaine, may have held more territory, but England now had, in the name of his descendant Henry VI, its greatest ever domination and control of France.

Bedford was, however, periodically needed at home. The ill health of Exeter, who had been appointed to the governorship of the infant King, meant that, in England, the first years of Henry VI's reign were dominated by the feud between Humphrey of Gloucester and Bishop Beaufort. Gloucester, like all his brothers, was a learned and cultivated man—the gift of his manuscript collection was to provide the basis for the foundation of Oxford University's world-famous Bodleian library—while his uncle Bishop Beaufort was a supreme politician and administrator, and thus of vital and continuing importance when it came to arranging money and supplies for the French Wars. But the men had counter-balancing weaknesses. Gloucester was temperamental and vainglorious—his issuing of a challenge to Philip, Duke of Burgundy, to settle a territorial dispute by personal combat, which was accepted, had threatened to bring about the collapse of the Anglo-Burgundian alliance until Bedford stepped in. Bishop Beaufort was less hot-headed, but inclined to be ruthless, manipulative and grasping on behalf of himself and his Beaufort relations (*see family tree, pp. 190–91*). Gloucester believed that he should have been made sole regent and effective ruler in England; while Beaufort, as a former Lord Chancellor of both Henry IV and Henry V, felt he should dominate the Council—though it should be said that his overbearing ambition and relentless quest for a cardinal's hat had at various times made him fall foul of both monarchs.

The mutual loathing between uncle and nephew was fuelled by increasing fears for their personal safety. The Bishop, as principal councillor, had infuriated London's citizenry both high and low. The former by his seeming to favour foreign merchants; the latter by his strictly enforcing the Statute of Labourers, which kept wages down and tied workers to a particular occupation and to a particular master. This animosity reached crisis point at the end of October 1425, when hundreds of armed followers of the Bishop on the one side, and the Duke and Mayor of London on the other, confronted each other on London Bridge. A pitched battle was only prevented by the persistence of the Archbishop of Canterbury and the King's cousin, Prince Peter of Portugal, who went eight times between the two parties in their efforts at mediation.[11]

Beaufort implored Bedford to return and restrain Duke Humphrey, which he duly did. Bedford ignored the placatory gifts offered by the Mayor and city,[12] and further showed his displeasure by personally escorting Beaufort back to London and summoning Council meetings and a February 1426 Parliament, to take place well away from the capital. The crisis atmosphere of the latter occasion at Leicester Castle is captured in the name contemporary chroniclers gave to it: 'The Parliament of the Bats'—each side armed with clubs, due to the banning of other weaponry.[13] There, in a vicious denunciation, conducted in front of the four-year-old King, Gloucester sought to destroy Beaufort. These were not minor charges: Beaufort stood accused of seeking, in reverse order, to kidnap Henry VI, murder Henry V and usurp Henry IV![14] Their ferocity was met with outraged denials and bitter counter-claims by Beaufort that Gloucester had sought to assassinate him.[15] Venomous as Gloucester's charges were, he could not prove them. Nevertheless, Beaufort was for a time forced from office, though appeased the following year in Calais when he finally received the cardinal's hat he had long craved.

Beaufort's removal was not, by any means, a victory for Gloucester. It merely entrenched the power of the Council. This was made finally and humiliatingly clear to the Duke at a Council meeting of 1427, where every single member formally affirmed that, during the King's minority, kingly power 'stands in his lords assembled in Parliament . . . and especially in the lords of his Council and not in one singular person but in all these lords together'.[16]

In the longer term, this did nothing to resolve the fault line stemming from the absence of a single, universally recognized regent. The crisis of the

1420s would be repeated in 1432 and 1433, when Gloucester would again achieve temporary dominance in the absence of both Beaufort and Bedford, but lose control once more through seeking his enemy's annihilation rather than his tactical demotion. The feud between Beaufort and Gloucester would also broaden, extend and poison future generations.

There was also to be one pre-eminent victim of the two men's vicious power struggle. Their mutual outpouring of vitriol, sustained throughout the 1420s and into the 1430s and beyond, was bound to have a lasting effect upon a young and impressionable mind: that of the King. As a minor, Henry VI was not trusted with wielding power but was expected to play a part that was both symbolic and participatory. While he was very young, even as a toddler, he participated in all the great ceremonial occasions, bestowed seals of office on his officers of state and rode in parades through London. He presided over his first opening of Parliament at the age of three. Most importantly, he was present for the set-pieces of vicious personal hostility acted out by his warring relatives.

Towards the end of 1429, Bedford and the Council asked Henry, who was then seven, to assume the central role in the most important ceremonial act of any king's reign: his coronation.

Display was at the heart of medieval kingship. Ceremonial went beyond mere celebration of regality, it was a key element of it. The greatest ceremony Henry VI would undertake, as for every English monarch from William the Conqueror on Christmas Day 1066 to the present, was his coronation. This was held in Westminster Abbey, scene of the most expensive ongoing building project of the Middle Ages.[17] Impressive enough today, in young Henry VI's time its interior was enriched throughout with colourful wall paintings, and its central focus, the tomb of Saint Edward the Confessor, glittered with gold plate and precious jewels. It was the burial place of Kings Edward I and III, Henry III, young Henry's father Henry V and, of course, Richard II.

Perhaps the greatest testimony to the memory of Richard II, the monarch usurped and murdered by Henry VI's grandfather, is the survival today of his *Liber Regalis*, one of the world's most valuable books. Meaning both 'The King's Book' and 'The Kingly Book', Richard commissioned it for the crowning of his consort, Anne of Bohemia, in 1382.[18] It is a remarkable document, providing the order of service for the coronation of every subsequent king and queen from Henry IV to Elizabeth I, and has remained the basis for all coronation liturgies up to the present day. Moreover, it contains the key elements of the service dating back to the Saxon King Edgar's coronation in 973. For a fifteenth-century king, the *Liber Regalis* contained a double compact stretching back hundreds of years. On the one hand it was a compact between the king and his people; on the other between the king and God.

The coronation ceremony for Henry VI, along with the days leading up to it, was conducted on the firm fabric of established precedent, but embroidered with added elements designed to extend and deepen this dual compact. One such novelty was unmistakable: the new King, born on 6 December 1421, was not quite eight when he was crowned on 6 November 1429. He was then, and remains to this day, both the youngest ever king of England and the youngest to be crowned.

In Henry's infancy, administrative power might have rested with his Council, but, even at that tender age, his symbolic power was exceptional and it was that which the Council sought to amplify and exploit. Power was fortified and sustained through ceremony, through its symbolism and display, but it was also created by it. The coronation was part of the process of investing the person of a king with a vastly increased power and authority. And that power would be transferred to those who acted in his name, either directly, or, in the case of a minor, through a regent or a Council of Regency. A crowned king had greater worldly authority and, even more importantly, the anointing gave him divine authority; both were granted for life.

The Council was in urgent need of that authority now. The situation in France was deteriorating; the Council required extra resources in terms of service and funding and to galvanize those who would provide them. It needed a propaganda coup to match that of the Dauphin, now Charles VII. For in July 1429, he had been crowned in Reims Cathedral, the traditional place of coronation for the kings of France.

The dual purpose of Henry's coronation was made clear through the incorporation of French rites and symbolism in an arduous series of ceremonies of new scope and magnificence that would stretch over three days.

God and the institutions designed to serve Him were, as outlined in the
Liber Regalis, central; but those of 'man' were also given an expanded role,
with a look back to the Saxon kings, an emphasis on the collective support
of the nobility, and an increased and calculated recognition of the importance of the wealth and power of the merchants of London.

Thus the established formal entry of the monarch into London was
not considered to be enough for Henry VI. The seven-year-old boy's
grand entrance commenced on 4 November at the Royal Borough of
Kingston-upon-Thames,[19] where seven tenth-century Saxon kings had
been crowned. The Lord Mayor and aldermen of the City of London,
attired in judicial scarlet,[20] then joined the procession, escorting the new
monarch to the Tower. Before spending the night there, as was customary,
Henry first created no fewer than thirty-two new knights of the chivalric
order of the Bath.

On the morning of 5 November[21] he showed himself to the cheering
crowds of London; while the city's most important citizens staged elaborate
pageants in celebration, he rode the three or so miles to the abbey under a
canopy supported by four young noblemen. The route the procession followed is still recognizable today: from the Tower of London he proceeded
through Cornhill, Cheapside, Saint Paul's, Ludgate Hill, Fleet Street, the
Strand, and then down Whitehall. Then it was over a small bridge and into
the water-surrounded Palace and Abbey of Westminster. There was then,
finally, some concession to his age, as he was excused the all-night vigil
that was mandatory for adult kings.

The following day, 6 November, was the Feast of Saint Leonard, now
venerated as the patron saint of prisoners.[22] Henry walked to the abbey
beneath a canopy of dark blue silk: the royal colour of France. In addition
he wore the same device on his scarlet cloak as that used by his French
grandfather, Charles VI: the broomscod or pod of broom seeds that also
linked him to his Plantagenet forebears.

Once inside the abbey he was led up a richly carpeted stairway to a
specially constructed, silk-covered platform between the high altar and the
choir. As Gregory tells us, here seated, 'he beheld the people all around seriously and wisely', and Archbishop Chichele of Canterbury proclaimed to all
sides: 'Here cometh Henry, King Henry V's son, humbly to God and Holy
Church, seeking the crown of this realm by right and by descent. If you are

well pleased with him, say "Yea" and hold up your arms'. And then 'all the people cried with one voice: Yea! Yea!'[23] The young boy had his rich robes removed and, in silken undergarments, had to prostrate himself before the high altar for a long time before being re-clothed and swearing his coronation oath. An oath that would bind him for ever, by his assenting to a series of questions and affirming that he would keep the laws of England and especially the laws of Saint Edward.

Yet more prostration with prayers and anthems followed and then the most important part of the entire service: Henry, seated in Edward I's coronation chair—still in use today—was anointed with the sacred Oil of Saint Thomas Becket from a golden ampula. Oil that, it was said, had been given miraculously to the saint by the Virgin Mary during a vigil of prayer. Lost for centuries, the ampula was rediscovered by Richard II, but triumphantly first used by Henry IV. It was to the kings of England what the Oil of Clovis had long been to the kings of France.

With the anointing achieved and God's enduring approval of the new monarch conferred, there followed the presentation of the royal ornaments: the sceptre with the cross was placed in Henry's right hand and the gold rod in his left, while the heavy crown of Saint Edward was placed on his head. This was the only point during the service where the young boy had to be supported 'with two bishops standing by him, helping him to bear the crown, for it was over-heavy for him, for he was of tender age'.[24]

After the Mass, Henry progressed with his nobles and his clergy to the shrine of Saint Edward. There was a final divestment of clothes and regalia, before the revestment in robes of state and the return of the regalia. He was then crowned with the crown created by Richard II and led in triumphal procession through the Abbey 'with great glory'.

This summary cannot do justice to what was an extremely long ceremony—the most important occasion in the reign of any king of England. Just over fifty years before, it had been too much for ten-year-old Richard II. Though he was later to become such a lover of ceremony, the young Richard had been so exhausted that he had been excused the Great Banquet that followed in Westminster Hall. Not so Henry.

Vast course followed vast course, each one accompanied by 'subtleties'—large, incredibly elaborate pastry confections rich in symbolism. One, for example, showed the patron royal saints of England and France—

Saint Edward and Saint Louis—together with the young King, all dressed in armour. Another showed the Virgin with the baby Christ on her lap, offering Henry, supported by Saint George of England and Saint Denis of France, not one crown but two. The symbolic meaning would have been perfectly obvious to the assembled guests, who were the nobility and privileged gentry, the higher clergy, the justices and chancery officials, the Mayor of London and 'his aldermen and other worthy commoners of the City of London'.[25]

Even for one who had grown up with lavish ceremonial, the whole event must have been a tremendous test of stamina as well as an assault on the senses for the seven-year-old King. Moreover, an appearance of royal dignity throughout was crucial.

Yet he remained calm, still, impassive and regal. He behaved magnificently. Young Henry had played his part well. The event's success was measured by the largest parliamentary grant of taxation since 1418 in order to fund an expedition to France involving seven dukes and earls and an army, with the young King as its titular head, of a greater size than that for the re-conquest of France between 1417 and 1421.[26]

His uncles and his Council were united in delight with the young King's performance. So was his 'master' or tutor, Richard Beauchamp, Earl of Warwick. One of the great servants of the house of Lancaster, a close and conscientious military and diplomatic aide of Henry V, whom he resembled in outlook and competence,[27] Beauchamp had been entrusted by the Council in the summer of 1428 with the task of instilling kingly virtues in the six-year-old monarch within the confines of a new male-dominated environment.[28] Conscientious, with a great loyalty to Bedford and above all to the Council, he certainly seemed to be the ideal candidate for the role.

The great event in the Palace of Westminster was, however, a rehearsal for one even greater. For the extravagant ceremonial of Henry's coronation in England was expected soon to be overshadowed by his subsequent coronation in his other kingdom, France.

The Dauphin's own coronation, at Reims, had been an act of great daring as the cathedral city was only just outside the expanded area of English control. But almost any risk would have been worth taking, for through coronation and more importantly, anointment, the Dauphin could claim that both tradition and God were indelibly on his side. He also had support from another and exceptional source: a teenage shepherdess and prophetess who could at will see the Archangel Michael and Saints Catherine and Margaret 'wearing golden crowns on their heads'[29] and talk to them whenever she wished, 'as a friend might talk to a friend'.[30] Furthermore she claimed that she acted in obedience to God's commands and with appropriate foresight.

In other circumstances she would have been accused of being possessed by the devil and tried for heresy, but she came through a great number of tests to convince a succession of listeners of increasing importance. Finally, this girl, Joan of Arc, appeared before the Dauphin himself. He was a man of great shrewdness but one with a profound interest in anyone that he felt could 'predict' the future; Joan first told him that Orleans would be saved and that he would be crowned at Reims, and then convinced him that it would happen.[31]

Her presence at the head of French troops proved inspirational. She was to the fore when the French relieved the large city of Orleans from its siege by the English in May 1429. She was there at the capture of Jargeau and of its English commander, the Earl of Suffolk. She was not involved at the Battle of Patay, where an English army under noted commanders Talbot and Fastolf was routed and the former captured. But she rode at the head of the French troops that followed up this devastating blow, gaining the easy submission of a chain of Burgundian garrisons that, in turn, opened the way for the Dauphin to enter Reims on 16 July. The next day he was anointed with the holy Oil of Clovis and crowned as Charles VII.

Orleans to Reims is just under 140 miles. Reims to Paris is around 80 miles. Burgundian fortresses continued to fall with alarming speed, and within a month the way to the capital itself seemed open until, in mid-August, Bedford blocked the advance at Senlis, just 25 miles to the north-east of Paris. He was assisted by three thousand troops from England recruited by Cardinal Beaufort. These men had been intended for a crusade against the heretic Hussites of Bohemia as part of Beaufort's plans for retirement from English affairs of state; by diverting them for the use of his country, he destroyed any hopes of a papal career, but he resurrected his English one.[32]

This success did not end the campaign, however. In early September

Joan and the Duc d'Alençon took an expedition to the very gates of Paris itself. It was easily repelled, as Charles VII had known it would be. The Anglo-Burgundian alliance was maintained, the cautious Charles withdrew to his own heartland at Bourges and, with that first defeat, Joan's aura of invincibility began to be tarnished. She may have been raised to the nobility by Charles, but now had no voice in affairs. On her own initiative, she led a mercenary force out of the town of Compiègne on 23 May 1430 but, through mischance rather than treachery, was captured by the Burgundians. Her military career was over. She was ransomed to the English, but it was overwhelmingly Burgundians and Frenchmen from the areas of English rule who were to try her and find her guilty of heresy. She was burnt at the stake in Rouen, on 30 May 1431, just over a year after her capture. By that time the young Henry VI and his court had also been at Rouen for nearly a year.[33]

Henry, with an army of around seven thousand,[34] had landed at Calais on 23 April 1430, Saint George's Day. In spite of the size of this force, a coronation at Reims was out of the question. Notre Dame was to be the cathedral of coronation, but even the route to Paris was blocked. It was fully three months before even the first leg of the journey, from Calais to Rouen, was considered completely trouble-free for the young King. There, under the tutelage of Richard Beauchamp, he stayed for sixteen months.[35] With the King was the King's Council, commanded once more by Beaufort, who as well as gaining a vast grant from the Westminster Parliament, acted as banker to the expedition. Bedford's powers were subordinated to those of the Council and he ceased to be styled as regent. Though he greatly resented this,[36] there was no Gloucester-style reaction. Instead he concentrated on securing the route to Paris, but it was not until November 1431 that this was finally achieved.

On 2 December, young Henry finally entered the city of Paris; on 16 December he was anointed and crowned by Cardinal Beaufort at Notre Dame in a ceremony that was more lavish than that at Westminster, but rather too 'English' in other ways; for the Bishop of Paris was supplanted by Beaufort and the majority of the peers of France were absent. Whereas at the 1429 coronation feast in Westminster every care had been taken to include the guests correctly, here the officials from the City of Paris, from the University and Parlement took offence at their treatment. Perhaps worst of all for the Parisians was the food, which had been cooked four days earlier and was described as 'shocking'.[37]

By early January, the King and his entourage were gone, leaving the Parisians with a truly gargantuan bill. Barely stopping at Rouen, the English expedition was back in England in early February. The short-term objective of matching Charles VII's anointment and coronation had been achieved. However, Henry VI was never again to cross the Channel to set foot in his French kingdom.

Through military, administrative and diplomatic brilliance and sheer hard work, Bedford had managed to maintain the English position. But the strain had taken its toll. In 1435, worn out, not least by his efforts to keep the Duke of Burgundy neutral, Bedford died. The alliance of Burgundy was lost and so within a year was Paris and the Île de France. Yet Calais, under the command of Edmund Beaufort, the Cardinal's nephew, held off an attack from the newly aggressive Burgundy. Similarly, Normandy and strategic territories around it were preserved by the twenty-four-year-old Richard, Duke of York, who arrived in June 1436 and took administrative command, sensibly leaving the military tasks to his brother-in-law Richard Neville, Earl of Salisbury, and to the recently ransomed Talbot. A long period of stalemate was about to begin.

Three

――◈◈◈――

AN ABSENCE OF KINGSHIP— MAJORITY

Within a year of his return from France, the young King was show-ing some independence of spirit. In late November 1432, as Henry's eleventh birthday approached, Richard Beauchamp appealed to the Coun-cil for additional corrective powers. The tutor complained that his increas-ingly unruly charge was 'more and more to grudge with chastising and to loath it' and he feared that the boy might 'possibly conceive displeasure or indignation against those who would take upon them to chastise him for his defaults, which without due assistance is not easy to be borne'.[1]

As an anointed king, Henry was beginning to be perceived very differ-ently from his former, mere childish, self. His wilfulness could be construed as betokening an, as yet, misdirected and unguided show of willpower. It would not be long before he took up the reins of kingship, and those who established themselves as his closest advisers would have a crucial advan-tage over their enemies. In the light of what had gone before, it is not sur-prising that Gloucester sought to increase the authority of the young King in order to undermine that of the Council. But in the light of what was to follow, it is ironic that it was Gloucester, not Beaufort or Suffolk, who first sought to exploit 'the dependence of the monarchical system upon the pri-vate person of the king'.[2] Yet the King himself was not ready. When Bed-ford was in England during the Parliament, once again as pacifier between Gloucester and Beaufort, the drift of power to the King's private person had been reversed.[3] But after Bedford's return to France and, above all, after his death, the situation began to change permanently.

From late 1435, Henry increasingly took on some of the less challenging kingly duties, such as reading petitions and indicating his views.[4] In May 1436, Beauchamp resigned his position as the Henry's guardian, possibly 'out of weariness with the King's "simpleness"'[5] and was not replaced.

Then in November 1437, after some attendance at Council over the previous two years, Henry was deemed to have reached his majority. The adult medieval king had an array of institutions at his disposal to assist him in his responsibilities: for the waging of war, the administration of justice, the distribution of offices and patronage and the maintenance of the proper state and estate of a monarch. But the personal active, interested and disinterested intervention of the king was necessary, because it provided the oil that lubricated the machinery of government. Under Henry V the machine had run smoothly. How would the young King do?

The early indications were not good. Henry VI did not exhibit the personality of a king. Indeed, he showed little personality at all. There was an immediate avalanche of gifts of lands and office to the favoured, including his great-uncle Cardinal Beaufort. It had to be tactfully pointed out to the King by his Council that, in some cases, these grants were not legally his to give to whom he chose. Some restraint then ensued, for a time.

Henry did undertake royal progresses, though they tended to be mainly around London, the South East and in the Lancastrian heartlands in the Midlands; but he did not, as was usual, personally administer royal justice. He was not interested in administration at all.

As for his French kingdom, the King's general inclination was, with Beaufort, for a policy of peace. Initially, though, this could waver, as his relations with the more bellicose Gloucester continued for a time to be good.

Early in 1440, Gloucester launched his final campaign against Beaufort,[6] taking advantage of the Cardinal's loss of prestige following the failure of his recent peace negotiations with the French. With the King looking on, first in Council and then in Parliament, Gloucester presented a venomous and detailed range of charges covering Beaufort's entire career, designed, as before, to destroy the Cardinal's reputation and to initiate an impeachment on the basis of corruption and defrauding the Crown.[7] Once again Gloucester's attempt to wrest control from Beaufort and the Council was to come to naught. The charges were not taken forward.

Shortly afterwards, Beaufort did indeed take a step back from the forefront of affairs, but not as a result of Gloucester's attempt at proscription. Though age played its part, the Cardinal's reduced role came about primarily because of the emergence of a new group at Henry's court, one which had no interest in maintaining the dominance of either Gloucester or Beaufort.

For in the extraordinary and unprecedented absence of any intervention by the now officially adult King, the exercise of real power had been moving decisively elsewhere, to those with constant access to him, under the leadership of William de la Pole, Earl of Suffolk.

Suffolk was to become a marquess in 1444 and a duke in 1448 with, most importantly, the wealth to support the titles. However, he was not, at the beginning of his career at least, one of the leading peers of the realm. Indeed it could be held against him that his ancestry, a mere three generations of it documented, was of uncertain, perhaps even peasant origin.[8] Though he had had the honour as a very young man of fighting and being wounded before Agincourt, he had shown no great military prowess in the French Wars during the 1420s. In fact, his active service came to an end after he was besieged in the walled town of Jargeau by Joan of Arc and forced to capitulate. The night before his surrender was remarkable, not for any heroic acts of defiance, but rather for his taking the opportunity to father a child with a French nun.[9]

Having been expensively ransomed, he returned to England in 1430 and it was then that his full range of opportunistic talents began to show. First he made an extremely good marriage to Alice Chaucer, the great poet's granddaughter and dowager Countess of Salisbury. Then, with the support of both Cardinal Beaufort, to whom Alice's father was extremely close, and, strikingly, Gloucester, with whom he had a rapport, he very quickly joined the Council. His attendance there was assiduous for the remainder of the King's minority.[10] To this he added, in 1433, the seemingly lesser role of Steward, in charge of running the King's household. By the time of the King's majority, he had gained the support of the Lord Chamberlain and was thus in control of both 'Upstairs' and 'Downstairs'.

As the King took his first faltering steps in government, Suffolk was constantly on hand. His genius lay in his patience, in moving slowly but remorselessly: he maintained his position in the Council as an upholder of collective responsibility, while simultaneously, through domination of the royal household, strengthening his control of the King's day-to-day affairs. And in East Anglia, where both had substantial landholdings, he merged his financial interests with the King's, under his own direction.

Beaufort may have moved into the background, but there was still the troublesome influence of Gloucester with which to contend.

This influence was eventually destroyed, not by Suffolk, nor by Gloucester's own quarrelsome actions, but by those of his wife Eleanor. Some said that Lady Eleanor Cobham had bewitched the Duke. He had happily put aside his existing wife with the aid of a legal technicality, in order to marry Lady Eleanor in 1428. From 1435, on the death of Bedford, the new Duchess clearly saw herself as wife to the possible heir to the throne. Her desire to know whether she might become Queen grew overwhelming. Astrology was a widely accepted and practised way of divining the future. But in matters touching the King, it was dangerous territory. When it became known in 1441 that her own expert astrologers, all priests, had forecast Henry's death, they and she were put on trial. That two of the judging panel were Cardinals Beaufort and Kemp could not have helped her case. She was found guilty of witchcraft: not of forecasting the King's demise, but of conspiring to bring it about. Her three associates suffered agonising deaths; Duchess Eleanor, the first lady of the realm, was forced to do public penance, walking barefoot like a common prostitute on three successive market days to London churches. She was then divorced by the Duke and imprisoned for life.[11] Any residual influence Gloucester might have had was henceforth at an end. The Duke's many enemies might have achieved their purpose, but the prestige of the court as a whole was badly tarnished. Observers could only conclude that something was badly amiss. There was also to be a long-term consequence for Henry's Kingdom of France.

From this point forward, the power of the cautious Suffolk steadily advanced. Continuing to act scrupulously within the Council, he was quietly strengthening his domination of the royal household and entrenching his position close to the King. Most of the great magnates of the land, such as the Dukes of Exeter and Buckingham and the Earls of Salisbury and Northumberland, acquiesced to his influence. Thus by the early 1440s power lay with Suffolk and a small inner circle who enjoyed constant access to the King. This inner ring was served by increasing numbers of satellites all seeking to join it. The size of the royal household grew exponentially, as did the number of grants of land from the King's estates. The royal debts, estimated at £164,000 in 1433, were up to £372,000 by 1450; this at a time when the regular annual income of the Crown was less than £33,000 per annum.[12]

Thankfully it was at a time of decreasing expenditure on the French Wars. The position there had stabilized. The defection of Burgundy and the death of Bedford, both in 1435, had indeed been major blows, with the following year's consequent loss of Paris and the Île de France. But England had managed to hold on to Calais; and this had brought Gloucester a temporary prestige when he had led the expedition to relieve it. For a while it had given strength to his pro-war arguments.

Whether waging an aggressive French war was a viable option or not, with Gloucester's disgrace it ceased to be considered. Suffolk and thus the King were in favour of peace. They wished to extend what had been a period of truces into something more permanent. It was a position that the wily Charles VII and his ministers were able to exploit from a position of strength and through the dark arts of diplomacy and negotiation.

It was with peace in mind that in 1444 the King was betrothed to a French princess. This was not, however, a marriage such as that of Henry II and Eleanor of Aquitaine, bringing vast lands to the English Crown. Margaret of Anjou would bring no lands at all. Her father, René, had a full range of exotic claims with titles to match—King of Jerusalem, King of Sicily and King of Sardinia—but these were titles without territories. What would have impressed Suffolk more was that René, married to the sister of Charles VII, was also a close adviser to the French King. In that fact, at least, a man very like himself.[13]

Though the marriage in 1445 was at the time popularly celebrated as likely to produce an heir and a satisfactory peace, it became clear that a 'dowry' had indeed been offered . . . but, astonishingly, by the English. It was Maine: the key French province that Bedford had secured to protect Henry V's reconquest of Normandy. But, as with the Munich Treaty in 1938, one side was seeking a solution, the other to make a ploy. The cession of Maine was seen by the English as the final part of their successful peace negotiations, by the French as an intermediate strategy. And as the talks dragged on in fits and starts and the English were seen to have breached ancillary terms, by 1447 Maine's cession became the key not to peace but to a continuing truce. This had been a catastrophic misjudgement. As Henry V and Bedford had known well, Maine was the gateway to the plains of Normandy—and now that gateway was wide open to the French.

Charles VII may have been talking about peace, but he was busily preparing for war. He now had the resources for a breakthrough, having forced through a new compulsory tax grant. He had at his disposal a well-equipped professional army, with the latest technology, in the form of effective siege cannon; so advanced were his preparations in this regard that it was said 'never in the memory of man did a Christian king have such a numerous artillery at one time'.[14] When the moment arrived, he would have the means to reduce Normandy's fortresses.

Gloucester was also aware of Maine's importance. He may have been sidelined and humiliated, but his opposition to the peace policy was well known. Suffolk feared that Gloucester would, at the very least, become a figurehead for opposition. In February 1447, a parliament was called in what was for Suffolk the highly friendly territory of Bury Saint Edmunds. Gloucester came to it with troops and was arrested by the collective force of the Dukes of Somerset and Buckingham, the Earl of Salisbury and Viscount Beaumont.[15] If it was Suffolk's intention to put him on trial for treason, then Gloucester's sudden death made that unnecessary.

It is probable that he died from natural causes. Though how 'natural' a stroke[16] might be considered, when brought on by the stress of finding himself in the very situation he had tried to inflict upon his enemy Cardinal Beaufort, is debatable. (Beaufort survived him, if only by just over six weeks.) But Gloucester's convenient death, in suspicious circumstances, was to generate all kinds of rumours. In the words of one chronicler: 'Many tales were blown about the land, some saying that he was stuffed between two feather beds, some that [in the manner of Edward II] a hot spit was put in his fundament; and some that he was drowned in wine and afterwards dried again'.[17] Far from extinguishing his influence, Gloucester's death and the persecution of his bastard son Arthur and many of his associates only served to fan the flames.

Though the confusion of Henry V's deathbed instructions and the actions of Beaufort and the Council had given Gloucester much cause for complaint, he had in life been an immensely disruptive force. The quarter-century of vicious vendetta waged between himself and Beaufort, and acted out in public, had had an effect on the young King which was soon to take an extraordinary turn. Yet within a few years of his death, Gloucester would be celebrated in popular opinion as 'Good Duke Humphrey', immortalized in popular verse and song, and transformed into a rallying point for a popular uprising of unprecedented coherence and lasting significance.

In 1449, England's alliance with the Duchy of Brittany was lost through a combination of French strength and English diplomatic misjudgement. The English Duchy of Normandy was left completely exposed to the French attack that followed at the end of July. Fortress after fortress was reduced through the devastating power of the French siege cannon. Or, shamefully, they fell with scarcely a fight. Rouen was surrendered at the end of October. Caen, the remaining centre of government, went the same way the following 1 July. There had been only one major battle: a devastating English defeat at Formigny in April. The English army's commander, Sir Thomas Kyriell, was taken prisoner along with all ransomable men-at-arms. The common soldiers, regarded as having no value, were slaughtered in an orgy of bloodlust. Agincourt, in its full ghastliness, was avenged.[18]

In August 1450 Normandy was lost for ever. By then, its commander, Edmund Beaufort, Duke of Somerset, was already back in England. Gascony—the lands that Eleanor of Aquitaine made English by her marriage to Henry II three hundred years before—was virtually unprotected following the withdrawal of resources to the north and fell rapidly the following year. This left Calais, a tiny enclave in the Flanders territories of the Duke of Burgundy, as the solitary remnant of England's empire on the Continent.

Calamitous as was the impending loss of Normandy, it was the reaction to it which was most devastating for Suffolk's government. Well before the final military defeat, political retribution came. On 6 November 1449, on the exact day of the twentieth anniversary of Henry's coronation in Westminster, parliament assembled. Suffolk sought much needed funds to retrieve the situation in France and the dire necessity for parliamentary grants was outlined. But, for the first time since Henry V's consolidation of Lancastrian rule, these were not forthcoming.

Instead the House of Commons was determined to call the government to account. Any open criticism of Henry was unthinkable: it would have been treason. Instead the focus for their ire was Suffolk. The House moved for his impeachment on 27 January. The first line of attack concerned the conduct of the war. To the fore was a 'confession' from one of the inner core of the administration: Bishop Moleyns, the Privy Seal, had been set upon by mutinous unpaid troops in Portsmouth and, perhaps in a vain attempt to save his own life, had accused Suffolk of treason with the French. This tiny unsubstantiated thread was added to a whole tapestry of charges, the worst of which was that Suffolk had planned since 1447 to assist a French invasion, to kill the King, to have his son betrothed to Henry's wealthy cousin and conceivable heir, Lady Margaret Beaufort, and to make his son king instead.

The charge of treason against Suffolk was nonsense. Suffolk, for all his faults, was not a traitor. But England was a country fearing the permanent loss of its French territories and the greatest national humiliation since the Norman Conquest. Worse still, it feared a greater reversal: its own invasion by France.

The Commons presented the initial bill of impeachment to the Lords, followed by further charges including, for the first time, a condemnation of Suffolk's government at home. The Lords agreed several times that Suffolk had a case to answer, but the King blocked all judicial action until, on 13 March, Henry finally allowed Suffolk to be brought before him and the Lords. Suffolk vehemently defended himself and, rather than asking for the customary trial by his peers, put his fate in the hands of the King. On 17 March, against all precedent, Suffolk was banished for five years, commencing from 1 May. On that day, he set sail for what he expected would be a short exile in Burgundy.

Though Suffolk had escaped the Tower of London and the normal operation of the law, he did not escape justice of a rougher sort, nor, in a piece of symbolism that would not have been lost on him, did he escape the 'Tower'. Off the coast of Dover, his ship was waylaid by a privateer. The master and sailors on board the eerily named *Nicholas of the Tower* ignored the safe conduct granted Suffolk by the King. None of his own protected him but instead stood witness to what followed, reporting that the *Nicholas*'s sailors said that 'as the King did not wish to punish these traitors, that they recognized no such King; that the Crown of the realm was the community of the realm and that they would now make another person from outside the kingdom the king in his place'.[19] That they were so clearly referring to Richard, Duke of York, does not of course mean that he instigated the event.

There was then a hiatus until two days later when a mock trial was held on deck. As the men on Suffolk's own yacht watched, he was 'tried' and sentenced to death. He was taken into a small boat where, with respect to his aristocratic position, a sword was prepared to execute him. Unfortunately for Suffolk, his executioner was not a skilled professional but 'one of the lewdest of the ship'.[20] The sword was rusty and it took half a dozen blows to sever his head from his body. The body was then taken to Dover Sands and left there. It is a tale which has about it the air of myth, particularly as the manner of Suffolk's death very closely resembled that of Pompey the Great. But as the *Paston Letters*—a treasure trove of fifteenth-century correspondence—show, these were the details that were recounted within days of the event and were heard by a horrified political nation.[21]

Further shocks lay in store, both from within the accepted political order and without. The former included an attempt by the Commons to gain the return of all lands granted by the King to Suffolk and his associates. The attack from outside the political order was focused on London. In 1450, up to forty thousand people lived in the City of London itself and its immediate suburbs such as Southwark. This was the economic and trading hub of the nation and probably four to five times the size of York, the next largest city.[22] Of an estimated fourteen thousand adult males living there, only four thousand could be regarded as men of property, freemen or citizens, with a say in choosing the city's mayor from amongst the twenty-five aldermen. To be an alderman you needed to be seriously rich and almost exclusively from one of the established merchant companies, such as the Mercers or Goldsmiths. The occasional unattached artisan freeman might be elected but this was a rarity, and the frustration at this exclusion could express itself in violence. Far more volatile however were the ten thousand unenfranchised—including labourers (both skilled and unskilled), apprentices, the retainers and servants of magnates with nearby town houses and, lastly, vagrants.[23] This volatility could be a danger to almost anybody, as Cardinal Beaufort had found, and it was a major ongoing concern for the Court of Aldermen. There was also the fear of incursions from outside and the destruction that could be caused by an angry collective mob: with the example of the Peasants Revolt of 1381 still very much in mind.

In the summer of 1450, that fear again became justified. In May, the very month of Suffolk's death, traditional seasonal gatherings to celebrate Whitsun started, in Kent, to transform themselves into a mass movement.[24] Though it was well disciplined and included many members of the minor gentry in its ranks, it turned to an ex-soldier of lower rank but commanding presence as its leader. That man, of mysterious background, called himself Jack Cade, Jack Amend-All, or Jack Mortimer—the latter name highly suggestive of a link with the Mortimer background of Richard, Duke of York. As the premier lord of the realm, albeit absent from the King's counsels in Ireland, York was viewed as a potential saviour, whether or not he wished it.

By 11 June a force of thousands had camped on Blackheath. Their grievances arose partly from the collapse in France and the resulting dislocation to trade. Kent was a major outlet to the Continent and would have been disproportionately affected by, for instance, the halving of imports of wine in 1450.[25] Their grievances were also partly political: held chiefly against James Fiennes, Lord Saye, Treasurer of England, Chamberlain of the Household, Warden of the Cinque Ports, and direct if distant ancestor of actor Ralph. Fiennes, a close ally of Suffolk, had treated the counties of Kent and Sussex as a personal fiefdom.[26] With his son-in-law Crowmer, he had trampled on the rights of the minor gentry and better-off yeomen farmers. But these were men who saw themselves as worthy of social respect in their small towns and villages. They were taxpayers who expected to be the agents of administration, justice and military recruitment—not its victims. They were part of a chain of service and protection—of 'good lordship'—rising up through gentry and lords to the king himself. And they saw themselves as 'the commons of England' with the right to complain against injustice and to petition the king in defence of the common weal—'the general good'—on the basis that there were matters of concern to all who had a stake in society.[27]

Their grievances might have been local, but they understood that the ultimate cause of them was national. As expressed in their Proclamation, issued on 4 June,[28] their criticism of the Suffolk regime was in no way parochial. Declaring themselves his 'liegemen', they appealed to the King as the 'true commons'.

Taken out of context, their assertions might be seen as revolutionary. But that would be completely wrong. They were in fact conservative. They looked to the national level as the ultimate cause of their grievances at the local level in Kent, but for redress they sought the restoration of the King's 'true blood'—including the Dukes of York, Exeter, Buckingham and Norfolk—and the dismissal of the 'false progeny and affinity of the Duke of Suffolk'. They urged the return of 'good counsel' at the national level and 'good lordship' at the local. Here are their chief points:

> We believe the king our sovereign lord is betrayed by the insatiable cov-etousness and malicious purpose of certain false and unsuitable persons who are around his highness, day and night, and daily inform him that good is evil and evil is good . . .
>
> [They] assert that at his pleasure our sovereign lord is above his laws, and that he may make them and break them as he pleases . . . The contrary is true . . .
>
> [They] say that the king should live upon his commons, and that their bodies and goods are the king's . . .
>
> We seek remedy for this: that the false traitors will allow no man to come to the king's presence for any reason, unless there is a bribe such as ought not to be . . .
>
> [It] is a grievous thing that the good Duke of Gloucester was impeached of treason by one false traitor alone and was then so soon murdered that he might never answer the charges. But the false traitor [William de la] Pole [Duke of Suffolk] was impeached by all the com-mons of England . . .
>
> [The king's] false council has lost his law, his merchandise is lost, his common people are destroyed, the sea is lost, France is lost, the king himself is so placed that he may not pay for his meat and drink, and he owes more than ever any King of England ought, for daily his traitors about him, when anything should come to him by his laws, at once they ask it from him . . .
>
> [The king's true commons] desire that he will dismiss all the false progeny and affinity of the Duke of Suffolk, who are openly known,

and that they be punished according to the law of the land. Moreover, the king should take about his noble person men of his true blood from his royal realm, that is to say, the high and mighty prince the Duke of York, exiled from our sovereign lord's presence by the machinations of the false traitor the Duke of Suffolk and his affinity. He should also take about his person those mighty princes the Dukes of Exeter, Buckingham and Norfolk, together with the true earls and barons of this land. Then shall he be the richest Christian king . . .

[The king's] true commons desire the punishment of the false traitors who plotted the death of the high, mighty and excellent prince the Duke of Gloucester . . .

[They] desire that all extortions be laid low . . .

Finally they made an appeal as men from Kent: '[We] move and desire that true lords and knights be sent into Kent to enquire of all traitors and bribers, and bring true justice', having first given assurance: '[We] will have it known we will not rob, thieve or steal but, when these wrongs have been amended, then we will go home . . .'

It was a devastating critique of the government both of county and country. The rebels wanted to see the King. This they did not achieve. However, having issued their proclamation and having met Archbishops Stafford and Kemp they did begin to disperse. By the time the King was brought to meet them, all had departed. Fortunately so, because he came with armed men. Henry was at last to appear on the field of battle, but appallingly, it was for the purpose of attacking his own subjects who had tried to exercise their right to petition.

That, however, should have been the end of the rising, had it not been for agents of Fiennes and Crowmer who started harrying the rebels. Worse, they introduced a rule of terror in Western Kent with the declared intention of turning the county into a deer forest.[29] This 'chevauchée'—rapid, organized killing and destruction of the type practised by Edward III against the French a century before—was as foolish as it was appalling.

What was novel about the protest was its articulacy and coherence, something that had been lacking in the 1381 Peasants Revolt.[30] The petitions of 1450 were framed by educated men representing those who felt they had a stake in society. They were seeking the better exercise of existing forms of government and in no way constitutional change—that was not their place or their role. However, these were not the landless peasants of the past, there to be harried by their thuggish lords; they were men with a 'voice' in their own small towns and villages, if normally a quiet one at a regional and national level where they looked for leadership from their local 'good lord' and, ultimately, the king.

That their own position and, even more, that of their forefathers had changed was due to the most cataclysmic event ever to afflict this country. It had first traumatized and then transformed England. It began almost exactly one hundred years before: it was the first visitation of the Black Death.

One of the greatest dangers to life and limb in the mid-fifteenth century was from the collapse of old buildings. Even prosperous towns were scarred by sudden gaps in streets, where houses had once been but where there were now empty spaces, stripped of all the materials which had once created a home. These gaps were a legacy of the Black Death, the devastating pandemic that had originated in China, spreading along the trade routes to reach mainland Europe in 1346. It struck England in 1348 and within two years had killed around 40 per cent of a population of around six million.[31] Additional outbreaks continued to strike down the population until by 1400 it was half what it had been before the plague hit. There were further outbreaks during the fifteenth century, though none with the virulence of the first, but a particular prevalence of the disease amongst children and adults of child-rearing age kept the population pegged at the low level of 1400.[32]

The spread of this plague was due to a number of factors. There had been previous plagues, but in one sense this was a new disease, as the last one of any significance had occurred hundreds of years before. It was ubiquitous, spreading along the networks of trade and human contact, from city to town, even to the smallest hamlet. Moreover, it was portable, transmitted by fleas carried by the black rat (*rattus rattus*) which, having killed their hosts, transferred themselves to humans. Remarkably adaptable, it came in three separate forms: bubonic, the most common, with a name derived from the inflamed swellings or buboes in the groin, armpits and neck; septicaemic, where the infection was so massive that it entered the bloodstream and the victim died even before the buboes appeared; and pneumonic, where the bacteria was passed from human to human in breathable droplets.[33] These forms of the plague were seasonal, bubonic and septicaemic being particularly prevalent in the summer, pneumonic in the winter. The causes were a mystery to medieval man and are not conclusively understood even today. Indeed, over the past decades some medical research studies have put forward the case that the Black Death was not a plague at all but an epidemic of pulmonary anthrax or perhaps an ebola-like virus.[34]

While even the most elevated families were not safe from the Black Death—Edward III's daughter Joan and daughter-in-law Blanche of Lancaster died, as did two Archbishops of Canterbury—it did show some respect for class. Amongst the peerage and gentry the death rate was an estimated 27 per cent of their number; within the parish clergy, this rose to 42–45 per cent; but amongst the great mass of the population—the peasantry—the rate, and hence the national average, according to manorial records, was around 50 per cent (with variations from area to area of between 40 and 70 per cent). It seems that more space per person and stone walls and floors to keep the nimbly climbing and nesting black rat further away would have afforded some degree of protection to the fortunate minority.[36] For some families and communities the death rate was comprehensive, leading to the desertion of villages and to a vast number of houses in towns with no surviving relative to inherit.

The pandemic completely changed English society. From a clearly hierarchical, feudal system, one evolved where obligations of duty and service remained but in a more nuanced and complicated form, less rigidly enforced than before. Money rather than feudal obligation had increasingly become the medium for transactions involving labour and goods. This was accompanied by a change in the language, with French gradually being replaced by English in matters of administration and culture.[37]

This did not happen overnight, of course. The initial reaction of the King and nobility was to seek to enforce their traditional rights, to maintain the minimal rate of reward for those who worked their land and to

keep them tied to the estate. This, together with the Crown's attempt to
maintain its revenue by widening the tax base with a Poll Tax, were major
causes of the Peasants Revolt of 1381.

But, during the decades that followed, and in the face of the practicalities of the situation, compulsion was largely abandoned. Scarcity of labour
helped promote its transferability: in short, if peasants wished to do so, they
could move to a new area beyond the reach of their lord, where they would
have no trouble finding work.

Of course, many stayed and took advantage of the new order. Landowners gradually abandoned feudalism and the sharecropping principle
whereby they provided land and seed and took a percentage of what their
tied labour force produced; instead of farming everything themselves they
began to rent out much of their estates, with the less productive land
being set aside or turned to pasture. This in turn changed the peasantry:
some retained their economic dependence on their social superiors, but
as servants rather than serfs; many became farmers themselves, increasing
their holdings until, over a period of years and a few generations, they had
turned into yeomen and then minor gentry; the less entrepreneurial or less
fortunate became waged labourers, with no land to call their own, but in
most cases enjoying a far better standard of living than their ancestors.[38]

It was a much more productive system, better able to support a vastly
greater number of sheep and consequently to produce the country's most
valuable commodity: wool. Furthermore, this did not occur at the expense
of the population as a whole. Everyone, no matter what their class, benefited from a better diet—even the beggars. The latter also had some sort
of safety net, courtesy of alms from the houses of the great and from the
monasteries and churches which owned roughly a third of all the land.[39]

Dietary improvements were vital for producing a population capable of
long-term sustained effort. It was even more essential for that part of the
population employed in soldiering, where a prodigious amount of strength
was required even to undertake the regular and routine practice of archery
and stave-fighting. And it was in the area of preparation for combat, including the recruitment and maintenance of troops, where a sense of social
obligation remained particularly strong. In the absence of the authority of
the King, all looked to the protection—the 'good lordship'—of the local
lord during troubled times.

The moronic aggression of Fiennes towards his own people was a spectacular example of bad lordship. In the 1440s, he had taken advantage of a power vacuum in Sussex and, most particularly, Kent, to build a regional domination. He sought to rule through fear. But in a part of the country uniquely destabilized by the collapse in France, his tactics promoted anarchy rather than security. This was especially so in June 1450. Men turned again to Cade.

By 29 June the rebels were back at Blackheath. This time the rebellion took on a harder edge and there was a disturbing new development. As Isobel Harvey, the leading expert on the revolt, makes clear, it was at this very point that in and around Blackheath retainers of the King himself and his magnates threatened to join the rebels unless those royal servants now deemed to be both dishonest and public traitors were immediately arrested.[40] Fiennes was denounced together with Bishop Ayscough of Salisbury and other members of the Suffolk inner core; though by this time, the hated Ayscough may have already been dead, 'hacked to death by his own flock'[41] and 'despoiled to the naked skin'[42] at Edington, as news of events around London spread west. By order of the King, and for their own safety, Fiennes and Crowmer, the Sheriff of Kent, had been committed to the Tower. As to the general safety, that was devolved to the Mayor and aldermen. Henry had cast away the opportunity to emulate his predecessor Richard II, who as a fourteen-year-old had charmed and disarmed the dangerous insurgents of the Peasants Revolt. Instead, having ordered an inquiry and ignoring the pleas of the Mayor, he left for the Duchy of Lancaster stronghold of Kenilworth near Coventry.

By 1 July the rebels had moved to Southwark and on 3 July they forced their way over London Bridge and looting began. That day, the inquiry commenced at the Guildhall. Cade's rebels had been denied access to the King's judgement, a crucial part of the ideal of the common weal. They were almost denied access to their hated target Fiennes, as Henry once again sought to protect a member of the inner circle on whom he had become so dependent. He tried to have Fiennes secretly released from the Tower, only to be thwarted by the Duke of Exeter, the Constable of the Tower, for reasons of his own.[43]

The rebels took 'justice' into their own hands. Fiennes was denied his demand for the judgement of his peers and the inquiry, overawed by the rebels, turned into a trial. Its decision was swift and the next day Fiennes was beheaded. Crowmer was taken by the Essex men and executed at Mile End.

From the moment the protest movement had gained access to London it had started to change shape. Whatever voice of restraint might have existed among the minor gentry behind Cade, it was drowned out as the mass cries for justice changed to the call for looting, pillage, arson and murder. There can be no doubt that the more unstable elements within London itself seized the opportunity for instant profit and to settle scores.

Cade was no longer the gallant captain. In vile scenes, Fiennes and Crowmer were reunited: their severed heads were made to kiss. Cade then rode around the city of London with Fiennes's body attached to his horse,[44] before it was taken away to be quartered.[45] Cade himself took to theft on a grand scale, loading a barge with loot as his mob swarmed through the gateways of London and then back out, staggering under the weight of their trophies.

This continued for three days, until, on the evening of 5 July the Mayor and aldermen, backed by a great number of Londoners and commanded by Lord Scales and their own captains, veterans of the French Wars, sought to re-establish control. After a battle on London Bridge that lasted from nine o'clock at night until nine the next morning,[46] the rebels were driven back into Southwark and the entry to the bridge barred.

The next day the two Archbishops and William Waynflete, Bishop of Winchester, met with Cade in Saint Margaret's Church, Southwark. Pardons were granted to Cade and three thousand others who were desperate to ensure their disassociation from the descent into barbarism. Almost all the pardons were respected, that to Cade was not. He was hunted down, mortally wounded and captured, but died en route back to London. There he was decapitated and quartered. The body was then roughly reassembled, with its head sewn on to its chest. This was to ensure that it would be recognized when it was dragged through the filthy streets of London.

What had begun as an ordered petition of grievances had, through the crass inaction of the King and even crasser mishandling of the situation by Fiennes, degenerated into something disgusting and degrading. The political and commercial nation was profoundly shocked.

The minor gentry and yeomen of Kent who had taken part in the march to London were appalled at the way their dignified protest had been completely overshadowed by the horrors of what followed. They welcomed the re-establishment of order, and lent their support to the judicial commissions which brutally punished the unpardoned or defaulting rebels and brought a 'harvest of heads'.[47] Yet there remained a vacuum of 'good lordship', which a great lord might fill; one was to do so with panache ten years later.

In London and the South East the undercurrent of scarcely contained turmoil continued, fed by unrest among the unsettled population, displaced soldiery returning from the French Wars, and retainers from the households of the great magnates, whose riotous behaviour was perhaps less anarchic and more targeted than it at first seemed. There were to be further short, sharp eruptions in 1450 and 1451, but this time the great lords—who had been judiciously absent in June and early July 1450—saw to it that the insurgents were put down firmly. But though there was no further massive eruption on the scale of Cade's revolt, the fear of another uprising was ever present. This contributed to a febrile atmosphere at the upcoming parliament, where the great nobles began to surround themselves with an ever-increasing number of personal bodyguards.

There can be no doubt Cade's rebellion had a marked effect on one crowned person in England: the Queen. King Henry might have been safely ensconced in the Midlands during the anarchy of early July, but Queen Margaret was at Greenwich. It has been suggested that she played a small part in negotiating the pardons. Whether she did or not, her later actions were to demonstrate a marked apprehension about London—enough to make her move her court away from the capital. This in time was also to make London markedly apprehensive about her.

And as speculation continued as to who had fomented the rebellion, the finger of suspicion came to point at a man who was not even in the country when it happened, who would not cross from Ireland to England for a further two months. That man was Richard, Duke of York.

Four

AN ABSENT-MINDED KING

With the fall of Suffolk's household government there was a vacuum at the centre of the polity. With whom would power reside? Might the King at last intervene? He was by this time approaching thirty—almost twice the age at which illustrious predecessors such as Edward I and his own father had taken a major, if not crucial, role in governing the country.

It could not happen. Henry's total mishandling of the challenge posed by Cade had shown that. It is doubtful whether Henry ever fully considered the nature of his kingship but, as will be seen, he had an alternative approach, one that Suffolk had been happy to indulge.

Henry's divergence from his expected role was not due to any lack of instruction: his tutor, Richard Beauchamp, Earl of Warwick, had been one of the most learned men of the age. Nor was it for lack of ongoing supplication by his subjects. Their expectations were clearly laid out in *The Mirror for Princes*, presented to the King with all tact and deference in the late 1440s.[1] Such *Mirrors* were common in the courts of Europe at this time. They were designed to outline the nature of good kingship and, of course, how well the recipients of the *Mirror* were conforming to these precepts. Henry's own *Mirror*, written by a learned churchman, was designed to be the King's own personal spiritual guide to his Christian quest for personal salvation in the face of the worldly temptations of 'a great and powerful King'. In describing the challenges Henry faces, the author praises the King's peace initiatives, but says that if Henry's French subjects and followers do rebel then he should lead a well-trained army to the battlefield. He goes on to stress the dignity of a prince and his responsibilities: to heed the law in order to preserve peace; the imperative of maintaining justice; of being advised by wise and experienced councillors; and of pursuing a non-partisan distribution of patronage. But this is a distinctly one-dimensional piece of work: it details what all kings were expected to do, but cannot furnish examples featuring Henry. Although in no way would this book have been designed to be critical but—and here is the nub—it does make it very clear that the ultimate salvation of Henry's soul would depend upon the faithful exercise of these duties. For him, as for all medieval kings, mere godly devotion and prayer were not enough.

At least the author of the *Mirror* did not have the embarrassment of having to pen a eulogy to the King at the time of Cade's rebellion. This was the problem faced by John Capgrave, an Augustinian friar from the wealthy port of King's Lynn. His *Book of the Illustrious Henries* can be almost exactly dated, as it expresses the hope that 'London will spew out her foulness and welcome Henry back'.[2] Adulatory of Henry VI's predecessors, the section on the reigning King is merely lukewarm; indeed, the Victorian editor of the book, wishing to know more of the reign and person of Henry VI, is moved by the banality of the section to remark: 'it is not a little provoking that the writings of a contemporary Historian should throw little or no light upon it'. Like the *Mirror*, the *Book of the Illustrious Henries* is full of hopes. Though it describes many noble deeds, there is none performed by Henry himself. Beneath the formulaic eulogy, its summary of Henry's accomplishments is stark: personally devout; marriage to Margaret; founding of King's College, Cambridge, and of Eton College.

Even these last two great institutions, dedicated to him as founder though they are, were largely finished by later monarchs. The resulting edifices were but pale imitations of what Henry himself had originally intended. These—Eton in particular—were the King's own great projects: 'the primer notable work purposed by me after that I . . . took unto myself the rule of my said Realms'.[3] Many are amused by the popular perception that Eton was founded as a school for poor scholars, but in reality provision for the poor scholars was just a small part of Henry's plans for the great cathedral of Eton. And Henry had a multitude of plans; constant change and amendment led the works to be started then rejigged and even pulled down—seven years' worth of construction in one instance—as Henry's enthusiasm was channelled by Suffolk's clique into a right royal medieval equivalent of a construction project from Hell.

With all of the clique closely involving themselves in the project—Suffolk himself, Moleyns, Ayscough, Fiennes et al.[4]—chaos on a grand scale ensued. In the *Domesday Book* of 1086, William the Conqueror had managed to establish an inventory of the ownership, extent, value, population and stock in all but his four most northern counties.[5] Henry VI's grand project advanced without accurate measurements for the country's largest existing cathedrals! As these were subsequently and sporadically established, the building at Eton had to be continually re-planned, first to make it as long as Lincoln Cathedral, then as wide as York Minster. For Eton was to be the largest church edifice in the kingdom and, even more importantly, letters written to Rome show that it was intended to have a greater power to grant indulgences for plenary remission of sins than any of the King's other churches in England or France. In short, it was to be the most important ecclesiastical building in the realm, to eclipse even the glorious Westminster Abbey itself, which had been largely rebuilt at near ruinous cost by Henry III.

It is difficult to disagree with Bertram Wolffe that Eton, just across from Henry's birthplace at Windsor Castle, was planned by the King to be his own magnificent final place of rest.[6] It requires only a further small step of the imagination to surmise that the lasting impression left on the seven-year-old boy by his Westminster coronation—reinforced by the second ceremony in Notre Dame—was a bastardized merging of the spiritual and the material. The duties and responsibilities listed in his coronation oath, the symbolism of his ritualized Saxon-style election to kingship as the leader of the noble class as a whole, and his role as the protector of his people, all seem to have passed him by.[7] It is as though, when prostrate before the ornate tomb of Saint Edward the Confessor in the Saint's own abbey, he had started to imagine an even greater destiny for himself.[8]

The Eton College chapel of today is based on just the choir of the original projected building—and aptly named in comparison—so Henry failed in this, as in just about everything else. However, an understanding of what appears to be a singular focus amidst a more general lack of focus is the key to an understanding of him. The effort given to these projects by Suffolk and co.—at a ruinous cost that was condemned by Parliament in 1451[9]—is extremely instructive. In order to maintain the continuing trust of the King, and thus their control over him, his revenues and patronage,

Suffolk's clique closely assisted him in his 'primer notable work'—or what might otherwise be described as his hobby.

Henry's enthusiasm for the project can be charted through his constant enquiries to his secretary, Bishop Thomas Beckington, as to whether papal bulls had been published granting rights and indulgences; and through the acts of gratitude when they were. Fortunate indeed were Thomas Carver in 1444 and Gloucester's bastard son Arthur in 1447, when their horrendous executions were commuted as part of the celebrations of good news from Rome.[10] In a personal monarchy, the personality of the king is everything. If one accepts that Henry had any control over his destiny, then it might be argued that a prefix of 'vain' should be added to Bruce McFarlane's famous summing up of Henry as inane and then insane.[11] However, whether vanity could be ascribed to someone who not only lacked control of events but increasingly appeared to be losing control of himself is a moot point.

For, as to the last part of McFarlane's conclusion, in August 1453, coincidental with the final loss for all time of England's French empire and a schism in the English nobility, Henry did go insane. To the divinely anointed and intensely religious King, these setbacks, following so closely on the disasters of 1450, represented nothing less than a personal rejection by God. Henry's breakdown was total. He was deprived of movement and speech, a condition that lasted for a period of seventeen months.

Historians have traditionally skirted around the root causes of Henry's madness: both his great 1980s biographers Ralph Griffiths and Bertram Wolffe believed that the evidence of his symptoms was insufficient and that we must judge him purely by his actions.[12] They felt that to understand him we must look to the King's administrative behaviour as shown by the vast wealth of documents bearing his seal and, sometimes, his signature. But over the past twenty years, Henry's notional administrative role has become more shadowy, because, as John Watts has shown, this was a king whose public actions really can be attributed to his ministers.[13] As with the later 'denunciations' of York and the Nevilles at Saint Albans, the words of the administrative record are not necessarily those of Henry himself.

Henry was still, however, a public ceremonial figure. He was closely observed by his contemporaries: by foreign diplomats who had a duty to send detailed reports to their masters; and by churchmen with close access to him, one of whom wrote a particularly useful memoir. Even the observations about the King in the parliamentary record and court documents reporting slanderous words against him can prove revelatory.

These detailed descriptions indicate types of behaviour that can be better interpreted today. Over the past two generations, psychiatric understanding has progressed so markedly that it provides the analytical tools for leading psychiatrists to make a more definitive judgement on Henry's condition. In the view of Dr Trevor Turner and Dr Nigel Bark of the Royal College of Psychiatrists, expressed both personally and in their published articles, Henry, as described by contemporaries, exhibited symptoms that are substantially indicative of schizophrenia. Doctors Turner and Bark, with many years of practice between them, Dr Turner in the UK and Dr Bark in the US, illustrate this conclusively in their respective articles— 'Schizophrenia as a permanent problem: some aspects of historical evidence . . .'[14] and 'Did schizophrenia change the course of English history? The mental illness of Henry VI'.[15]

The identification of schizophrenia is of primary and central importance in understanding Henry's character, and even more so for appreciating the nature of his kingship. That Henry's illness was schizophrenia would explain the nature of his complete mental breakdown in 1453, as well as illuminating the cause and effect of his own actions and of those with whom he came into contact throughout his entire life.

From his grandfather Charles VI, Henry inherited both the Kingdom of France and the illness which would overwhelm him. In Charles's case, it was episodic, came in an acute paranoid form and manifested itself in a particular delusion that was little known in the Middle Ages and is even less well-known today: Charles believed that he was made of glass. He was terrified by the approach of other people and of himself knocking into hard objects and his body shattering. This was reflected in the abnormal behaviour he showed and in the postures he adopted in order to protect himself.

In Henry's case, the seventeen-month breakdown that incapacitated him in 1453 was catatonic. As the contemporary chronicler Abbot Whethamstede reported, Henry had no sense of time nor memory from the onset of the attack. With no control over his limbs, he could neither stand upright, nor walk, nor indeed move unaided from one place to another.[16]

These symptoms lasted, to a greater or lesser degree, from August 1453 to Christmas 1454 and are, as described, completely commensurate with the symptoms of catatonic schizophrenia.

The King's residual faculties were minimal: he could drink and eat—or rather, he could be fed—and he could stare. For those around him, it must have been acutely disturbing to see the King remain mute and contorted for hours on end, staring fixedly yet completely devoid of facial expression or emotion. It would have seemed extraordinary that they were unable to elicit any recognition from those staring eyes, even when his baby son of two months was presented to him during the Christmas and New Year period of 1453–54, the only sign from Henry being a single flickering eye movement.

In an age when medical treatment was still based on the ancient Greek principle of balancing the four humours of blood, phlegm, yellow and black bile, there was no separate psychological focus. As for the ultimate cause of his condition, at the time it would have been seen as an act of God. Those around him might try to keep his true condition secret, first at the hunting lodge near Salisbury where he was initially afflicted and then at Windsor Castle, but this was to prove an impossible task.

One eyewitness account came from a delegation of peers and bishops that called upon the King, after the death of Cardinal Kemp, on 22 March 1454. They urgently needed Henry to nominate successors to both Kemp's pivotal roles: as Chancellor and Archbishop of Canterbury. Without a chancellor the basic administration of the country could not function; and with an adult monarch on the throne only he could nominate a successor. There was no precedent for this situation nor any other conceivable course of action: some sign of the King's intent had to be gained by any means possible. Thus only three days after Kemp's death, ten senior clerics and peers, including the Bishops of Winchester, Ely and Chester and the Earls of Warwick and Shrewsbury arrived at Windsor. Keen that it should be seen that they had done everything to gain a decision from the King, they made a report to Parliament. This, in modern translation, is an extract of what was placed on the parliamentary record:

> And then considering that it pleased the king's highness not to give any
> answer to the articles, the said bishop of Chester, by the advice of all
> the other lords, declared and pronounced the other matters contained

in the said instruction to the king's highness; to which matters, or to any of them, to any prayer or wish, doleful encouragement or exhortation, nor any thing that they or any of them could do or say could they get any answer or sign, to their great sorrow and distress. And then the bishop of Winchester said to the king's highness that the lords had not dined, but they would then go to dinner and wait upon his highness again after dinner. And so after dinner they came to the king's highness in the same place where they were before; and there they moved and roused him by all the ways and means that they could think of in order to have an answer of the aforesaid matters, but they could obtain no answer; and from that place they willed the king's highness to go into another chamber, and so he was led between two men into the chamber where he lies; and there the lords moved and roused the king's highness a third time, by all the means and ways that they could think of in order to have an answer of the said matters, and also desired to be informed by him if it should please his highness that they should wait on him any longer, and to have answer at his leisure, but they could obtain no answer, word or sign; and therefore with sorrowful hearts they came away. And the said bishops of Winchester, Ely and Chester, the earls of Warwick, Oxford and Shrewsbury, Viscounts Beaumont and Bourchier, the prior of St John, lords Fauconberg, Dudley and Stourton, and each of them, prayed that the said instruction and this their report might be enacted in this high court of parliament on record.[17]

They could not rouse him because Henry was catatonic. The paralysis of the monarch now aptly mirrored that of his monarchical authority.

This attempt to pinpoint the exact nature of his illness is not prurient. If he was not in any way ill before 1453, there can be no mitigating explanation for his previous negligence of his duties. Yet modern medical research gives us such an explanation. Traditionally, schizophrenia has been viewed as an illness initiated by a sudden crisis, without antecedents. That opinion has been revised under the influence of research conducted over the past half-century, on both sides of the Atlantic.

The research findings derive from detailed interpretation of statistical analysis of large groups in the UK and of close observation of smaller numbers in the United States. The former is based on three UK birth cohorts—1946, 1958 and 1970—with, to date, detailed examination of the first two;[18] the latter on a form of study unavailable until the last fifty or so years, involving observation through viewing US home movies of the childhood years of people who were later diagnosed as having schizophrenia.[19] Both types of study show that those with later-onset schizophrenia can exhibit antecedent signs when young; abnormal movements and expressions in comparison to those of their classmates and siblings; and abnormal behaviour showing an anxiety for acceptance that can lead at crucial stages—such as the ages of seven and eleven—to ungovernable hostility on sensing rejection, to be followed by an increasing sense of social withdrawal, so that they appear as anxious bystanders at events. Richard Beauchamp's call for greater powers to control Henry at the age of eleven is indicative of such behaviour in Henry: there is no contradiction that he should be so aggressive then and so passive later. Most importantly, the children in these studies can be described as 'psychologically thin-skinned', so that situations of extreme hostility and conflict may hold lasting terror for them and cause them, in later life, to protect themselves from similar scenarios. In this context, one can see why the viciousness of the vendetta between Gloucester and Beaufort, played out before Henry as an infant, child and minor, could have had a lasting impact on him: how it could have led to a desire to avoid all conflict; how it would mean that, on achieving his majority, he would give everything to anyone who asked, rather than suffer a moment's discord. It also explains why he would wish, indeed would need, to be protected by an inner clique based in his household and with privileged access to him. For it would be they who would carry out the administration of government on his behalf, first under Suffolk and then under Somerset.

It would also explain why that clique, in order to maintain this vital contact with him, were all involved in his one central area of focus: religion and the building projects connected with it. An intense interest in religion, even reaching the level of what some might now consider to be religious mania,[20] was completely normal, indeed lauded, at the time: an exemplar being the King's father, the great Henry V, who was remembered as 'Henry the Pious'. But the personal piety of a ruler, as epitomized by Henry V, was supposed to inspire and inform active government of his country. His personal piety was just one part of his good kingship. A dereliction of duty in one ruling with divine authority might be seen as both an offence against man and, ironically, against God.

In this context, Henry VI's acute religiosity from the moment he achieved his majority, both needs and has another explanation: it is that an unusually intense interest in religion during the later teenage years can be a classic indication of what is described as 'prodromal' or incipient schizophrenia. Indeed the religious belief can develop to a point where the sufferer from schizophrenia has, in his own mind and separated from all around him, a unique relationship with his god. The only difference in Henry's case being that a unique relationship with God was exactly what a medieval king was expected to have. Given Henry's position, it would have been remarkable if his illness had not engendered an acute religiosity. Auditory hallucinations would naturally be interpreted as the 'voice of God', supporting 'the delusion' of a unique relationship.

Henry's religiosity is honoured in a precious memoir of the King by a man who knew him well. Its title sums it up: *A Compilation of the Meekness and Good Life of King Henry VI Gathered by Master John Blacman, Bachelor of Divinity and afterward monk of the Charterhouse of London.*[21] Blacman was a fellow of Eton from 1443 to 1454. He was also Warden of King's Hall, Cambridge before resigning the wardenship and his other livings in 1457–58 and becoming a monk. Most importantly, the bulk of the memoir covers Henry's life between 1443 and 1452, i.e. during the years immediately before his breakdown. It is a singular and crucial work, the only extended contemporary account of the King's personality, and comes from someone who both had repeated access to Henry himself—as a priest to the King[22]—and also to advisers very close to him. In addition to Blacman's own observations, it features those of royal chaplains and, importantly, of Bishop Ayscough.[23] Most significant are the impressions of Blacman's own patron, William Waynflete, who was Provost of Eton between 1442 and 1447 and Bishop of Winchester, for he was, 'of all Henry's bishops, perhaps the one closest personally to him'.[24]

Blacman's own prime consideration, as his final monasticism showed, was not this world and the duties of kingship but the contemplation and preparation for the next. He offers Henry as a paragon in this respect. But the lasting importance of the memoir is in ways that Blacman could never have intended. In seeking to portray Henry's extraordinary religiosity, Blacman demonstrates the King's complete abandonment of his kingly duties and also unwittingly offers a compelling description of a man exhibiting the symptoms of incipient schizophrenia.

That this should be so is explained by the acutely 'mystical' nature of the religion that Blacman and Henry shared. This was strongly Carthusian, influenced by the 'Devotio Moderna' from the late fourteenth century, with its renewed emphasis on the importance of the contemplative life. It also owed much to the religious writings of Richard Rolle, a hermit—albeit an exceedingly well-to-do and well-connected one—who fell victim to the Black Death in 1349. In the early fifteenth century Rolle's writings circulated among educated people. Indeed, he was read more widely than any other vernacular writer of the period.[25] Rolle, following in the footsteps of Saint Paul, extolled the sensory and mystical experience of God's love, of 'a warmth', a 'sweet smell or taste', and 'the angelic chorus of the saved in heaven'.[26] He also praised the ways of the hermit, of one cut off from social interaction. In Rolle's own words: 'Let nobody deny that one who continues to sit in solitude for the sake of charity will be seized, not by a bodily singing but surely by a singing in the spirit livelier than I will be able to preach'.[27] In an age when death of family members, friends and neighbours was a near everyday occurrence and when, as with the plague that took Rolle himself, it could come suddenly and with extreme virulence, then a belief in the confirmation through individual physical experience of a loving God and a better world everlasting must have been exceptionally comforting to the vast majority of believers. But for Henry and a tiny minority, there was an additional element of comfort: this was that the physical, sensory nature of the religion provided a relieving outlet for both prodromal and developed symptoms of schizophrenia.

It is totally understandable why the very intensity of Henry's religious expression appeared so 'saintly' to Blacman. Witnessing that Henry 'was wont almost at every moment to raise his eyes heavenward like a denizen of heaven or one rapt, being for the time not conscious of himself or of those about him, as if he were a man in a trance or on the verge of heaven',[28] he interpreted this as confirmation of the King's true piety.

Without Blacman's mystical religious starting point, Henry's behaviour was viewed very differently by others. But descriptions of it demonstrate the same fundamental problem of untreated incipient schizophrenia. For instance, Henry greatly confused foreign embassies in the 1440s and early 1450s, a time when he still received them. The observations of a French embassy in 1445 were of a king who seemed to have done little more than dress in various opulent costumes, 'grinning broadly and crying "Saint Jehan, grant mercis!"' whenever Charles VII's name was mentioned, and then, when the ambassadors wanted to leave, crying out 'no', but just continuing to grin, saying nothing.[29] Here Henry would seem to have demonstrated schizophrenic symptoms of 'formal thought disorder', an inability to think coherently. Individual elements of this include: 'thought block'—a sudden halt to conversation; 'thought insertion'—where speech would begin again in an unrelated way, as if suggested by another source; and 'thought broadcast'—where the sufferer of the illness would not feel the need to speak because others could read his mind. Here, Henry seems to have shown all three.

Henry was less expansive to Hans Winter, the Prussian agent in London in 1450, who, having recently met the now nearly thirty-year-old King, described him as 'very young and inexperienced and watched over as a Carthusian [monk]'.[30] The 'Carthusian' characterization is telling, as Henry V's two successful foundations, for the Carthusians at Sheen and the Bridgettines at Syon, were both enclosed, sealed off from the outside world. Blacman would have approved of the description, as he himself wrote of Henry: 'Even when decked with the kingly ornaments and crowned with the royal diadem he made it a duty to bow before the Lord as deep in prayer as any young monk might have done'.[31] But Blacman gives us far more in his accounts of Henry. He describes what might be taken to be hallucinations and 'passivity experience', of Henry feeling that an outside presence was controlling his actions and feelings. Once again, these accord with classic symptoms of incipient schizophrenia.

And for the much devotion which he always had to God and His sacraments, it seems not unsuitable that he should often have been enlightened by heavenly mysteries and comforted thereby in his afflictions. He is reported by some, in his confidence, to whom he was used to reveal his secrets, to have often seen the Lord Jesus held in the hands of the celebrant and appearing to him in human form at the time of the Eucharist. Again when he was at Waltham he told someone privately (though others also standing behind him heard it) of a repeated revelation from the Lord vouchsafed to him three years running at that feast of St Edward which falls on the vigil of the Epiphany, of the glory of the Lord appearing in human form, of His crown, and of a vision of the assumption of the Blessed Mary both corporal and spiritual.[32]

Blacman applauded Henry's eschewal of regal behaviour: 'This pious prince was not ashamed to be a diligent server to a priest celebrating in his presence, and to make the responses at the mass . . . He did so commonly even to me, a poor priest'.[33]

Also at the principal feasts of the year, but especially at those when of custom he wore his crown, he would always have put on his bare body a rough hair shirt, that by its roughness his body might be restrained from excess, or more truly that all pride and vain glory, such is apt to be engendered by pomp, might be repressed.[34]

Although Blacman obviously approved of a king who acted according to his own monkish precepts: 'a diligent and sincere worshipper of God was this king, more given to God and to devout prayer than to handling worldly and temporal things',[35] he unintentionally reveals far more to us of Henry's state of mind.

He shows us a king who had absolutely no interest in the business of government. Consider, for instance, an incident that occurred at Eltham in the period before the King's breakdown:[36]

The Lord King himself complained heavily to me in his chamber at Eltham, when I was alone there with him employed together with him upon his holy books, and giving ear to his wholesome advice and the sighs of his most deep devotion. There came all at once a knock at the king's door from a certain mighty duke of the realm, and the king said: 'They do so interrupt me that by day or night' with hardly 'a moment to be refreshed by reading of any holy teaching without disturbance'.[37]

Bishop Ayscough, before his murder early in 1450, was both Keeper of the Privy Seal and, unusually for a bishop, Henry's confessor. It was this which made him such a major figure within Suffolk's regime. Blacman would have been well known to Ayscough and the priest inadvertently shows the success of the Bishop's guidance of Henry, political as well as spiritual, in the revelatory observation from the King himself, that: 'The kingdom of heaven, unto which I have devoted myself always from a child, do I call and cry for. For this kingdom which is transitory and of the earth I do not greatly care'.[38]

Abbot Whethamstede of Saint Albans, a chronicler who had known the King from the cradle and thus was well placed to comment on Henry's development, came to the same conclusion, though he expressed it more cruelly. For even his prudent praise of Henry in the late 1450s, as a simple and upright man, was tempered with 'chidings that he could not resist those who led him to unwise decisions and wasteful prodigality';[39] this becoming, within a couple of years when the Abbot's circumstances changed, the much more trenchant 'his mother's stupid offspring, not his father's, a son greatly degenerated from the father, who did not cultivate the art of war . . . A mild-spoken, pious king, but half-witted in affairs of state'.[40] It was the contemptuous judgement on a priestly king by a very secularly minded priest.

Though many of the contemporary chroniclers might justifiably be accused of having a Yorkist bias, their criticism of Henry is consistent. They are united in describing his childlike foolishness, even when the King was well into his twenties. The same accusation was levelled by a growing number of commoners. Thomas Carver, the bailiff of Reading, preached a sermon to an audience which included the King himself in 1444, along the lines of 'Woe to thee O land when the king is a child'; and almost paid for it with his life. Such criticism began to spread in the late 1440s and Henry's government was extremely sensitive to it. Documents from the King's Bench record the case of a London draper who said that Henry was 'not in his person as his noble progenitors have been, for his visage was not favoured', that he had a face like a child and 'is not steadfast of wit as other kings have been before',[41] Indeed 'men as far apart as Cley in Norfolk and Brightling in Sussex in 1449 and 1450 expressed opinions that Henry was a natural fool and no fit person to govern'.[42]

The schizophrenic nature of Henry's breakdown in 1453 and his inability to govern afterwards has been posited for some time. But now we are able to explain his incapacity before the breakdown. The research work into the formative years of those who later have fully developed schizo-phrenia shows a disease that is debilitating even in terms of its childhood antecedents. It is now well established that young modern-day sufferers are particularly sensitive to what psychiatrists describe as 'high emotional expression', to situations of great stress produced by a family environment of extreme conflict. They tend to withdraw from social engagement, to dis-tance themselves from the cause of conflict and from all but a few trusted, calming people. Henry VI's behaviour exhibits all these symptoms and from this we can see a tragic situation unfold, for Henry himself and for his country. Here was a boy damaged by being forced to witness the vicious vendetta of those closest to him. Here was a man trapped in a position for which he was totally unsuited, but from which he could not escape. Most importantly of all, here was a king expected to rule his country, who never, at any stage of his life, had the capacity to do so.

Five

⤙◈◈◈⤚

A QUESTION OF HONOUR

In the months after Cade's rebellion, in the late summer of 1450, there began another oscillating struggle for supremacy between two great magnates whose mutual hatred was visceral. They were clearly seen to be the political heirs of Gloucester and Beaufort, but with one key difference: not just one man but both had a conceivable claim to be heir to the throne. This made their rivalry more intense and finally, more deadly. One of these men was Richard Plantagenet, Duke of York, the other was Edmund Beaufort, Duke of Somerset. At the core of the antipathy between them was the military collapse in France and the vacuum of authority following the death of Suffolk and the implosion of the household clique in 1450.

Traditionally it was thought that York and Humphrey of Gloucester were close during Gloucester's lifetime. It is now thought that was probably not the case.[1] What is certain is that the petition delivered during Cade's rebellion had thrust York into the role of Gloucester's heir. Position at birth, the death of a succession of near relatives with no direct descendants and a strategic marriage could propel the beneficiary of such good fortune to a massive landholding; this had been the case with York.

York's early years had not been so blessed. His mother was already dead when, not yet four years of age, he lost his father, the Earl of Cambridge, in the worst of circumstances. This was the man whom, on the eve of departure for the Agincourt campaign, Henry V had executed on charges of conspiracy. In different times and with a different king, the son, too, would have been permanently disinherited and thus would have vanished from history; but on his return to England Henry decided to take into account the fact that the boy was related to a hero as well as a traitor—his father's elder brother, Edward, Duke of York, had died at Agincourt—and so the rehabilitation began. In due course, he was permitted to inherit his uncle's title and lands, and yet more land came his way on the death of his childless maternal uncle Edmund Mortimer, Earl of March (that same Mortimer who had alerted Henry V to Cambridge's conspiracy).

York's Anglo-Welsh estates were spread far and wide across the country—this would in time give him a strategic problem—but, taken together with further holdings in Ireland, his landholdings were so vast as to be exceeded only by those of the King himself. His 'insider' position was cemented by marriage to Cardinal Beaufort's niece, the beautiful Cecily Neville, known as the 'Rose of Raby' after her childhood home. A dedicated servant of the regime in his young adulthood, York was noted more for his administrative abilities than any great military prowess. Twice in charge of Normandy, he served ably in difficult circumstances.

With the death of Gloucester, York was unofficially presumed to have become the new heir to the throne. Though unlike Gloucester he was not given official recognition as 'heir presumptive', there was a clear legitimate descent from Edward III's fourth surviving adult son, Edmund of Langley, that placed York next in the line of succession. Had succession through the female line been permitted, York—through his mother's descent from Edward III's second son, Lionel of Clarence—would have had a stronger claim than the King himself. But, of course, it was succession through the male line that mattered and Henry VI's direct descent from Edward III's third son, John of Gaunt, gave him clear precedence.

In all, there were three candidates with a claim to succeed Henry, though the prize they sought was certainly not the throne itself but primacy as the recognized heir. With Henry still childless after five years of active marriage, this was a position that needed resolution.

The closest English royal male relative to the King was the 'violent and stupid'[2] Henry, Duke of Exeter, grandson to Henry IV's sister Elizabeth. By this stage he was married to York's eldest daughter, but no closer to York for that.

Edmund Beaufort, Duke of Somerset, the third contender, boasted an all-male descent from John of Gaunt and was, by 1450, second only to the King in that respect. There was, however, an impediment: as a Beaufort, he was a grandson of Gaunt and Gaunt's mistress Katherine Swynford. Katherine went on to become Gaunt's third wife and their children were legitimized by Richard II in 1397. But their right to succeed had been specifically precluded by Henry IV in 1407, in order to protect the succession of his own progeny; it seems that, even then, the machinations of Bishop Beaufort on behalf of his nearest family had been viewed with suspicion.[3] Nevertheless, in theory at least, that exclusion could be reversed, as it was not necessarily binding on Henry IV's successors[4] (see family tree pp. 190–91).

Certainly Somerset seems to have harboured ambitions to bring about such a reversal. Twenty years before, when he was merely heir to an earldom, he had been daring enough to dally openly with the long widowed and sexually charged Catherine de Valois, Henry VI's mother.[5] The Council, realizing that if Edmund Beaufort took on the role of stepfather to the young King it would threaten their own position, instigated a parliamentary statute relating to the remarriage of the queens of England. Their efforts to keep Edmund Beaufort in check were prescient for two reasons: when Duke of Somerset he did indeed establish a psychological hold over the still childlike Henry VI in the 1450s; and shortly after the statute, and in defiance of it, dowager Queen Catherine secretly married—for love, and most unsuitably—not Edmund Beaufort but the athletic Welsh squire, Owen Tudor. Whether Beaufort would have risked the extreme penalties for making an unmarried dowager queen pregnant is unlikely;[6] but the liaison was to be remembered and would set a question mark against his relationship with a future queen and his exact relationship to her son.

In the 1440s, machinations on behalf of his nephews by the elderly Cardinal Beaufort—who though eclipsed by Suffolk, was still regarded by him as a man of residual importance—had led to his nephews John and Edmund both taking on crucial roles in France. These had affected York's own position, as John had campaigned outside York's authority and Edmund had succeeded York, but there is nothing to suggest that York reacted with any animosity. On his return to England, York became more involved in Council matters than ever, and when he departed to take up the lieutenancy in Ireland in June 1449, 'Duke Richard did so as a loyal and well-regarded member of the Lancastrian establishment'.[7]

Edmund Beaufort's actions in Normandy during 1449 and 1450 changed everything. He was the man in command when the English dominion in France dissolved. In terms of military disaster, he was following in the footsteps of his elder brother John, his immediate predecessor as Duke of Somerset. Indeed, John's 1443 campaign had been such a catastrophe that he was called home in disgrace, debarred from court and eventually took his own life.[8] Edmund's fate could not have been more different. Having negotiated his own personal safety, first at Rouen and then again at Caen on 1 July,[9] he abandoned what was left of Normandy to its fate and returned home. Yet, within two months Edmund Beaufort, Duke of Somerset, was playing a crucial role in Council with a place at the centre of Henry's government in England.

For one man this was anathema. If his disgust at Somerset's general cowardice was not enough, York had a particular reason to be appalled at the fate of Rouen, for he still held the position of captain of Rouen and as such was responsible for the officials there. He had given his assurances that their positions, lives and lands would be protected. As a trusted figure within the Suffolk regime and a recipient of its largesse, he had done so in good faith, but Somerset had breached that faith and besmirched York's honour, as well as betraying his country.[10]

The crucial importance of this in understanding the future actions of both men cannot be overstressed. It may seem strange to the modern mind that so much time should be taken, let alone blood spilled, over the settlement of a matter of honour; or that York's sense of grievance should increase with each instance of justice for Somerset being postponed. But that is the point: York did not have a modern mind. Chivalric honour mattered intensely to him. Unlike his elder son, Edward, York did not have an easy rapport with people, and certainly not his peers. He was, however, fanatically loyal to his advisers and immediate subordinates.[11] Though not immune to indecision, he was a man who, once he had decided on action, could be as remorseless as his youngest son, Richard III.

In the cause of bringing Somerset to justice, York was prepared to use all relevant tools to hand—not Cade and the mob, perhaps, but certainly the House of Commons. As late as 1445, York had been so highly regarded within the Lancastrian inner circle of nobility that his eldest daughter was chosen to marry Henry, Duke of Exeter, the King's closest male relative. In September 1450, he cast himself out of that circle when he crossed from Ireland without the Council's permission, citing his authority to act in an emergency. His landing was opposed by agents of the Crown, for they attributed to him a more far-reaching agenda, and the manhandling he received while escaping their clutches gave him further furious incentive to act.

So began the first moves in a struggle for supremacy that would become a vendetta which would ultimately engulf the entire nation.

That York could feel himself so dishonoured by Somerset's betrayal of the Rouen officials goes, once again, to the heart of the nature of social obligation and the concept of 'good lordship'. The furious reaction of the men from Kent[12] towards Fiennes showed the anger of dependants towards a 'bad lord'; York's outrage was that of a 'good lord' who had been prevented from fulfilling his obligations to his dependant liegemen by a third party—Somerset.[13]

The trading of reward and protection in exchange for service was not restricted to the rank and file at the bottom of the chain. The system operated from the very top of society, from the king himself and down through the nobility. Under Henry V the system had worked well, with the nobility serving as a senior officer class for military service in the wars with France, and this practice continued under Bedford. There was nothing new about the nobility fulfilling a martial function. Warfare had long served as a useful setting for social competition: combat brought potential reward, prestige and honour; it also brought potential death, defeat, dishonour and the financial penalty of having to find ransom for one's release—the latter being a fate that befell Suffolk, Talbot and Fauconberg, amongst others. Importantly, though, this test of valour and fortune was comparative, with Englishmen pitted against foreigners and not directly against fellow Englishmen.

Where there was no active war, as during the peace treaties and negotiations of most of the 1440s, then this focus for noble reward and endeavour was removed. Suffolk's answer to this—indeed, his means of consolidating his position—was through a policy of rewards for all, or at least for all those he considered of importance. In the 1440s his regime created a rash of new titles to reward its inner circle and to curry favour with the nobility as a whole. The rank of baron, previously used merely to denote someone who had been summoned by the king to the House of Lords, was formally recognized as a rank of hereditary dignity, the fifth and lowest stratum of the peerage. One of Suffolk's household clique, Lord Beaumont, became a viscount in both England and France, in a grandiose attempt to bring heraldic unity to Henry VI's two kingdoms: his was the first English viscountcy, creating what remains to this day the fourth rank of the peerage. Marquessates, a short-lived and unpopular creation of Richard II that was, by one rank, superior to an earldom, were now revived, with Edmund Beaufort being the first so dubbed when in 1443 he became Marquess of Dorset. At the very highest level of peerage, Suffolk himself became, in 1448, one of the first non-royal dukes.[14] That dukedom may have been seen as a step too far by the higher nobility; certainly that was the perception at the time of his downfall, two years later. But throughout the 1440s he had for the most part been successful in maintaining their support by bestowing honours or generous grants of land and royal patronage in the form of high office and wardships. Suffolk's overall strategy had been to use the Crown's resources to reward as many people as possible and thus avoid conflict amongst the territorial magnates. Where such conflict proved unavoidable, the aim was to further strengthen the stronger of the two parties, underpinning those who would lend their power to prop up the regime. The system worked as a temporary expedient. But eventually it helped precipitate Suffolk's fall, and with him gone it broke down completely, being, as it was, financially ruinous for the Crown.

Somerset tried to revive Suffolk's approach to patronage, while York sought to bring it to order through 'Resumptions', the rescinding of grants and their return to the Crown. These actions resulted in major conflict within the ruling elite, a struggle for central political control and, as both cause and effect of this process, the outbreak of violence in the localities between warring magnates and, at a lower level, between their surrogates.

This vast outpouring of patronage served to make mighty subjects mightier, yet at its heart the problem was not one of the 'overmighty subject', rather, as McFarlane neatly put it, of the 'undermighty ruler'.[15] A wise, strong king who was respected and feared, such as Edward I, Edward III, or Henry V, would have been able to ensure that all his subjects would obey his word, his administration and his law. But the weak, non-functioning

Henry VI could not do so, and, in the long term, his surrogates were limited in their effectiveness because they lacked the authority that was uniquely held by an anointed and crowned ruler.

The mightiest subjects, however, were very mighty indeed.

They each had their own advisers and their own courts, which became centres of social prestige and display. This in an age which, like our own, though subject to short-term economic and financial dislocations, could also be very prosperous for the well-placed. And it was ostentatious wealth: the great magnates found opportunities for display in all areas of their lives, from their titles, their holdings of buildings and land, their manner of dress and that of their womenfolk, in the personal ceremonies of their households and in the superior nature of what they ate and drank. They did not only dress like peacocks, but, with the birds cooked, stuffed and reassembled in their finest plumage, they ate them too.

The aristocratic lifestyle was what set one apart from one's social inferiors. It is evident from a visit to the Neville stronghold of Middleham Castle near Ripon, that life for the aristocratic few was so designed that almost literally, as well as figuratively, the feet of lords and ladies need never touch the earthy ground. This was achieved through having covered upper-level wooden bridges linking the accommodation areas of the outer ranges to the public areas of the Keep and with mounting blocks at the bottom of staircases where horses would await noble riders.[16]

This privileged lifestyle brought with it duties and responsibilities. A lord's prestige would be measured by his ability to behave according to his status, by the numbers of his personal servants and by their standards of dress and behaviour. He would also be judged by the generosity and quality of his hospitality.[17] With the increasing international availability of novel and scarce commodities, a great lord would need to keep up with changes in consumption. He might enjoy ale, but that was a drink for Everyman and therefore deemed inappropriate, in a social context, for the aristocracy and gentry or for those who aspired to climb the social ladder. Thus, just as rich merchants would consume wine in taverns rather than ale in alehouses, aristocrats, in order to underline their higher status, would opt for expensive sweet wines such as rumney and malmsey from the Eastern Mediterranean and seek out scarce furs such as marten in place of the all too common squirrel.[18]

Charles VI, King of France

Henry VI inherited both the Kingdom of France and his schizophrenia from Charles VI, his maternal grandfather.

Henry V, King of England

Hero of Agincourt and poised to become King of France. His untimely death brought, within months, the succession to both kingdoms of his baby son.

Christine de Pisan in her study

This extraordinary woman gained financial independence through a diverse range of writing, from poetry and romance to military theory. The accuracy of her pithy summary of the key elements needed for victory in battle was to be chillingly demonstrated at Towton, more than three decades after her death.

The birth of Henry VI, 1421

Baby Henry with his mother, Queen Catherine. Henry VI was born and is buried at Windsor.

Nine-year-old Henry VI with St Catherine and the Madonna and Child

This is an illustration from Henry's own psalter.

The tomb of Richard Beauchamp, 13th Earl of Warwick and tutor to Henry VI

The tomb of Henry V's great lieutenant has been rightly described as a medieval masterpiece. A dispute over the vast Beauchamp inheritance was to destabilise the Lancastrian polity. On the tomb's facing side are five male figures in mourning: four of them were to be killed or executed at different battles within eight years; the fate of the fifth was decided at another battle ten years later. They are identified in 'Selected Places to Visit and Related Organisations' (p. 221).

John, Duke of Bedford, Regent of France

The elder of Henry V's two surviving brothers and effective ruler
of the English Kingdom of France for most of Henry VI's minority.
His victory at Verneuil was second only to Agincourt in terms of
contemporary importance. Bedford had to return periodically to
England to manage a visceral antipathy between his younger brother
(Humphrey of Gloucester) and their uncle (Henry Beaufort), one
that was to have lasting consequences.

Humphrey, Duke of Gloucester, Protector but not Regent of England

A learned but vainglorious man, who was later to be characterised as 'Good Duke Humphrey' in Yorkist propaganda.

Jan van Eyck painting of a cardinal dated 1430–5

Long considered to be a portrait of Cardinal Albergati, the historian Malcolm Vale has controversially re-identified the sitter as Henry Beaufort. What is incontrovertible is the clear superiority of Burgundian art at this time.

(left) **Ralph, 1st Earl of Westmorland**

Founder of the Neville family's fortunes, with sons

(below) **Joan, Countess of Westmorland**

Half-sister to Henry IV, full sister to Cardinal Beaufort, with daughters

(above) **Eton College**

The schoolyard at night, with the chapel to the right. The statue in the shadows is of Henry VI, the school's founder.

(below) **The Chapel of King's College, Cambridge**

Henry's other great foundation

The defeat and massacre of the English at Formigny, 1450

The siege of Caen, 1450. Note siege cannon.

What they ate with their guests was defined by its succulence and quality, but above all it must be food that would be out of the reach of their social inferiors, whether through its scarcity and price or its restricted nature. Thus on meat days, lighter meats would be preferred and include birds and wildfowl, game and, most impressively, venison from their own estates. If the more generally available meats were served, then it would be of younger specimens: veal rather than beef, lamb rather than mutton, and piglet rather than pork. On the religiously prescribed fish days of Friday or Saturday, in Lent or on days immediately before church festivals, they would dine on freshwater fish from their own ponds and streams, or the finest seafish, though the Church was sufficiently generous in its rules that anything thought to come from water, such as ducks and barnacle geese and even aquatic mammals such as beaver could be acceptable, for these were not perceived as 'flesh'. Vegetables were sparse and primarily in sauces, and the small amounts of bread served were made with the best wheaten flour. In addition there would be morsels of fine dairy products such as cheeses. Consumption of dairy products tended to be greater in houses headed by women, where there was concern for nursing mothers and infants; there is evidence that cheese might be another element on 'fish' days.[19] The final course would consist of fruit, whether fresh fine pears from local orchards, or dried figs, dates and grapes from the Mediterranean, along with nuts, in small quantities. The Mediterranean was also the source for an increasing range of spices.[20] These tended to be used to enhance flavour and certainly not, in a wise household, for disguising a lack of freshness.

The diet of lower status household servants and retainers was different but in no way insubstantial. On meat days there would be vast quantities of the stuff with more beef and mutton than pork in the later Middle Ages. The household records of Richard Beauchamp show that, in 1420, an ordinary member of his household would have consumed the larger part of a pound of beef and two-thirds of a pound of mutton in each of their two main daily meals. This alone would add up to 1,150 calories per meal. Members of the gentry in the same household would also be entitled to one and a quarter pounds of piglet pork and a pound of poultry—an additional 2,864 calories—at each of the meals. This is not counting the bread and ale. And of course, there was breakfast too. It is estimated that the daily calorific content of food available for each adult member of the gentry within this household would come to about 13,000.[21] A considerable amount, when one considers that the daily intake of today's Boat Race rowers approaching the race is up to 8,000 calories and that of Tour de France cyclists on the most arduous days in the mountains is around 10,000—and these tend not to be meat-based diets. In reality, it is extremely unlikely that such massive portions would have been consumed by any individual; most would have passed part of their allotted portion down the line to retainers in an extending chain of interdependence. Even so, here was a lot of potential energy that could be expended in hunting and military training. If taken on board, it would need to be used up, particularly if the well-fed gentleman hoped to fit into his armour.

This amount of food was available because it could both be afforded and produced. There was also an understanding that those who were undertaking strenuous work would require more of it. Studies of harvest workers in Norfolk have proved both these points. Whereas in 1256 their daily allowance of ale was 2.8 pints and they ate bread that was made almost entirely from barley, in 1424 that had risen to 6.4 pints of ale a day and bread was made exclusively from wheat. As for meat, that rose from less than 2 per cent of calories consumed (the bulk of their daily intake coming from the barley bread) to just under 24 per cent with an estimated 1,169 calories from a total of 4,968, and whereas before, the meat content had consisted of a few bits of bacon, it was now made up of beef and mutton too.[22] A century earlier this sort of daily calorific intake would have been restricted to fighting men; accounts listing provisions for Edward I's army of English troops in Scotland circa 1300, show an allocation of approximately 5,500 calories.[23] Of course, England and Wales were far from uniform, socially and economically. There were still pockets of poor peasants scraping along on a diet of pottage—an oaten gruel that would also contain dried peas, beans and very occasionally small scraps of meat. Poor peasants, however, would not be the type of men who would be called upon to fight at Towton.

The men who took to the battlefield would have had some connection to the great lords, either as members of their household, their tenantry, or through some link to a wider affinity of men who would have taken the lord's food and drink.

For the lords themselves, the connection did not come cheaply: the vast outgoings commensurate with their rank required a vast income. And the higher the rank, the greater was the pressure. This, of course, had been part of the Suffolk principle of promotion; his own rise to the title of duke, for example, demanded that he be supplied with the wherewithal to support the dignity such a rank required. This interconnection between a rank and its cost goes some way to explain the rash adventurism and ill temper of the Duke of Exeter in the 1450s, for he had the royal genes necessary to support a dukedom but not the resources to match.[24] It illuminates a whole series of incidents involving English-based Anglo-Norman landowners whose holdings were lost in 1450. The more astute, like Sir John Fastolf, had sold up during the 1430s and 1440s. Of the remainder, there were some who had vast estates elsewhere, such as the Duke of York, so that the loss of their French lands did not present a debilitating problem. However, there were others—including, ironically, the Duke of Somerset—for whom the loss was more serious. In Somerset's case it provided the motivation for an ill-fated attempt in 1453 to secure part of a large inheritance in order to compensate.

An estate was at the centre of the 1453 wedding-party battle between the Nevilles and the Percys. It was instigated by Thomas, Baron Egremont, second son of the Earl of Northumberland, an ungovernable hothead who has been pithily summarized as 'quarrelsome, violent and contemptuous of all authority'.[25] Though there had been long-running aggressive competition between the two families, the violence was sparked by the Percys' fear that the marriage being celebrated that day between a Neville and a Cromwell would lead to the manor of Wressle, which had formerly been theirs, passing permanently into Neville hands. For an explanation of Lord Grey's actions at the Battle of Northampton in 1460, one need look no further than his desire to secure the manor of Ampthill against a further assault by Exeter.[26] Finally, to read the *Paston Letters* is to understand the overriding importance to the Paston family of securing the inheritance of Sir John Fastolf's estate and the manors it contained.[27] Manors and the land attached to them were the source of the required dual benefit of wealth and prestige: in the mid-fifteenth century it was very much a case of 'manors maketh man'.

The great territorial magnates also had houses in London or just outside. Here opulent open house could be kept. It was later written of Richard Neville, Earl of Warwick that:

The Earl was always held in great favour by the commons of this land, by reason of the lavish household he kept wherever he was. When he came to London he kept such a house that six oxen were eaten at breakfast and every tavern was full of his meat. And anyone acquainted with his household could have as much boiled or roasted meat as they could thrust upon a long dagger.[28]

This must have intensified the distrust and disgust of his aristocratic competitors, who would have seen this behaviour for what it was: the creation of a backdrop of prestige in order to widen his 'affinity'—the circle of influential or simply useful men that could be called upon to advance or just protect his interests. Warwick was merely employing, in London, the methods generally adopted within the country at large. The great magnates relied upon a web of interconnected interests to ensure that large numbers of men could be conjured up at short notice. Under the rule of a strong, active and unifying king such as Henry V, the magnates and the great urban centres would put their men at the monarch's service. In the absence of such a figure, these forces would be put at the independent disposal of the great lord himself as part of what has come to be known as 'Bastard Feudalism'. And in March 1461, exceptional circumstances would come into play, with the great lords raising vast numbers of men for two competing kings.

In the summer of 1450, Somerset wasted no time stepping into Suffolk's shoes as chief minister for he knew this was his only hope of avoiding Suffolk's fate. The residual acolytes of his predecessor's regime naturally served his successor and King Henry welcomed the familiar presence of a close relative. The administrative functions provided by the Council continued and were strengthened: the veteran Cardinal Kemp, who had served at the side of Lancastrian kings from 1417—and until Suffolk sidelined both him and Cardinal Beaufort—returned to the fore as chancellor.[29]

The combined strategy of Council and Household for the restitution of authority was straightforward: with Suffolk's inner clique of lesser lords and of bishops destroyed, there was a need for all the great lords of the realm, in form at least, to become, in lieu of the King, once again the practitioners of government rather then merely its pensioners. And the foremost of these was York.

If it was hoped that embracing York into the fold would neutralize the threat from that quarter it was a flawed strategy, for it failed to take into account the psychological make-up of the man. Up to 1447, when he was nudged aside for Somerset as lieutenant in France,[30] York had been a regime 'insider', one of the beneficiaries of Suffolk's munificence. Though he may have been slow to take up his new position in Ireland, neither that posting nor the fact that he was owed vast sums of money by the regime formed the basis of his grievance. To York what mattered most was the satisfaction of his honour. And that required Somerset to be brought to justice for the betrayal of York's liegemen in France.

The Crown's desperate need for money, due to the legacy of debt amassed by the war and Suffolk's government, gave him leverage. York may not have been instrumental in the rising of the 'commons of England' during the disciplined first part of the Cade rebellion, but he was certainly at the heart of what happened next. When a new parliament had to be called in order to raise money, the very first action of the House of Commons was to choose York's own chamberlain, Sir William Oldhall, as Speaker. Its next move was also instructive: the call for the posthumous rehabilitation of Good Duke Humphrey. The popular identification of York with Humphrey, Duke of Gloucester, was complete.

There followed a spate of popular actions, with a mob of ex-soldiers and London citizenry, doubtless in cahoots with a coterie of York's own men, engaging in the riotous destruction of a number of courtiers' houses. This gave York the pretext of an 'emergency' to have Somerset brought before the lords 'in Parliament assembled', to be charged with the 'culpable loss of Normandy'.[31] Such was Somerset's unpopularity, had York not ensured safe passage to the Tower, his rival would very likely have been killed by the mob.

All of this was possible because York had the support of a sufficient number of the great lords—the Duke of Norfolk, the Earl of Devon and, temporarily at least, the Neville Earls of Salisbury and Warwick—both to start proceedings against Somerset and to lend a firm base for government. Yet there was one crucial element lacking and by January, Somerset had been released and restored to his position in control of the King and the country.

The missing element was the support of the King. When Parliament went into recess, York's platform there was removed and the magnates who had supported him, almost without exception drifted away. Whereas Somerset's regime of household officers and long-term councillors such as Chancellor Kemp, having put down a small populist uprising in Kent, stood solid. It also had the quicksilver support of the nobility.

Once again York's position showed strong parallels with that of Gloucester, but not in the way he would have liked. He commanded great support among the populace and this had been increased rather than diminished by his readiness to take firm punitive action against unruly elements within it. But, to the majority of the nobility, that popular support identified York as a potential instigator, with many assuming that he must have had a part in Cade's rebellion, for all that he could not have directed it from Ireland. Indeed, it was the desire to defend his honour in the matter of Cade as well as the matter of Somerset that had brought him back to England in the first place.

York's position and his personal authority might give him pre-eminence in a crisis, but as John Watts puts it: 'The lords, once again under Beaufort presidency, responded to York as they and their predecessors had responded to Gloucester, by upholding the common rule of the peers against a more individual authority resting on a mixture of royal blood and popular agitation'.[32]

Over the next two and a half years, York endured a period of intense frustration as all his attempts to play an active role in the country were thwarted. His enemies saw to it that he was denied access to the King and those who supported him came under attack. When, in June 1451, Thomas Yonge, the Bristol MP and York's personal lawyer, presented a petition that the Duke be recognized as heir presumptive, the response was Yonge's committal to the Tower. In November, Speaker Oldhall fled to sanctuary in the Church of Saint Martin-le-Grand near Saint Paul's and was then indicted for treason.

In early 1452, in an effort to end his exclusion, York took up arms to force access to the King in order to petition him. The target of his aggression was unchanged; as he proclaimed to the citizens of Shrewsbury when recruiting there, Somerset's removal was vital to the interests of the country: 'Seeing that the said Duke ever prevails and rules about the King's person, and that by this means the land is likely to be destroyed, I am fully decided to proceed in all haste against him, with the help of my liegemen and friends'.[33]

By the end of February, York's army was at Dartford. The King's only slightly larger force was at Blackheath. York was accompanied by the thuggish Earl of Devon and one other peer, Lord Cobham. Every other available peer and councillor was aligned with the King and Somerset. On this occasion, however, there was to be no confrontation. After the mediation of bishops and lords, York, Devon and Cobham were granted an audience with the King. But it was a trap. Somerset was with the King and he had York disarmed and put under house arrest in Baynard's Castle, York's London home. York's leaderless troops melted away and the commons of Kent were by now too cowed to rise on his behalf.[34] Two weeks later he was forced to make a humiliating public repentance in Saint Paul's. At this point he retired to his estates, moving between Ludlow, Bewdley and Fotheringhay.[35]

Somerset, by contrast, strengthened his position at the centre of government. In the wake of the loss of France, the 'common weal' revolt of Cade, the mob killings of the King's chief ministers and the call for vengeance by York, he had pulled off the amazing feat of restoring the government's authority. By 1453 he had succeeded in giving the King at least the appearance of governing. The county of Kent, in particular, was privileged with a number of Royal Assizes, where, in the King's presence, often savage justice was dispensed. For all but those found guilty, this was met with general approbation: at long last the King appeared to be ruling. And this revival of fortunes extended across the Channel, with the position in Gascony suddenly transformed: the people of Bordeaux, far preferring English rule to French, revolted. Parliament, now more pliable, voted a large subsidy to send an army under that revered old warrior John Talbot, Earl of Shrewsbury, to reinforce the King's loyal Bordelais subjects.

Somerset had shown himself to be commanding, competent and politically astute. He had also set about cementing his own position as well as the King's. The marriage of his niece, Margaret Beaufort, to the elder of Henry's Tudor half-brothers, Edmund, recently elevated to be Earl of Richmond (the younger, Jasper, was made Earl of Pembroke) helped strengthen the dynastic ties.[36] But having achieved his pre-eminence, Somerset's ambition led him to pursue an inheritance claim against the counter suit of a young Beaufort relative. It was to prove a catastrophic mistake.

The Collegiate Church of Saint Mary, Warwick, houses a chapel that is considered second only to Westminster Abbey as 'the most lavish family burial chapel in the country'.[37] And of all the jewels contained within, the greatest is a fifteenth-century tomb, hailed by Simon Jenkins as 'one of the masterpieces of medieval art',[38] for its intricate stonework and a superbly crafted effigy made of latten, an alloy akin to bronze. Importantly, it is almost complete, having survived the desecration and destruction of the Reformation in the sixteenth century and the civil wars of the seventeenth. Fortunately for us, the chapel was protected by powerful patrons: the earls of Warwick.

The tomb is that of one of their number, Richard Beauchamp, 13th Earl and the former tutor to the King. On its four sides are beautifully carved gilt bronze statuettes of his children and their spouses: dukes and duchesses, earls and countesses—the top echelon of the nobility that served the Lancastrian regime. Indeed, these were people at its very heart. With this in mind, one side's five individual figures of men in mourning clothes are particularly striking. These five shared a chilling fate: they either died in battle or were captured and executed immediately afterwards. But they died not in one event but in five separate engagements, four of which took place over the course of just seven years; the fifth, a decade later.

The Chapel of Our Lady—or the Beauchamp Memorial Chapel, as it is commonly known—is a tribute to a highly important and extremely wealthy man. It is also a testament in stone to the collapse of the common purpose of the noble class, marking the final disintegration of the cohesion instilled by Henry V. That collapse was the fatal flaw of Somerset's regime in the early 1450s.

Richard Beauchamp had been a pillar of the Lancastrian polity. At the time of his death in 1439, Beauchamp had been serving his king as lieutenant-general and governor of the Kingdom of France and the Duchy of Normandy. In addition to the landholdings and wealth that had come to him on the death of his father in 1401 and of his mother in 1407, supplemented through marriage and further inheritances, four decades of faithful service to the House of Lancaster had been richly rewarded, making him one of the wealthiest men in the country.[39]

He left a vast inheritance. After the early death of his only son in 1446 and of that son's only child, a three-year-old daughter, in 1449, it also became an extraordinarily complicated one. A full point-by-point account of its interconnecting intricacies is magisterially explained on six consecutive pages of A. J. Pollard's recent biography of the 16th Earl.[40] The cogent points may be less fully, if rather less expertly, set down as follows: Earl Beauchamp married twice, firstly to a rich Berkeley heiress with whom he had three daughters and secondly to the fabulously wealthy Despenser heiress who presented him with a son and a daughter. When that son and his infant daughter successively died, there was a case that the daughter of the second marriage, as nearest in blood, should inherit almost everything with the exception of one half of the Despenser estates, of which she was only joint heir. That was to be the least of her entitlement in the view of her young husband, the 16th Earl. He would spend the next four years fighting to enforce the claim.

There were some minor challenges from the daughters of the first marriage, but the major one came in 1453, when the husband of one of the daughters decided to act on behalf of his under-age ward, the heir of the second half of the Despenser estates. That husband was the powerful Duke of Somerset. But Richard Neville, the young man he challenged, was also from the Beaufort core of the Lancastrian establishment and was more than Somerset's match when it came to decisive and ruthless action; indeed, Richard Neville, 16th Earl of Warwick was to become the most famous earl of all, remembered for posterity as Warwick the Kingmaker.

Warwick had, completely illegally, occupied that large second half of the Despenser estates, taking in Cardiff and Glamorgan. Operating on the principle that possession is nine-tenths of the law, he garrisoned Cardiff Castle and disobeyed all instructions to give way, even when they were issued in the name of the Crown.[41]

Important in itself, this activity coincided with three shattering events. Firstly, there was the outbreak of open warfare between the two great families of the North, the Nevilles and the Percys. Secondly, the devastating defeat and death of Talbot at the decisive Battle of Castillon in Gascony, which marked the final demise of England's French empire. Finally, there was the madness of the King.

Although the King was suddenly completely incapacitated in 1453, the basic day-to-day administration of the country by the King's Council continued under the direction of the ancient Cardinal Kemp, Archbishop of Canterbury and Chancellor. In this it was supported by a series of Great

Councils of nobles. Though Somerset sought York's exclusion, he was over-ruled, his power base having been weakened by the sudden failure of his policies and by a host of enmities, both old and new. On 21 November, Somerset was again accused of treason, this time by the Duke of Norfolk, and once more sent to the Tower.[42]

In March 1454, Kemp's death and, with it, the suspension of the crucial executive function of chancellor, brought all administration to a halt. Hence the desperation with which the delegation to Windsor Castle sought any sign from Henry that he would nominate a successor. After their inability to gain a response, the only hope of providing stability and effective action at a time of continuing threat from France and upheaval at home was to set up some form of regency. There could be only one compelling candidate. Just two years after the complete debacle at Dartford/Blackheath, another movement of the York–Somerset see-saw brought York back into supremacy once again, with his appointment as Protector. This time it was with the full and permanent support of the Neville Earls of Salisbury and Warwick.

On one level this was extremely surprising. Warwick's father—Richard Neville, Earl of Salisbury—may have been the Duke of York's brother-in-law, but with the pattern of aristocratic inter-marriage that fact did not count for much. One of Salisbury's sisters had even married the Nevilles' arch rival, Henry Percy, Earl of Northumberland. At one time or another Salisbury had four dukes, one viscount and four earls as brothers-in-law or sons-in-law. Salisbury's children had twice married into the enormous Beauchamp inheritance: his daughter to the short-lived Henry, only son of Earl Richard, the great Lancastrian servant; his son, the Kingmaker, to Henry's sole full sister.[43]

The Nevilles had steadily progressed to the very epicentre of the Lancastrian regime. Following initial service to John of Gaunt, Duke of Lancaster, much greater advance had come under Henry IV when Salisbury's father, Ralph Neville, Earl of Westmorland, first abandoned Richard II, then played a major part in defeating the Percys twice and securing the crown of the usurping King Henry. Ralph's second marriage, to Joan Beaufort, Gaunt's daughter and Cardinal Beaufort's only sister, had brought the family closer in blood to the Lancastrian Henries. Thus, even when Henry V, as part of his reuniting of the noble class, restored the Percy earldom of

Northumberland, the Nevilles' power remained undimmed. For the children of the second marriage, such as Salisbury, this remained so even after Ralph's death in 1425, when Cardinal Beaufort made sure that there was no difficulty with the junior branch receiving the major share of the inheritance. There were also glittering marriages for the children, or at least advantageous ones, with Salisbury's militarily brilliant younger brother, the diminutive William 'little' Lord Fauconberg being married off to a fabulously wealthy heiress who had been an imbecile from birth.[44] In just two generations, the Nevilles had thus moved from the edge of the nobility to its very heart, which provoked noticeable, if constrained, Percy resentment.

The elder Richard Neville, Earl of Salisbury, born in 1400, became a Warden of the West March at the age of twenty, guarding the border with Scotland for Henry V. In 1429, after the death of his father-in-law, he gained the earldom of Salisbury and the vast Montagu estates. In 1437 he was appointed to the King's Council. Thus by 1454, Salisbury personally had spent over three decades serving the Crown as part of the Beaufort inner circle. Yet now he put himself outside it. That he did so was purely in support of his son's dispute with Somerset over the Beauchamp inheritance. Unlike York, whose chief aim was the messianic one of good government, the Nevilles acted completely out of self-interest: to secure the inheritance, and to settle scores with the Percys.

That open warfare had broken out between these two great families of the North, the Wardens of the West March and the Wardens of the East, was due to the fatal flaw in Somerset's regime: it held power at the centre by not adjudicating on disputes between magnates in the localities. Without that firm hand, one that would undoubtedly have been exercised by an active king, the Northern dispute continued to simmer and flare up into raid and counter-raid led by hot-headed younger sons: Sir John Neville on the one side, Egremont for the Percy opposition. By October 1453 a pitched battle between Nevilles and Percys and their large armies of retainers, with Salisbury and Northumberland at their respective heads, was only prevented by the intervention of the Archbishop of York.

This was, by some distance, the most dangerous dispute over property and influence in the country at that time. But there were others: for example, that between the equally matched Earl of Devon and Lord Bonville, his long-time rival in the West Country.

It is difficult, however, to condemn totally Somerset's general policy of non-intervention in noble disputes. On one of the rare occasions that he did intervene, taking a firm line against the Duke of Norfolk's warlike activities in East Anglia, it led to an alienated Norfolk denouncing Somerset for assuming 'over-great authority in this realm' as well as for the old charge of responsibility for the French defeat.[45]

Norfolk did not complain when his ally York seized the opportunity offered by Somerset's removal to assume the greatest authority in the realm. This was officially sanctioned on 27 March 1454, when York was named Protector.

That summer yet another noble dispute flared up: the Duke of Exeter—who had frustrated claims to pre-eminence of his own and was also in dispute with Lord Cromwell—combined forces with the equally foolhardy Egremont in open rebellion in Yorkshire. The Duke of York acted decisively: the rebellious troops were dispersed and Exeter was removed from sanctuary and imprisoned in Pontefract Castle. Egremont had escaped for the time being but his freedom was short-lived. In October, he was captured in a skirmish and, unable to pay levied compensation, was thrown into the debtors' prison of Newgate.[46]

In November, at a Council meeting, there was a further attempt to have Somerset committed to trial. The Council as a whole delayed once more. This was to be crucial. By Christmas the King was lucid again and by early in the New Year York had ceased to be Protector. At a Council meeting on 4 March, the restored Somerset was absolved of all blame and regained the crucially important position of Captain of Calais.[47]

So things stood until, early in April of the next year, 1455, a Great Council was summoned for late May. It was to take place at Leicester, an area of traditional strength for the Duchy of Lancaster. Perhaps this might have brought about the arbitration that York and Somerset had nominally agreed to accept, but with the fate of Duke Humphrey in mind, York and his Neville allies called up their armed retainers and, instead, on 22 May they gathered outside Saint Albans, sealing off the road to the North.

Six

A QUEEN TRANSFORMED

THE DUKES OF YORK AND LANCASTER
1455-59

After Saint Albans, the King was in York's power but the country was not, as it would only recognise the power of an anointed king. Within this vacuum of authority, great men of the realm followed the lead given by York at Saint Albans and sought to settle personal disputes by violence. Nowhere was this worse than in the West Country, where the long-standing quarrel between York's erstwhile ally the Earl of Devon and Lord Bonville escalated. It is worth relating one incident at length, as recorded in a petition for redress. It was outbreaks of lawlessness such as this which persuaded a reluctant peerage again to make York Protector, after Saint Albans, in order to restore order.

> The Thursday the 23rd day of October the year of your noble reign 34th, [Nicholas Radford] was in God's peace and yours in his own place called Uppecote in the town of Cadley in the same shire. There came, on that same day and year, Thomas Courtenay late of Tiverton in the said shire who was a knight, son to Thomas Earl of Devonshire, Nicholas Philippe otherwise called Nicholas Gye late of the same town and shire who was yeoman and with him, Thomas Philippe late of the same town and shire, also holding the title of yeoman, John Amore otherwise called John Penyale late of Exilond (Exe Island) in the same shire who was a tailor—(and 94 others)—with other riotous persons whose names had been unknown, arrayed in the manner of war, that

is to say, with jacks, sallets, bows, arrows, swords, bucklers, halberds, long daggers and other weapons defensible, greatly against the peace of you Sovereign Lord at midnight of the same Thursday. They then that said place assaulted and beset it all about. The said Nicholas, along with his wife and all his men were, at that time, in their beds and the misdoers, as soon as they had beset the place, they made there a great shout and set the gates of the place on fire. Nicholas Radford awoke, hearing a great noise and stirring about within his quarters, arose and opened the window of his chamber and, seeing the gates on fire, asked who they were that were there and whether there were any gentlemen among them. Nicholas Philippe, one of the aforementioned individuals, answered and said, 'here is Sir Thomas Courtenay'.

That same Sir Thomas Courtenay, hearing the said Radford speak, called to him, saying in this wise, 'Come down Radford, and speak with me.' And then Radford, knowing the voice of Sir Thomas Courtenay, knight, answered, saying to him these words: 'Sir, you will promise me on your faith and truth, as you are a true knight and gentleman, that I shall have no bodily harm, nor shall you hurt any of my goods, then I will come down to you.' Sir Thomas Courtenay, knight, answered the said Nicholas Radford once more, and said to him in this wise, 'Radford come ye to me, and I promise you as I am a true knight and gentleman you shall be safe in regard to both your body and your goods.' Whereupon the said Nicholas Radford, trusting faithfully in that promise, came out of his chamber with torch alight, and did set open the gates and let him in—and then cramped in with him in his place the misgoverned individuals. Radford, seeing so many within his place, was sore afraid, and said to Sir Thomas Courtenay knight, 'Sir what do all these people here?' and he answered again and said 'Radford, you shall have no harm', and thereupon the Sir Thomas Courtenay bade Nicholas Radford bring him to the chamber where he lay. Radford did so, and there Sir Thomas C. both ate and drank, and thence came out into the hall, with Radford accompanying him, and there they stood together at a sideboard, and drank of the latter's wine. There the said Sir Thomas Courtenay subtly held the said Nicholas R. with tales, while his men broke up the chamber doors and coffers of the said Nicholas R. and then and there the said misdoers above named, along with others, feloniously robbed the said Nicholas Radford of £300 and more in money numbered from his trussing coffers, and other goods and jewels, bedding, gowns, furs, books and ornaments of his chapel, to the value of 1000 marcs[1] and more, and the goods they trussed together and carried them away with Radford's own horse.

Through further rifling, they found the said Nicholas Radford's wife in her bed, sore sick as she hath been for two years and more, rolled her out of her bed, and took away the sheets that she lay in and trussed them with the other stolen goods.

Afterwards, Sir Thomas Courtenay left his talking with the said Nicholas R. at the sideboard, and said to the said N. R., 'Have do, Radford, for thou must go with me to my lord my father', and Radford said he would go with him, and bade his servant make him and his horse ready, and his servant answered him, 'Sir your horse is stolen and charged with your goods'. Hearing this, Radford said to the said Sir Thomas C., 'Sir, I am aged, and may not well go upon my feet, and therefore I pray you that I may ride'. Sir Thomas Courtenay answered him again in this wise, 'Radford thou shalt ride. Come on with me'. And he went forth with him a stone's cast and more from his place within Cadley, and there the said Sir Thomas Courtenay, knight, met with the said Nicholas Philippe, Thomas P. and John Amore and forthwith spurred his horse and rode away, saying, 'farewell Radford'. The said Nicholas P., Thomas P. and John Amore and others turned upon Radford, and then and there the said Nicholas P. with a glaive smote the said Nicholas Radford a hideous deadly stroke across the face, and felled him to the ground, and then the said Nicholas Philippe gave him another stroke upon his head from behind so that the brain fell out of the head. And Thomas Philippe with a long dagger smote Radford from behind in his back, right into the heart. And so the said Nicholas P., T. P. and John Amore thus gave Nicholas Radford several deadly wounds, and then and there feloniously and horribly slew and murdered him. And the said Sir Thomas Courtenay knight, Nicholas Philippe, Thomas Philippe and John Amore and the other misdoers above named, there feloniously procured, stirred, consented and abetted with the others to carry out the horrible murder and felony in the above manner. And forthwith, after the said horrible murder and felony thus done, the said Sir Thomas Courtenay with all the other misdoers rode to Tiverton, Devonshire where the Earl, on the Friday next after that feloniously passed Thursday, comforted and harboured Sir Thomas Courtenay, N. P., T. P., and J. M. [sic] and other misdoers above named, along with the misdoers with the goods, knowing them to have done the said murder, robbery and felony in the above manner.

And the next Monday after the infamous Thursday, Henry Courtenay late of Tiverton in Devonshire, himself a squire, brother to Sir Thomas C., knight, and godson to Nicholas Radford, with several of the misdoers, came to the place where the body of Nicholas Radford lay, in the chapel of that man's estate in Cadley, and there and then the said Henry C. and those misdoers took upon themselves the office of coroner without authority, with one of them presiding over an inquest into those that murdered Radford, he called them by such strange names as no man might know them by. The misdoers, by such peculiar names as they were called, scornfully appeared, and made such a presentment of events as pleased them and thus it is reported that they should find Nicholas Radford guilty of his own death, in great contempt and derision of your laws. And after that, Henry and several of the misdoers with others amounting to a great number, constrained certain persons there that were servants to Nicholas Radford to bear his body to the church . . . And there the misdoers took Radford's body out of the coffin that he was laid in, and rolled him out of his sheet in which he was wound; and there and then cast the body all naked into the pit, and cast upon his body and head the same stones as Radford had recently put aside for the construction of his tomb, and the corpse horribly broke and quashed, having been shown no more compassion, no more pity than if it had been a Jew or a Saracen; this was one of the most heinous examples that have been seen or heard before in this realm of yours. And thereupon of your most benign grace for the confirmation of your laws and for the repression and prevention of such foul and horrible murders, robberies and felonies in eschewing of perilous example that by likelihood should ensue, if the murder, felony and robbery pass unpunished, may God defend us.[2]

The incident was an extreme example of the divorce between idealized concepts of behaviour and what was actually happening. In this instance the Earl of Devon's son, Sir Thomas Courtenay, broke his word in 'faith and truth' as a 'true knight and gentleman' (not once but three times). His own actions, together with those of his brother and their followers, went against every concept of chivalry and all conventions of civilized behaviour. Shockingly, they gave recognition to institutions and concepts of justice, even as they subverted them. Devon and his sons were thugs. The rest of Radford's property was put in the safekeeping of the Dean of Exeter Cathedral and though it was kept in a church, the Earl of Devon threatened to break the doors down unless the Dean unlocked them. He thought nothing of storming the cathedral with armed men, removing a clerk in the middle of celebrating Mass, beating him up and then imprisoning him until he was paid off.[3]

Appallingly, the Courtenays and their followers acted with impunity. There was an initial corrective from York, strong enough to alienate them and to join them to the court party. But there was no real punishment. Indeed, the reverse, as Sir Thomas married a cousin of Queen Margaret and received a comprehensive pardon in 1457.[4] It was emblematic of the merging of national and local disputes—the Courtenays' arch rival Lord Bonville having aligned himself with York—and of the sacrifice of formal and informal restraints on behaviour to the greater interests of security and survival.

That the institutional constraints were crumbling away was bitterly if colourfully captured by the contemporary chronicler John Hardyng in a poetic address dedicated to the King: 'The law is like a Welshman's hose; it is the right shape for each man's leg. So supporters subvert it and twist it and its might is crushed under foot and the rioter's rule might completely take the place of your law'.[5]

Once again York's Protectorate was short-lived. By February 1456, most of the Lords were suspicious of York's attempts to introduce reform of government in collaboration with the Commons in Parliament. Without the support of his fellow peers, the institutions of government naturally flowed back towards the monarch, or at least away from York. As for the King, Henry could henceforward barely function even as the figurehead he had been for Somerset between 1451 to 1453. His illness had left him a tired, broken man, increasingly in the shadow of his Queen. From this point on, York's chief antagonist would be Margaret of Anjou.

Sir Thomas Malory's *Morte d'Arthur* is thought to encapsulate the very essence of medieval chivalry. But the story, conceived and written in the 1450s and 1460s is far more complex than that. It is a celebration of the ideal of chivalry, but, with strong asides from the author, it is also a lament to its absence at the time of writing. Malory had many months to contemplate his task as he spent long periods in prison during those years. His alleged crimes were the complete antithesis of chivalric behaviour. Beginning with an eighteen-month spree in the early 1450s, he was accused of: leading twenty-five others in an attempt to ambush and murder the Duke of Buckingham; committing rape and extortion; cattle and deer rustling from Buckingham's estates and violent robbery against two sets of monks, from the priory at Monks Kirby and from Combe Abbey. He was captured and charged at Nuneaton in a court presided over by the vengeful Duke of Buckingham himself and was sent for trial at Westminster, a trial that never took place. Instead, for Malory, the rest of the decade consisted of imprisonment, punctuated by periods of freedom, either through being bailed by powerful supporters or through his own daring escapes. He was released early in the 1460s, only to fall foul of a different set of authorities later in the decade and it was in prison once again, probably this time in some comfort in the Tower of London, that he finished his masterpiece. However one looks at it, the case of Sir Thomas Malory is far from the ideal world of the early days of Camelot. If he was guilty, it shows a knight who possessed not a shred of knightly virtue. If he was not—and his modern biographer Christina Hardyment makes a good case for him, though she accepts 'the deer poaching'—then this was yet another example of the law being abused and used as a weapon in the hands of a powerful magnate, with the assistance of a new breed of unscrupulous lawyer.[6] Either way, it showed how distant this age was from the chivalric ideal.

As the actual practice of chivalry began to disappear, its stylized trappings and forms became grander. This process would continue in Tudor England and would be repeated in all the other great kingdoms of Europe. Its outer expressions, in hunting, in jousting, in heraldic badges, in household ceremonies and in the vast conspicuous consumption of everyday living were increasingly just part of social competition and display.

By the time of the battle of Towton, a core element of chivalry—its operation as a code of conduct between knights—was defunct. The increasingly vengeful behaviour of both sides in the coming battles saw to that. Thus chivalry, in terms of what has been elegantly expressed as the insurance policy of the knightly class on the battlefield, had gone.[7] There were also more long-term causes relating to the nature of warfare itself. It had become both more impersonal and with that more 'democratic'. In the earlier Middle Ages, battles were generally encounters between knights on horseback.[8] By the late fourteenth century and into the fifteenth, the nature of battles had changed: one only had to think of the renowned English victories in France—Crécy, Poitiers and above all Agincourt—to realize that. If you, or your horse, were likely to be felled by a plebeian arrow then it made sense to fight en masse and on foot.

By Towton, there was no longer 'a code in which a key element was the attempt to limit the brutality of conflict by treating prisoners, at any rate when they were men of "gentle" birth, in a relatively humane fashion'.[9] Defeat and capture did not, as in France, mean release on the payment of a ransom. By Towton, the ideal was to profit by the death of one's aristocratic competitor. By then the aristocracy was no longer a collaborative class. The united, unified elite of Henry V, itself a reconsolidation of what Edward III had created, was gone.

York's Protectorate was formally ended on 25 February. This was the third time that he had been displaced. On this occasion, however, he did not withdraw completely from the exercise of authority. A more inclusive administration ensued—inclusive but not collaborative. Rather like modern politics, there were people of differing interests and approaches who detested each other, but who were temporarily united under the pressure of a common enemy, giving them the opportunity to hate each other even more. There were real fears of an invasion from France; and in the summer there would be an actual invasion from Scotland, France's 'auld ally'.

But in the meantime there were other pressing matters. On 9 February, the House of Lords debated the sighting of what would later be known as

Halley's Comet. No doubt with some trepidation, as comets were seen as harbingers of upheaval: in Christendom at this very time, Alfonso Borgia as Calixtus III added a prayer to the Ave Maria, 'Lord save us from the devil, the Turk, and the comet.'[10] It was a time of great tension; York and Warwick rode that day to Parliament with four hundred armed and armoured men.[11] Whether it was in response to a real or imagined plot cannot be known.

After Saint Albans, York had decided to entrench his position once and for all. A Parliament had been summoned just four days after the battle. Of course he had wanted to gain protection for himself and his allies, but he had also been determined to bring final stability to the government, with himself as its provider in its absence from the King.

The vehicle used was the House of Commons. The very first symbolic act had been the final rehabilitation of the Duke of Gloucester, with the proclamation that Good Duke Humphrey 'was the king's true liegeman until his death'. This had been followed by placing the blame for Saint Albans on the dead Duke of Somerset and two rather minor figures, a former speaker called Thomas Thorp and a royal household man named William Joseph, who had acted with malice culminating in an attempt, by force, to block the Yorkists' resort to the King.[12] It was, of course, a travesty of the truth.

A major part of this Parliament was involved, as in 1450–51, with an attempted Resumption of previous royal grants of land, sinecures and pensions. On one level it was understandable: the still crippling expenditure of the royal household needed to be brought under control. On a tactical level, however, it alienated a great number of the more neutral peers, partly because they had themselves received rewards from the generous hands of the Somerset regime, but also because they saw it as an attack on the royal prerogative. As a result, they withdrew their support for the Protectorate. Even worse, from York's point of view, the attempted Resumption had incurred not just the opposition but the permanent bitter enmity of the Queen.[13]

Margaret of Anjou may have been viewed with suspicion by the common people as a French Queen of England at a time of disastrous defeat in the French Wars, but she had been, right up to the end of those wars, a loyal, submissive, mediating and very traditional Queen. For the first eight years of her marriage there had, however, been one absolutely essential missing element: she had failed to produce an heir to the throne. But on 13 October 1453, during the early months of Henry's madness, Margaret had at last given birth to a healthy son, Edward. Despite later Yorkist slurs, there was no doubt that Henry was the father.

In 1454 Margaret put herself forward as a candidate for the regency, but it seems that she understood why York was made Protector. However, after Saint Albans and particularly after the move for a Resumption, her attitude changed completely. The envisaged Resumption of lands and revenues by the royal household was far more draconian than that of 1450. In an attempt to bring royal expenditure under the control of a Council dominated by York, the Yorkist-controlled House of Commons had attacked the dignity of the House of Lancaster itself. The lands of the King's two Tudor half-brothers, the Earls of Richmond and Pembroke, would be reclaimed, as would Henry's endowments to Eton and King's. The income received by the infant Prince of Wales from his estates would be that for a child, with the rest going to the royal household. Furthermore, the Resumption would include the management of the Duchy of Lancaster estates within a royal household to be controlled by York; they were no longer to be treated as the King's personal revenue. In addition to restricting the actions of the incumbent king, those of his son and heir would also be subject to Yorkist control. The Queen would countenance none of this.

Nor would the majority of the nobility. The avowed enemies of York and the Nevilles were joined in opposition by more moderate figures such as the Duke of Buckingham—a magnate who also had royal descent from Edward III and possessed landholdings almost as extensive as those of York himself. His was a personal loyalty to the King and Queen. It did not diminish when his Bourchier half-brothers, Henry Viscount Bourchier, Lord Treasurer, and Thomas Bourchier, Lord Chancellor and Archbishop of Canterbury, were removed from their pivotal administrative posts at Margaret's command in October 1456. Buckingham himself, with his son-in-law the new Earl of Shrewsbury (son of the warrior of Castillon) as treasurer and Bishop Waynflete of Winchester as chancellor now ran the basic administration of the country in attendance on Henry.

The executive power to issue royal decrees through the Privy Seal was also with Henry, or rather with Margaret, whose own personal chancellor, Laurence Booth, was made its keeper operating from the new base for the court deep within the Duchy of Lancaster lands at Kenilworth and at Coventry.[14] If York believed that the exceptional circumstance of the permanent incapacity of an adult King to exercise authority required a permanent solution, then so too did Margaret. Yet their motives and their approaches could not have been more different and more conflicting. Ultimately they were irreconcilable. They shared one ambition: each sought to have pre-eminent control.

York has traditionally been cast as someone whose focus was utterly self-interested, stemming from financial concerns, personal hatreds, dynastic ambitions, the fear of exclusion and the not inconsiderable aim of self-preservation.[15] He was surely more complex than that and consequently far more dangerous. He may have been a recipient of the largesse of the Suffolk regime and he did consider his own personal interests, but he would not have allowed any number of grants and gratuities to compromise his honour. It was what he believed to be the gross dishonour of Somerset's surrender of Normandy and, with it, the betrayal of men to whom he had given his promise of protection which initially stirred him to action. Furthermore he had been gravely insulted by accusations of treason and the slur of having sponsored Cade's rebellion, compounded by the opposition to his landing from Ireland in 1450. That Somerset should then be able to take on Suffolk's mantle at the head of the administration, rather than facing 'justice', led York to challenge the way the administration itself functioned.

However, this challenge outlived the death of Somerset and York's brutal achievement of the initial objective. Increasingly, it had become the remorseless York's aim to fill the vacuum of royal authority with his own. He wanted to dominate the Council and control and reform the Household as a ruler, rather than as a manager of interests as Suffolk and Somerset had done. Yet to do so he needed the complete control of the King and his seals of administration, together with the acquiescence of the greater part of the nobility. In the short term, through successive crises, York had gained control; in the long term he was perceived by too many of the peerage as the problem rather than the solution. They suspected him of ambitions to permanently change the nature of the monarchy and with it the position of the nobility; of an unscrupulous willingness to use the monetary and legislative power of the House of Commons; and furthermore as personally reckless, ready to unleash the physical threat of his own retainers and the common people. York saw himself as an authoritative figure, acting for the common good of all and restoring order by the most effective means to hand. His opponents saw him as a dangerous innovator, willing with the Nevilles to unleash the mob to advance their position.

The greatest of his opponents was the Queen, whose opposition spurred her to behave in a completely revolutionary way. From October 1456 onwards, she had control of the instruments of government. Not just the Privy Seal, but also, for much of the time, the supreme administrative authority of the Great Seal through the presence of Chancellor Waynflete and, additionally, access to finance through Treasurer Shrewsbury. Though she asserted the dignity of the King, she increasingly promoted a new pre-eminence: that of herself and her son. The civic records of Coventry show this: when a Great Council came to an end there in March 1457, it was made chillingly clear to the mayor and aldermen that the special honours traditionally due only to a king on his arrival and departure must hence-forward, and without fail, be shown to the Queen. Thus that September, to mark the Feast of the Exaltation of the Holy Cross, it was Margaret who made the triumphal entry into Coventry. We know that Henry was there, because a reference was made to him in a speech and because gifts were received, but it seems that his was a passive and silent presence.[16] Again in 1457, when Margaret heard that the chapter of Exeter Cathedral had failed to install the royal candidate despite being instructed to do so in a letter sent in the name of the King, a further letter was sent—this time signed by her, not the King—expressing 'our great marvel and displeasure if it be so'.[17]

The Queen was thus seeking to act as king. In this she was driven by her total focus on her son and the need to protect his inheritance. It has even been suggested, improbably, that in 1458 she vainly tried to get Henry to abdicate in young Edward's favour. Meanwhile, having resisted York's attempts to gain conciliar control over the Duchy of Lancaster, the Crown's own private personal domain, Margaret sought to use its base in rich lands in the Midlands to establish herself as the most powerful regional magnate in the country. As well as trying to contain the Duke of York by using, through proxy, the power of her husband, she was prepared to utilize the resources of the Duchy. In short, to defeat the Duke of York by being, in effect, the Duke of Lancaster.

It is possible that Margaret might have destroyed York in the autumn of

1456, had she had enough noble support. That she had not even attempted it was because York's and Salisbury's military prowess was needed to see off the Scots and Warwick's to protect the immensely important territory of Calais.

By 1458, England was more secure from outside invasion. Partly as a consequence, it was even less secure from internal division. Recognising this, an attempt was made to broker reconciliation between the irreconcilable parties by bringing them together at a 'Love Day'. To signal a new start, it would take place on 25 March—Lady Day, the Feast of the Annunciation of the Virgin Mary—which, until the calendar changed in 1752, was the first day of the New Year. Some have attributed this initiative to Henry, but it is more likely to have been organized by Chancellor Waynflete and the more moderate men of the Council.[18] As well as peace between Margaret and York, it was hoped that this gathering would draw a line under events at Saint Albans three years before, by assuaging the grievances of the three lords—Somerset, Northumberland and Clifford—whose fathers had been slain. These three had, according to the Yorkists, repeatedly attempted to settle the score by assassination. The Lancastrian lords had certainly organized gangs for the purpose of 'arresting' York, Salisbury and Warwick, commanding them either individually or collectively. Their ally Exeter had joined the plots.

Young Somerset, in particular, had cause to hate Warwick. Henry Somerset had been at his father's side at Saint Albans; having been badly wounded, he was placed under the 'protection' of Warwick until the Parliament opened. There can be no doubt that this was, in fact, custody. At the Great Council summoned at Coventry in October 1456, Somerset had to be restrained from physically attacking York. The next month in London he had tried to assault first Warwick and then Warwick's younger brother, Sir John Neville.[19]

Love Day sought to pacify the Lancastrian lords by having York, Salisbury and Warwick make reparations to them, with the only offer in return being a bond made by Egremont to keep his peace with the Earl of Salisbury for ten years.[20] The bitter foes walked side by side and hand in hand to Saint Paul's for a service of thanksgiving and, with the King and Queen back in London and its neighbourhood, celebrations continued for some weeks. None of the lords, however, had come to London alone—far from it. The Lancastrian heirs of Saint Albans and their allies had brought more than two thousand men; York and the Nevilles fifteen hundred. The two sides were separated by the walls of the City itself, with the Yorkists inside and the Lancastrians out. Even so, the Mayor of London raised a force of five hundred men to keep the peace.[21] The number of retainers brought by the leaders of the two sides for their own protection was a truer indicator of the state of affairs between them.

Love Day was doomed to failure. Proof of that came in November, when Warwick was almost assassinated in a highly dramatic manner at a Council meeting at Westminster. He had been called to the Council to justify his actions in Calais, probably with the intention of having him replaced by young Somerset. The meeting was scarcely under way when a clash of weapons was heard outside, coming from Warwick's men and soldiers of the royal household. Warwick himself instantly became embroiled with senior household officers and had to fight his way to his barge to escape.[22] Soon he was back in Calais, refusing all demands that he give up his post. Within months the King and Queen were in the Midlands, hastened on their way, without doubt, by ever-increasing lawlessness in London and the South East.

The country had been slowly dividing into two somewhat unequal halves. The Lancastrians could boast possession of the Crown itself through the King. They also had the Queen and the greater part of the nobility. This included men such as Buckingham, who though he had been involved in property disputes with Warwick at a local level, had previously been more patient nationally. A pivotal figure at court and in the Council, his attitude had hardened completely, both to Warwick in Calais and to his own brother-in-law, York.

The interdependence of the Lancastrian party was being reinforced by fresh marriage alliances in the manner of an arms race. Partisans were in control of the central administration and that of most of the shires. Yet they were administering in an increasingly ad-hoc and informal way through 'martial law, arbitrations, monetary bonds and sworn oaths'.[23] The traditional route of the law and the courts was avoided as it was considered too slow at a time of increasing lawlessness. Consequently, lesser men sought to resolve their disputes by force. They protected themselves by joining the affinity of men more powerful than themselves: it was a case where the enemy of the patron of one's enemy should be sought as one's friend. Enmity of one family for another at a regional and local level could dictate which national faction was favoured and could bring about changes of allegiance. The desertion of the court faction for the Duke of York by the former Beaufort insider Nevilles brought the Percys, their long-standing greatest enemies, back into the bosom of royal favour. The desertion from York to Lancaster by the Courtenays of Devon brought their hated rival Lord Bonville into the Yorkist camp. In the same way, men many layers down who had no existing affiliation joined the thousands who already did, and looked to a lord to protect their interests.

Queen Margaret had not felt strong enough in 1456 to settle accounts, but by June 1459 her position had consolidated. A Great Council was called at Coventry. York, the Nevilles, the Bourchiers and some others were deliberately excluded. It was a public acknowledgement that the confrontation which both sides had been anticipating and for which they had been arming themselves, was inevitable. York, Salisbury and Warwick called their own council, with their own forces, to meet in York's heartlands in the West Marches, at his fortress at Ludlow.

York, Salisbury, Warwick and their allies expected to assemble their forces at Ludlow, then head east together to the great royal castle of Kenilworth and, as at Saint Albans four years earlier, to capture and take control of the King—and if this meant they would first have to defeat their enemies in battle, so be it.

But this time the odds were stacked against the Yorkists. The King and Queen were in their Midlands heartlands and able to recruit more easily; whereas the Yorkists were widely separated. Although York was already at Ludlow, Salisbury was at his own great Yorkshire fortress of Middleham and Warwick was in Calais. They therefore had insufficient time to maximize their forces before moving to rendezvous with York. For Warwick, this was almost calamitous; on his march from London, where he had been allowed entrance for one night, he and a small group narrowly escaped capture by the vengeful young Somerset at Coleshill in Warwickshire. Meanwhile Salisbury was being tracked not by one large contingent, but three, nominally commanded by the King, the Queen and Prince Edward respectively.

It was the Prince's contingent, largely composed of men from Cheshire, that caught Salisbury's force at Blore Heath near Market Drayton. In the ensuing engagement, though significantly outnumbered, Salisbury beat off a much larger force and the Prince's commander, Lord Audley, was killed. Significant blood had been shed. There was also a cost to Salisbury as two of his younger sons were wounded then captured by Lancastrians and later imprisoned. Salisbury's contingent then continued its march and, under cover of darkness, evaded the converging Lancastrian forces. The account in *Gregory's Chronicle*, written after the event, added the colourful but no doubt fanciful detail that Salisbury's decampment was aided by an Austin Friar firing a cannon at who knows what during the night to give the impression that Salisbury had remained on the field.[24]

Warwick and Salisbury did make it to Ludlow and soon afterwards the combined force began its march towards the King. They were between Worcester and Kidderminster, still a long way from Kenilworth, when York's army sighted the Lancastrians. Realizing how heavily outnumbered he was, and hesitating to attack the King with Standard raised, York led his force back to Worcester. Here the three Yorkist leaders, after taking the sacrament, took an oath of loyalty to the King. Their protestations were ignored; the Lancastrians continued their advance. York then retreated to Tewkesbury while the King advanced to Worcester. It was probably from here that the Bishop of Salisbury was sent to offer a general pardon to the Yorkists, with one exception—the Bishop's namesake by place. For the Earl of Salisbury's action at Blore Heath, in opposing a royal army and killing its commander, was not forgiven. The more general pardon, as all must have known it would be, was rejected. As the King's forces continued their advance, York's crossed the Severn and returned to Ludlow.

There, at Ludford Bridge, alongside the River Teme, he spent the daylight hours of 12 October building a defensive position. His pursuers, at first slowed by their own need to rest and reorganize and then by York's forward traps and skirmishers, arrived at near nightfall to be greeted by Yorkist cannon fire over their lines.

Yorkist morale was not good. They were heavily outnumbered, possibly by as many as two to one. Yet they faced an even greater problem: the King may not have been in command—probably, as at the Battle of Saint Albans, it was the Duke of Buckingham—but he was, however, present and, most importantly, his Standard was clearly raised. This was not like Saint Albans, where the thin excuse of not being able to see that Standard had, in their own eyes at least, covered the Yorkists' actions. It was an important enough difference to give Andrew Trollope, Warwick's second-in-command, the excuse to cross to the enemy lines under cover of darkness and honour his long connections with the Beauforts. Trollope, the Master Porter of Calais, was an extremely talented professional soldier, thus to lose him was a great blow. An even greater blow was that he took a good part of the Calais troops and the Yorkist battle plan with him.

York, whose visceral hatred of Somerset had stemmed from what he regarded as the latter's dishonourable actions in Normandy, now did something deeply dishonourable himself. Taking with him his two eldest sons, together with Salisbury, Warwick and a few captains, he crossed the river into Ludlow and the castle. He had assured his remaining captains that the group was going to Ludlow Castle for refreshment. In fact they fled, leaving the bulk of York's army to their fate.

Buckingham and the Queen were merciful to those left behind. Fined and imprisoned they may have been, but they were generally later pardoned. It was not they but Ludlow itself which was the immediate target of Lancastrian vengeance. In another dishonourable act, one designed to utterly humiliate York through showing him incapable of ensuring the well-being of his servants and retainers at the very heart of his own estates, Ludlow was treated as an alien foreign town. *Gregory's Chronicle* describes the scenes that followed:

> The misrule of the King's gallants at Ludlow, when they had drunk enough of the wine that was in the taverns and in other places, they full ungodly smote out the heads of the pipes and hogs heads of wine, that men went wet shod in wine, and then they robbed the town and bore away bedding, cloth and other goods and defiled many women.[25]

The *English Chronicle* confirms that Ludlow 'was robbed to the bare walls'.[26] The rape and pillage of Ludlow was a clear and deliberate sign to York: he may have saved his own life but he had lost everything else.

At the Coventry Parliament that followed the Yorkist debacle, York's duchess, Cecily, was allowed to retain some manors but lost her freedom.

She was placed in the custody of her elder sister Anne, Duchess of Buckingham, and subjected to choleric lectures from her brother-in-law, the Duke.[27] As for York's vast English estates and those of Warwick and Salisbury, all were confiscated. Some were kept by the Crown and the rest granted to the trio's fiercest Lancastrian enemies.

York, with his second son Edmund, Earl of Rutland, escaped to Ireland. Warwick, Salisbury and York's heir Edward, Earl of March, had, with some difficulty, reached Calais, kept secure for them by Salisbury's brother, Lord Fauconberg. Reports on the fate of Ludlow would undoubtedly have followed them to their new redoubts. But the news of the rampage of undisciplined troops and the sack of an important town was greeted with trepidation elsewhere; not least by the citizens of London.

Seven

——◆◈◈◈◆——

'A WARWICK'

A NEW KIND OF LORD
1453–60

Warwick was allowed back into Calais because he had linked the interests of the port's merchants and its garrison with his own. Their support was crucial—and not just for his temporary survival. The Pale of Calais was an enclave eighteen miles long by eight to ten miles deep on the Channel coast, surrounded by the Flanders lands of the Duchy of Burgundy, close to its border with France.[1] With the loss of all England's other continental territories, it was the sole English-governed area on the mainland of Europe. As such, it now acted as the secure entry point for all England's trade, though it had already long served that purpose for one particular product, which was by some distance the most important: wool.

Wool and woollen cloth were England's main source of wealth, for farmers, landlords, cloth producers and merchants. Duties on its trade provided the government with its largest source of revenue. Other countries, such as Spain, might export more fleeces, but no other wool could compare with England's finest.[2] The bulk was now being made into cloth close to source, but much was still being exported to feed the looms of Flanders through one place: Calais. The trade was so important that, in order to ensure its quality and supply, it operated as a staple, or monopoly of the Calais-based Merchant Staplers. In order to protect it, the town had a garrison of around two thousand troops, the largest single permanent force in the pay of the Crown.

Such a huge body of men was massively expensive to maintain and, most significantly, to pay. At a time of extreme pressure on expenditure, complicated arrangements were adopted to ensure that payments did not fall into arrears. Unfortunately, they had done so in the early 1450s, at a time of great threat to Calais from the French and Burgundians, and at a time when York and Somerset were competing for power. York went so far in 1452 as to accuse Somerset of planning to surrender Calais to the French, as he had Normandy. That was not the case, as shown by Somerset's efforts to get the men's arrears paid, efforts that were repeated by York during his first Protectorate. In 1454, just as York, frustrated by all normal means, was seeking to finalise an arrangement to pay the money with Robert White, the Mayor of the Staple, the garrison took matters into its own hands. Under the orders of Lords Rivers and Welles, its Lancastrian commanders, the garrison did what it had done with success on four previous occasions in the fifteenth century: it seized, as a form of guarantee, all the Staplers' wool stored in the port. This complicated matters to the point that neither York nor Somerset, on his brief return in 1455, could resolve them. As York's grip on government loosened once more in the early part of 1456, he was desperate that his ally Warwick should take up the command before it was too late. When Warwick finally took up his post, he and York were, at last, able to satisfy the garrison. Their settlement was secured with funds from England, together with the crucial support of the Staplers, by this time desperate for political and financial security.[3]

When Warwick arrived in April 1456 it appeared his stay was destined to last only as long as it would take Queen Margaret to engineer a change. However, he was still in place on 28 August the next year, when the French under de Brézé raided and sacked Sandwich, then a major port. With English fears of a French invasion heightened, national security dictated that the incompetent and irascible Duke of Exeter be replaced as Admiral by someone with proven martial prowess. That man was Warwick.

In modern-day England there are two positions, aside from that of prime minister, which invite singular focus from the tabloid press in its role as the purveyor of popular sentiment. The first of these is the manager of England's football team and the second, to a lesser extent these days, is the captain of its cricket team: defeat in these roles invites crushing criticism, if not derision. Failure is seen as an affront to national pride. For all classes in the proud xenophobic England of the fifteenth century, where sport had

not yet become a means of sublimating the aggression that formerly made
the successful practice of war the measure of a nation's sense of well-being,
the loss of France had been a devastating blow to the national psyche. The
population was united in its desperate need for a national hero who could
be celebrated in verse and song. Warwick, with his naval exploits, made
himself that man.

He did so by piracy. Piracy that was necessary to keep the garrison
paid in the absence of proper or timely funding from England. Piracy that
was focused on the shipping of those who were unpopular with the Calais
Staple and their allies the merchants of London. Most unpopular of all
were the Germans of the Hanseatic towns and the Italians granted special
licences to avoid the wool staple (special licences that had been granted for
personal profit by the lords at court). Thus, when three of Warwick's ships
sailed up the Thames as far as Tilbury, seized three Italian vessels loaded
with wool and cloth and sailed them back to Calais, Warwick himself was
eulogized. The nation was even more ecstatic when, in the summer of 1458,
he captured the exceptionally valuable cargo of the Hanseatic fleet. These
exploits had great popular value, and Warwick was the master when it
came to capitalizing on this.

These and similar actions led to friction with Margaret's court party
at home and ended with the Council's call to account that almost cost
Warwick his life at Westminster in November 1458. These same actions,
however, helped to merge the Yorkist interests with the commercial classes
of Calais and London. Calais was to provide the Yorkists with a power base
alongside their landed estates in England and Wales during the difficult
years up to 1459. Crucially it was to do so when those estates were barred to
them after the action at Ludford Bridge.

Margaret's response to the news that Warwick, Salisbury and March
had rejoined Salisbury's brother Lord Fauconberg in Calais was maladroit
in the extreme: the Crown imposed an embargo on all trade with Calais
in the winter of 1459–60 and instructed the Staplers to trade elsewhere. It
was a misjudgement of fundamental and lasting importance. The Staplers
turned to the Yorkists for their very preservation and secretly loaned them
the enormous sum of £18,000.[4] The loan proved to be essential.

Somerset and Trollope managed to land troops and suborn that part of
the garrison occupying one of Calais's outlying fortresses at Guînes. From

here young Somerset launched attacks, but these were fought off by the majority of the garrison, whose loyalty had been secured by Warwick. Somerset was further frustrated when some of his ships were blown into the harbour of Calais itself, enabling Warwick to settle scores with the men that he knew had 'deserted' with Trollope at Ludford Bridge, by having them killed without hesitation. The remainder of the captured troops were recruited or pardoned.

Warwick's main concern, however, was not with defence. He was planning the reinvasion of England. In the spring of 1460 he consulted York in Ireland, and on his return in May forced an intercepting fleet under Exeter, reinstated as Admiral, to take flight. There were also two daring raids on Sandwich. The first was in January 1460 when, led by John Dinham, the raiders captured the Lancastrian fleet preparing to sail against Warwick and its commanders, Lord Rivers, in his bed, and his son Sir Anthony Woodville. Dinham, with commandeered fleet, commanders and all, sailed triumphantly back into Calais harbour. The second raid, under Dinham, Sir John Wenlock and Fauconberg, destroyed another fleet preparing to invade and, once again, captured its commander. This time the men under Fauconberg's command stayed behind in Sandwich, having seized the town and established a bridgehead for invasion. In 1455, before Saint Albans, Fauconberg had been a potential peacemaker, but his efforts to deliver York's petition to the King had been blocked.[5] He had been a skilful commander for York in France; he was to be so again, but now in England.

The Yorkists had prepared the ground physically, but they also needed to promote a moral justification for their invasion, in terms of defending the 'common weal'. This they began to do by written manifesto, and by word of mouth, acting through agents centred on their favoured territory of Kent with emissaries throughout the South East.

Though they had been denied access to revenues from their estates for some time, they had been able to secure personal loans from the merchants of Calais.[6] The negotiations would no doubt have been assisted by the extremely welcome attentions of the strapping and rakish young Earl of March to the merchants' own wives and daughters.[7]

The Yorkists also found an unlikely fellow traveller and provider of spiritual guidance in the person of Francesco Coppini, Bishop of Terni and Papal Legate. Coppini 'was small of stature and undistinguished in appearance, but he had a strong personality and possessed energy, vivacity and eloquence'.[8] A Milanese by birth, Coppini served both Duke Francesco Sforza of Milan and Pope Pius II. This was not difficult: they were allied to each other and also to Don Ferrante, the new King of Naples, all in a firm anti-French alliance. This was the point where Italian and English politics touched: a previous, unceremoniously ousted, King of Naples was none other than René of Anjou, Queen Margaret's father. René had been trying to regain his realm ever since, with the active assistance of his ruthless son, John of Calabria. The desire to prevent any possibility of René's dutiful daughter from offering assistance, perhaps even in extraordinary alliance with her uncle, Charles VII of France,[9] would in itself have given Coppini reason for an anti-Lancastrian bias. But it had been reinforced by the extremely cool reception he personally received at Margaret's court in 1459, when seeking support for the papal initiative of a crusade to liberate Constantinople from its Turkish occupation of, then, just six years. In contrast, returning to the Burgundian court at Bruges, he had been courted by Warwick from nearby Calais. By June 1460 he was with Warwick's invasion party.[10] And thus England, regarded by the Italians as an island on the edge of Europe best known for its wool and cloth, was to be affected by the backwash of Italian political intrigue.

The Calais earls landed with their troops at Sandwich on 26 June. Their numbers rapidly swelled with Kentish recruits, both those long pre-arranged and those responding to organized proclamations such as one pinned to the gates of Canterbury and addressed to the Archbishop.[11] The earls marched immediately to that city, covering the dozen or so miles by nightfall. After offering scrupulous prayers at the tomb of Saint Thomas Becket, they marshalled their forces. Two days later they moved on London. There was no opposition—far from it: men flocked to their banners. On the evening of 1 July they reached Blackheath.

With the court in the Midlands and no leading magnate in the capital, the Lieutenant Governor of the Tower, Lord Scales, sought to establish himself, as in 1450, as the city's captain. London's Common Council denied him and said they would be responsible for their own defence 'without any aid of lords'.[12] It was an empty boast. Their messages to Warwick that they would resist him soon changed to acceptance of his loyalty to the King. Meanwhile Lord Scales and party fortified themselves in the Tower. On 2 July, the earls left their army outside the city gates at Smithfield and established their headquarters inside, at the house of the Grey Friars at Newgate.

Once inside London, Warwick's ability to command key interest groups soon became apparent. The Common Council capitulated to Warwick's requests: a baggage train was provided, victuals produced for the Yorkists but denied to Scales in the Tower. Most importantly, a loan of £1,000 was granted,[13] thus creating a financial interdependence. It was not yet the chain of mutual interest that bound the Yorkists with the Staplers at Calais, but with most of the merchants of the Staple being Londoners and with them handling most of the export of the wool through the city,[14] it certainly increased a link that was already forged.

Then it was the turn of the bishops in convocation at Saint Paul's: either of their own volition, through Warwick's appeals or swayed by Coppini, they agreed to go with the Yorkists to the King as potential peacemakers if nothing else.

Finally, Londoners as a whole, both propertied and unpropertied, were decisively with the Yorkists. Partly this was solidarity with the men from Kent, such as had been shown, at least initially, to Cade. Partly it was due to long-standing grievances against the absentee court, especially amongst those Londoners who had been impoverished by dislocations in trade and economic activity dating back to the end of the French Wars. This mood communicated itself to the city authorities. It was a mood which became uglier, with a new-found hostility to Scales, who, in retaliation against the Earl of Salisbury's artillery, was firing wildly and murderously into the city.

All were brought together by Yorkist propaganda, skilfully promoted by Warwick. This seemingly modern element was a crucial element of Warwick's success. His dashing naval feats as Captain of Calais in the late 1450s had given him the status of a popular hero. His actions after his return from Ludford Bridge, including his subordinates' daring attacks on Sandwich and the humiliating and cruelly entertaining capture of his foes, had amplified that status many times. He was at this moment the most charismatic man of his age. Now he was in London, dispensing vast hospitality, having verses written and songs composed and sung in his honour, and being greeted with cries of 'A Warwick! A Warwick!' wherever he went.

As well as the backing of the professional troops of the Calais garrison, Warwick could now count on vast numbers of new recruits: men from Kent and Sussex that he had attracted on the march. These men were absolutely essential, because the Yorkists, denied access to their own lands, needed to create a wave of popular support on which they could surf: 'a popular uprising focused and directed by the great nobility', for which 'Warwick was required to metamorphose from great magnate into popular demagogue'.[15]

Demagogue or not, he certainly grasped the real distress brought on by commercial dislocation at the end of the French Wars, exacerbated by Margaret's trade ban against Calais. He knew how to identify the concerns of his audience and 'was much loved by the commons of Kent and of London' because he promised to reform the 'hurts and mischiefs and grievances that reigned in this land'.[16] In his manifestos of 1459 and 1460 he used the language of the common weal to appeal to 'the same local militias of "fencible" men, raised by their elected constables of hundred and parish, who had turned out in 1450'.[17] This was no rabble, but the type of husbandmen, yeomanry and minor gentry who had formed the disciplined element of Cade's rebellion.[18]

In the hero of Calais, they had a new 'Captain', and one who was able to ensure that this rebellion would not become subverted by a mob. It might seem amazing that Warwick, who had the ability to be both haughty and brutal to those he considered not quite his peers, could embrace those far lower down the social scale. It may be that it was Warwick's own self-worth, his sense of entitlement that stemmed from birth, marriage and inheritance and pointed to his being blessed by providence, that led him to go far further than the Duke of York, who was always an aristocratic reformer, and to 'place himself at the head of the true commons in defence of the common weal'.[19] In short, Warwick had done something unprecedented. He had created a new affinity, one not based on ownership of land but on 'good lordship' pure and simple. He was the 'good lord', stepping into a vacuum of authority and promising to deliver and maintain the kind of justice and security that it normally fell to kings to provide.

The new recruits flocking to fight for the Yorkist cause were happy to serve, for pay of course, but for something more, too: the joy of serving someone who was at once truly charismatic and yet who, as we can see in the Yorkist Manifesto of 1460, was articulating complaints against the maladministration of the law and the burdens of taxation from the perspective of the commoners themselves.[20]

Thus far Warwick had organised, choreographed and orchestrated the popular reception. On 3 July, before the convocation of bishops at Saint Paul's and to the great throng that packed the cathedral and spilled into the surrounding streets, in what might justifiably be described as the greatest theatrical performance of his career, he articulated the Yorkist case. The four Calais earls were, he said, true subjects of the King, come to reform the government and to remove the evil councillors around him. Those named included Beaumont, Shrewsbury and Wiltshire: though the last, true to form, had fled the country. That these names were cited, rather than the already well-known Yorkist foes of Somerset, Northumberland, Clifford, Exeter, Egremont and Devon, underlined Warwick's claim that their focus was not on settling old scores but on aiding the King and helping him to provide good government. Beaumont was indeed still a core adviser and Shrewsbury, a former Treasurer, had been responsible for routine administration with Chancellor Waynflete; but they were not hot-heads and certainly, in comparison to the others, would in past years have been considered moderate. Also named was Buckingham, illustrating that there was now no room for compromise on either side. The middle ground had disappeared.[21]

Then, in the final act of their theatrical performance in the cathedral, the four Calais earls, Warwick, Salisbury, Fauconberg and March, swore their allegiance to Henry before Almighty God and on the Cross of Canterbury. This was met with loud approval from the massed crowds.[22]

The next day's activity struck a darker note. On 4 July, as the advance guard under Fauconberg set off from London, Coppini posted a message to Henry at Saint Paul's Cross. If not quite the noticeboard of the nation, Saint Paul's Cross was certainly the place where important announcements would be displayed for maximum effect. This was no confidential plea for time to negotiate reconciliation. After the normal obeisances due to a crowned king, Coppini delivered a chilling warning:

> I beg you for the love of God, for the devotion you have always shown, which served for pious and holy things to the extent of its powers, and out of the pity and compassion you should have for your people and citizens and your duty, to prevent so much bloodshed, now so imminent.

You can prevent this if you will, and if you do not you will be guilty in the sight of God in that awful day of judgment in which I also shall stand and require of your hand the English blood, if it be spilt.

In order that there may be no excuse before God and man, I repeat that your servants who came from Calais expressed their readiness to do everything for the welfare and honour of your Crown and the unity and peace of your realm, which I approve, and I offer that I will propose and attempt all those things which seem honourable to your Majesty if you keep an open mind and remove suspicion.

If you will not listen to what is right and true I am guiltless before Almighty God and the Holy Apostolic See and all the community, both cleric and lay, by the evidence of this letter, which I have had published, and I have also sent it by a faithful messenger of your Majesty's household, and so I am guiltless of the blood of your people if it is shed through the fault or negligence of yourself or others, when this could be prevented in the way I have shown. I expect a speedy reply, because the danger is imminent and does not brook delay.[23]

Delay did not suit Warwick. It was essential for the success of the Yorkist strategy that they move quickly to meet the King's party for negotiation or for battle before the full resources and authority of the Crown could be mobilized against them. The King's move from Coventry to Northampton, in cutting the distance between himself and London by a full third, actually aided them.

Only nine days after the landing at Sandwich, the main part of the Yorkist army left London on 5 July, making rapid time to Northampton and travelling the sixty-odd miles by the evening of 9 July. This was fast movement for an army that faced so much rain and took with it so many clergy, among them seven bishops (including the Archbishop of Canterbury) who were sent ahead in an attempt to petition the King and to negotiate a compromise. Legate Coppini was also willing to travel in person to the battlefield to underline his threat of excommunication. The Yorkists had a greater number of peers than the previous year, with the Duke of Norfolk, Viscount Bourchier and the Lords Abergavenny, Audley, Scrope of Bolton and the new Lord Saye all joining Warwick, Fauconberg and March. But it was the spiritual firepower that was most likely to overawe the pious Henry. Partly for that reason, the Duke of Buckingham, once again the Royal Commander, blocked all Yorkist attempts at negotiation on the 10th. Thus, after a final vain representation by Warwick Herald, the earls' troops moved forward in driving rain at around 2 p.m., watched, it is said, by the Archbishop and the Legate from the Eleanor Cross, which today is one of only three originals surviving.

Buckingham had been able to draw up his forces on ground of his choosing and it was a strong defensive position that faced Warwick. The Lancastrians had the bend of the River Nene at their backs, giving cover at their rear but also, to some degree, at their sides as well. These were protected by ramparts and with covering cannon, and in the front by boggy ground that the approaching Yorkists would have to cross. With the support of archers shooting from a stationary position, the Lancastrian troops of around five thousand would seem to be more than a match for the advancing seven thousand Yorkists.[24]

The continuing rain hampered both sides. For the Lancastrians, it made the cannon useless: 'the ordnance of the king's guns availed not, for that day was so great rain, that the guns lay so deep in the water, and were so quenched and might not be shot'.[25] Artillery may have proved highly effective when used by the French, both in reducing the English fortresses in Normandy and fired from a fixed position at the Battle of Castillon, but as field weapons they were still in their infancy and, not for the last time in these wars, proved to be a hindrance. Yet rain also disfavoured the Yorkists, it made the difficult ground more problematic and the ramparts more slippery to climb. It is possible that the Yorkists would, over a period of hours, have ground down the enemy defences. Yet, as Warwick knew in advance, it was all academic—once again a battle was to be decided by treachery. This time it was to the Yorkists' advantage.

At a pre-arranged signal, the men wearing the badge of the black ragged staff of Lord Grey of Ruthin, a major local landowner commanding the Lancastrian right, started helping the Earl of March's men to climb up the sides of the steep ramparts and into their own lines. Once the breach was made, the whole Yorkist army followed. Within half an hour of the troops' first engagement, the battle was at its climax. Buckingham and his sons-in-law Shrewsbury and the Neville-hating Egremont were slaughtered outside the King's tent by Warwick's fearsome men from Kent.[26] As was Beaumont, the last of Suffolk's inner core of seven and the only one who had escaped the proscriptions and violence of 1450. A great number of the common soldiers were drowned in the River Nene, trying to escape.

The chaos of battle brought an unexpected opportunity for one man. Sir William Lucy arrived late on the battlefield to assist the King at a time when the battle was effectively over. It was not over for him. He was killed by John Stafford, who had a personal reason for action, as he soon demonstrated by marrying Lucy's widow.[27]

As for Grey's reasons for treachery, it is unlikely that he was moved by Coppini's threat of excommunication. In common with Trollope's abandonment of Warwick at Ludford Bridge the previous year, Grey's motives were not specifically related to the King. It seems probable that his incentive was related to his securing property against the continuing attentions of the Duke of Exeter, just as it had been with a previous conspiracy, his involvement in the murder of Speaker Tresham in 1450. He obviously believed that he now had a better chance of success with the Yorkists than with the King.[28]

With Buckingham dead, Queen Margaret herself and younger and more accomplished commanders would ruthlessly direct the Lancastrian cause. As for Henry, though treated with all due deference, he was effectively an honoured but captured guest of Warwick, and was escorted to London to the Bishop's Palace, within the walled precincts of Saint Paul's Cathedral, and certainly not to the Tower.

The Lancastrian defeat at Northampton had made the Tower's surrender inevitable and Warwick made an example of seven defenders. These included John Archer, a councillor of the Duke of Exeter, and also, in a popular move with Warwick's Kentish troops, the Sheriff of Kent. All seven suffered the agony of a traitor's death: being hung, drawn and quartered. As for Lord Scales, Warwick granted him a safe conduct. Or rather, it was given but not ensured: his barge, en route to Westminster, was intercepted by vengeful Londoners. Scales was killed and stripped and his body, 'naked as a worm' was found at the porch of Saint Mary Overy in Southwark.[29] It was felt by many that Warwick might have done more to secure his safety.[30]

*   *   *

After Northampton, Warwick governed England with the King's Council in the name of the quiescent Henry. No one was in any doubt that a more permanent solution would have to wait upon York's return from Ireland for what, it was assumed, would be his third Protectorate.

For York himself, the contrast between his reception at Beaumaris in 1450 and that near Chester ten years later could not have been greater. In 1450, he had hurried back without government authority and found remnant members of Suffolk's household government striving hard to prevent him landing. In 1460 the only authority that mattered to him was his own.

His return was leisurely: he did not land until nearly thirteen weeks after Northampton. His onward journey took him almost five. This had been less of a return, more a statement of new intent. In Ludlow, the scene of his humiliation a year before, he was treated royally by his own people. His progress became more splendid as he travelled east. He was preceded by a sword carried vertically, like the sword of state, and his arms were now the Royal Arms. These were mere hints of what was to come. At last he arrived at Westminster on 10 October, three days after Parliament had assembled.

It is said that if you want anything to seem spontaneous, then you have to organize it. Whether what happened to York when he arrived in Westminster Hall was due to bad organization, an inability to agree amongst the main parties or complete stage fright from the supporting cast has been a matter of great debate. For what York did next was to place his hand on the throne, as an assertion of his claim to it. But whereas when Henry IV had claimed an 'empty throne' there had been organized acclamation, now there was only silence.

It was broken by Thomas Bourchier, the Archbishop of Canterbury, who had been a Yorkist ally in the attempts to parlay before Northampton. The Archbishop's question: 'Have you come to see the King?' was met with York's haughty response, 'I know of no person in this realm whom it does not behove to come to me and see my person rather than that I should go and visit him.'[31] Then with ill grace York left the Hall. He ordered the seals on the doors of the King's apartments in the Palace of Westminster to be broken and then took up occupation.

How could York have so miscalculated? Almost certainly because there had been no calculation at all. Whatever may or may not have been agreed with Warwick in Ireland, York had concluded that the captive King Henry had, de facto, abdicated.[32] And that God and providence had approved his own rightful claim to the throne. York had not consulted his experienced personal councillors—such as Oldhall, Herbert and Devereux—from whom, in Ireland, he had been separated. He had not sounded out the views of the nobility as a whole, whose support for a peaceful deposition would have been imperative; nor even those of his allies Warwick, Salisbury and his own son Edward, Earl of March. He had not consulted, because he had not felt the need to do so. Separated by his months in Ireland, isolated from his personal advisers and his noble allies, he felt that he had merely to issue a personal challenge at the Parliament summoned under the name of Henry VI, in order to set in motion what was a re-run, or rather a corrective re-run, of the events of 1399. Indeed, 'York's confidence was such that he even arranged for his own coronation to take place on 1 November.'[33]

Just as he had at Dartford in 1452, York had both acted rashly and misjudged completely the level of his support. He did not even have the Commons on his side as he had had in 1455.

It was a calamitous error. That it did not lead to a complete unravelling of the Yorkist political coalition, so painstakingly created by Warwick, was largely due to Warwick himself and to Bishop Coppini, the Papal Legate.

Warwick, with fierce support from Salisbury and from March, York's own son and heir, finally persuaded the Duke to allow the matter to be referred to the Lords. However, there was another problem inherent within that, for what should have been initiated by York as an informal process to measure support had now become a formal one. There was also no available constitutional mechanism to negotiate the removal of an anointed and crowned king. Indeed, the whole point of anointing and crowning a king was to give his actions and those of his ministers the complete authority that came from the permanence of that position: exactly the reason for the coronation of Henry VI as King of England at the age of seven and of France at the age of just ten.

There was also no precedent for the scenario of 1460. Certainly, English kings had been intentionally removed since the Conquest: these were the unfortunate 'seconds' of Richard II, Edward II and, arguably, William II. But all, whatever the niceties of explanation afterwards, had been by force. And in every case, the kings previously had personally and actively sought to extinguish the rights, power and lives of a crucial section of the nobility and in such a way that they could, in retrospect at least, be presented as having broken the coronation oath. This could not be alleged against Henry, whom Pope Pius II would describe as 'more timorous than a woman, utterly devoid of wit or spirit',[34] and who was still ensconced in the Queen's royal apartments in the Palace of Westminster.

On 16 October, York's claim to the throne through direct descent from Lionel, Duke of Clarence—the second adult son of Edward III—was placed before the Lords. The assembled peers in their turn, through the Chancellor, declared this to be a matter beyond their jurisdiction and referred it to the only authority higher than themselves: the King. At this, Henry, showing some spirit, instructed the Lords to compose the arguments against it. This they were forced to do, having tried in vain to involve the King's judges, who also declared it beyond their jurisdiction, concerning as it did the peerage and the Princes of the Blood. The Lords collectively gave York the arguments for the status quo: based on previous oaths of loyalty, parliamentary acts and York's own use of heraldic arms, they even included a largely disregarded argument put forward on behalf of Henry IV, that his ancestor, Edmund Crouchback, Earl of Lancaster, was actually the elder son of Henry III, and thus Henry had precedence not through John of Gaunt but through Gaunt's wife Blanche of Lancaster. That is to say that if York was going to claim precedence through the female line, King Henry could also do so and trump him.[35]

York's response to the serious part of the argument, that his claim had in essence lapsed, was magisterial: 'Although right for a time rests and is silenced, yet it does not rot nor shall it perish.'[36] It was a right he was determined to pursue.

On the twenty-fifth, the assembled lords spiritual and temporal suggested a compromise. It was one that would effectively give York the powers, if not the name of king. Put to Henry by Warwick's brother George Neville, Bishop of Exeter and Chancellor, it proposed that the King remain so for his lifetime, but then York himself, or more likely due to his greater age, York's heirs would inherit. No one can doubt what the King was being asked to do: to disinherit his only son.

Henry was completely isolated, with his long-time attendants dismissed and replacements who were more gaolers than companions. His wife, son, the larger part of a supportive nobility and key advisers were denied him. During this period, he feared for his life, timorously avoided York in the Palace of Westminster and was even seen distractedly considering the position of his tomb in Westminster Abbey. There was no expectation of the superb memorial at Eton now. Perhaps worst of all, Legate Coppini intervened in the Pope's name, suggesting, no doubt, a great threat to Henry's soul in the afterlife. Certainly Pius II himself thought Coppini to have been decisive, writing 'by the wisdom of the Legate the dispute was settled'.[37] The priestly King would have been no match for the worldly priest. Faced with all these pressures, the increasingly pathetic Henry agreed to the compromise on the thirty-first. The next day, with his nobles, he processed to Saint Paul's and thus marked his public acceptance of the Accord.

It is hard not to feel pity for the King in this situation, one with which he was completely inadequate to cope and one from which he had no ability to escape.

Henry's new position was soon made painfully clear to him forcefully and physically, when on the night of the thirty-first he was removed 'against his will' from Westminster and taken back to the Bishop of London's Palace. George Neville later referred to Henry as 'that puppet of a king',[38] and this was exactly how York and his supporters treated their sovereign.

There was one final snare for the enfeebled Henry. The Yorkist lords introduced an article of faith which trapped him in a pact of mutual obligation. York and his eldest sons, the Earls of March and Rutland, 'made a promise and oath, according to the said agreement and settlement, on condition that the King, for his part should duly keep and observe the same settlement and act thereon, *which the King at that time promised to do* [author's italics]. And then the said duke and earls immediately requested that this condition, and also the said promise made by the King, might be formally recorded.'[39] Its full significance would be revealed in just a few months.

THE SUN IN SPLENDOUR

CIVIL WAR
1460-61

The Act of Accord did more than just look to the future in settling the succession on York and his heirs, it sought to make the Yorkist ascendancy permanent. Having sworn that he would do nothing to shorten Henry VI's natural life, York expected the same in return. He may not have been crowned, but York's person was now sacred: any plot to harm him would be considered treason.

York may not have had the title of king, but he expected to rule as one and in this he was strongly supported by Warwick. The Earl of Warwick may have had doubts about York replacing Henry as king, but he showed no reservations about pursuing the best way forward. Even before the June invasion from Calais, Coppini had been the recipient of Warwick's frank view of the King and his capabilities, as 'a dolt and a fool who is ruled instead of ruling. The royal power is in the hands of his wife and those who defile the king's chamber'.[1] This may or may not have been Warwick's real view of Henry's mental capacity from the moment he saw a catatonic king at Windsor in 1454. It was certainly his view in 1460.

The kingly power and the Crown's assets were henceforth, so the Yorkists believed, with them. York was given the Duchy of Cornwall and he and his sons were awarded vast sums of money taken from the revenues of the Duchy of Lancaster, not to mention the Principality of Wales and the Earldom of Chester, all to be under the supervision of the new Lord Treasurer—the Earl of Warwick. There was no longer any suggestion from

York, as in 1456, of restricting the Crown's power for the good of the common weal. This was no mere reversal of the forfeiture of their titles and estates suffered by the Yorkists after Ludford Bridge.

This was England's own particular version of the Treaty of Troyes, closely mirroring that agreement which had made Henry V heir to the Crown of France. As then, the previously accepted heir to the throne had been ruthlessly discarded. There was, however, one signal difference: this particular queen was not going to declare her son a bastard and give away his inheritance. The venom of this 'great and strong laboured woman'[2] towards York is still apparent in a letter to the City of London of several months later: '[York] of very pure malice, proposed to continue in his cruelness, to our utter undoing and that of our son, the prince, [has promulgated] several untrue and feigned matters and surmises'.[3] Foremost amongst these of course were slurs against the prince's legitimacy: what had been the stuff of popular ballad at the time of the 1460 invasion had become official Yorkist propaganda.

Both from York's perspective and according to the Parliament of 1460, the preservation of the public good and common weal was reliant upon York's repression of 'great rebellions'[4]—i.e. those in support of Margaret and the rights of her son. York was now the overriding legitimate authority and all who opposed him would be committing treason.

York left the capital for the North on 9 December. With him went Salisbury, Rutland and, at this stage, just a few hundred men. York had raised money for the payment of troops and purchase of supplies from London's Common Council. But he received only half of the money he requested for he refused to give them the securities they sought.[5] Warwick was to remain in London with the King. March, meanwhile, was in the Welsh borders, raising troops.

Had it been the normal campaigning season, York would no doubt have paused in a pro-Yorkist territory well south of the Trent, raising his own forces and waiting for his sons to arrive. But this was outside the normal season and usual weather for warfare. Driving rain hit them on the march and it was sufficiently bad for York to send his artillery train back southwards.[6]

There was a skirmish with Lancastrian troops at Worksop, probably under Somerset's command.[7] This further demonstrated Somerset's utter contempt for the Yorkists, for he thus reneged at the first opportunity on a remarkable agreement he had reached with Warwick. It was indeed singular, because the otherwise efficiently brutal Warwick, on returning in the autumn to Calais, had allowed Somerset to march out of Guînes on the understanding that he would not take up arms again.[8] It showed a remarkable underestimation of both the strength and hatred of the Lancastrians.

From Worksop, York's small army continued north and west to his northern redoubt of Sandal Castle at Wakefield. He was on his own lands, but surrounded, for the most part, by those of his enemies.

Historians have speculated about York's motives for advancing to Wakefield.[9] He probably did so for one of two strategic reasons. Either he intended to go there from the first and expected acquiescence in the Accord from all but the Queen, the Prince and a small group of Lancastrian diehards. Or he diverted from an initial intention to stay south of the Trent and was drawn to Wakefield to protect his estates and those of his loyal retainers from devastation by his enemies. In short, if the latter, to take on the protective role he had been forced to abandon so shamefully at Ludlow, just fourteen months before.

There may have been another, more immediate reason, that he made, in Legate Coppini's words 'a rash advance'.[10] He could have been taking advantage of a seasonal truce negotiated between himself and Somerset that was due to last over the Christmas period.[11]

If so, it was a grave misjudgement. Somerset and the older, experienced Trollope were extremely capable commanders—the contemporary Burgundian Chronicler Chastellain singled out Somerset for praise, as did Gregory,[12] while another chronicler was to describe Trollope as '*Magno capitaneo and quasi ductore belli*'.[13] To add to that, there was: 'A new style of military leadership among the Yorkists' opponents—devious, inventive and quick to exploit opportunities'.[14]

There had also been a fundamental change in the Lancastrian attitude. According to Professor Anthony Goodman: 'The complacency shown by York and Salisbury over Christmas may have stemmed partly from a failure to grasp that they were dealing with opponents no longer prepared to keep faith with them'.[15] In terms of 'faithlessness', one need look no further than

Somerset, Northumberland and Clifford, all of whom remembered how their fathers had been brutally killed at Saint Albans, and who were all currently serving with the Queen's army. The Queen herself was in Scotland, seeking aid and troops from Mary of Guelders, Regent and mother of the eight-year-old James III.[16]

The Lancastrian forces approached Sandal Castle on 30 December. It is not known how greatly York's numbers had grown since leaving London, but two recent specialists on the battle, Haigh and Cox, believe they had reached between five and six thousand,[17] the great majority of whom would have camped outside the castle, which during a truce would have been practicable. The exact numbers of both sides may be unclear to us. Most pertinently, however, the Lancastrian numbers, through a laxity in Yorkist scouting that was inexcusable even during a declared truce, were unclear to the Duke of York himself.

York may have reasoned that Sandal, which could only maintain around five hundred, and that with difficulty, would thus not be able to withstand even a short siege in winter. He may also have estimated the Lancastrian numbers on the basis of those he could see on the open ground before him. But it seems doubtful that the Battle of Wakefield was prompted by an attempted breakout from entrapment, as has been traditionally thought, or by the even more unlikely decision to commit all York's forces to defend a forage party.

York came on to the field of battle not under duress but in the expectation of an overwhelming victory. In so doing the Duke was not a victim of rashness but, for the final time, of his own overbearing sense of honour and rectitude. With the effective executive authority of a king, given to him by the Act of Accord, York had ordered additional troops under a Commission of Array: a form of recruitment that, short of treason, could not be refused. That such a commission should have been issued is not surprising, but the identity of its recipient certainly was:[18] Lord John Neville—not Warwick's brother, but the younger brother of Ralph, 2nd Earl of Westmorland. As a member of the disinherited elder branch of the Neville family, a victim of the machinations of Duchess Joan and her brother Cardinal Beaufort, Lord John Neville was a man who had everything to gain from the destruction of York and Salisbury. Yet York assumed Neville would recognize that he was acting with the full authority of the anointed Henry VI as well as himself and would have no hesitation in actively supporting him against the Queen and her 'treasonous' followers.

Thus when the arrival of the Lancastrians on the battlefield was followed, perhaps even after battle was joined, by the arrival of Lord John Neville with up to eight thousand troops,[19] York's confidence would have been high. He expected to have the advantage in terms of position and, logic would dictate, numbers, otherwise he would not have responded to the initial Lancastrian deployment by moving his own troops to well beyond the security of the castle.

Yet Lord John Neville's actions had not been coordinated with York in mind, but in consort with Somerset and the Lancastrians. The arrival of his troops at the Yorkist lines was not to support the Duke and the cadet branch Nevilles, but to entrap them.

The trap being set, it was then sprung. Within minutes the bulk of the Yorkist forces, including York himself, were surrounded and fighting for their lives, with York trying desperately and vainly to retreat. It is said that York was offered the chance to surrender. Like Somerset at Saint Albans five years before, he could have had little doubt what his enemies intended for him. Within just over half an hour, the battle and York's life were over.

Some Yorkists did escape the battlefield. York's second son, the seventeen-year-old Earl of Rutland, was caught by Clifford's troops near the Chantry chapel on Wakefield Bridge that survives to this day. There, no doubt relishing the symbolism of revenge on the son of the man he held responsible for the death of his father, Clifford stabbed Rutland to death.

Salisbury got further away but was captured and taken to Pontefract Castle. Somerset was prepared to ransom him, albeit for a 'great sum of money', but 'the common people of the country, who loved him not, took him out of the castle by violence and smote off his head'.[20] The mob acted, it is believed, at the instigation of William Holland, the bastard son of the 1st Duke of Exeter.[21] Certainly Warwick believed it, as three months later, when Holland was captured in Coventry, he saw to it that Holland was killed without hesitation.

York may have been dead, but the Lancastrian revenge was not yet complete. York and Rutland were decapitated. Their heads, together with those of Salisbury and his younger son Sir Thomas Neville, together with those of the more significant knights killed at Wakefield, were sent to the city of York, where they were mounted on poles on the top of Micklegate Bar. The Duke was given the added indignity of a paper crown.

Edward, Earl of March, York's heir, was recruiting in the West when he heard the dreadful news from Wakefield. Both he and Warwick, the surviving Yorkist leaders, regarded the Lancastrians as guilty of appalling treachery and of breaching all rules of chivalry. This might be thought extraordinary after Saint Albans, Northampton and even Blore Heath, and after the Yorkist 'treason' against the Crown and the 1460 Act of Accord. But Wakefield was added to the Yorkists' own list of festering resentments, to join the attempted assassinations of the late 1450s, the humiliation at Ludford Bridge, the rape of Ludlow, the despoliation of their estates and the displacement of their followers.

Whatever the Yorkist cousins' feelings, their position had become perilous. March urgently sought to gather troops while trying to anticipate the movement out of Wales of Jasper Tudor, Earl of Pembroke, the King's half-brother. Pembroke must not be allowed to break through towards London to join up with Margaret's forces. Warwick, in London, was once again the propagandist, this time seeking to energize London and the southern counties through promoting fear of the northern people about to move against them.

The Lancastrians were not fearful—far from it. They were exultant. Queen Margaret, who had proved herself to be a highly skilled organizer in the months after Northampton, immediately prepared to leave Scotland, accompanied by a number of Scottish troops.

When the 1460–61 campaign began the adherents of the two sides were spread across the whole country, albeit unevenly. Yet by January 1461 a marked regional divide had set in. There were still many potential Yorkist recruits in the North and, similarly, Lancastrians in the South. However, due to the different areas of territorial domination and both the need and the ability to recruit and provision, the army moving southwards across the Trent in support of Margaret and Prince Edward was largely one of Northerners.

In the Midlands, potential recruitment was more balanced. Certainly, the Queen had established herself in the late 1450s as a major power in the region. She had then been able to command in the name of the King and the royal prerogative; but the latter, with the passive Henry lodged in the Tower of London, was officially with Warwick.

With the Queen's army closing in, Warwick urgently set about arraying troops drawn from the towns and the counties of the South East, chiefly those around London. There had also been some recruitment in the prosperous areas of East Anglia, but here, as the *Paston Letters* show, the picture was more mixed.[22] As for much-needed finance, the Yorkists were able to call upon London's Common Council, which 'in defence of the realm' was willing to advance four times as much as they had to York only a short time before.

By 12 January, Margaret's army had reached Beverley, which they immediately pillaged. This was a different type of force to those that had fought the battles of 1455 and 1459–60, partly because the distance it had to travel from starting point to objective was so much further; partly because provisioning during winter was much more difficult; and partly because any connection that the common soldiers might have had with the local people they encountered lessened with every additional mile they moved south. Thus was created a swathe of despoliation up to thirty miles wide, as alien-looking and harsh-sounding men with incomprehensible accents demanded food and ale. Sometimes money was proffered. On other occasions, when towns and estates were targeted that were thought to be pro-Yorkist, then it most certainly was not.

And with the troops came anarchy. As one fearful chronicler from Crowland Abbey described, 'paupers and beggars flocked forth . . . in infinite numbers . . . and universally devoted themselves to spoil and rapine, without regard of place or person'. It was a fear accentuated by a sense of personal risk:

> For really we were in straits, when word came to us that this army, so execrable and so abominable, had approached to within six miles of our boundaries. But blessed be God, who did not give us for a prey unto their teeth! For, after the adjoining counties had been given up to dreadful pillage and spoil . . . that we may here confess the praises of God, in that at the time of His mercy, He regarded the prayers of the contrite, and in His clemency determined to save us from the yoke of this calamity.[23]

Those who had witnessed the depredations of Margaret's army, arriving as refugees in safer towns and villages, spread the fear with their tales of what had befallen them—or that was certainly the narrative increasingly promoted by Warwick.

Yet, because of the difficulties of marching in winter, the army's progress was slow. The distance between Beverley and London, as the crow flies, is just over 160 miles. Partly due to their circuitous route, after a full month the Lancastrian forces were still over 30 miles to the north of the capital. However, this length of time heightened the sense of dread that gripped the city, with Warwick busily fomenting it. It was a sign of his desperation, yet in portraying these fellow countrymen as aliens, Warwick dehumanized them in the eyes of his followers. This can be seen in a letter from Clement Paston, a student in London, to his brother, written on 23 January: 'In these parts, every man is well willing to go with my Lords here and I hope God shall help them, for the people in the north rob and steal and are set to pillage all this country and give away men's goods and livelihoods'.[24]

Papal Legate Coppini had a more particular fear—and with good reason. After his powerful support of the Yorkists the previous summer and his role in the disinheritance of Prince Edward, he could expect no mercy from Queen Margaret. This showed in the letter he wrote on 9 January 1461 to his subordinate, Lorenzo de Florencia, who had remained with the Queen:

> We are writing to you, as we cannot proceed in person to the Queen and the lords with her, as you know. First and foremost, as the basis of everything, we require you to declare and offer on your own behalf, that should it ever be found that we have excommunicated or cursed any one assisting her Majesty or being with her, or if we have ever committed or consented to such things, we will gladly be flayed alive or torn asunder, for we excommunicated no one, cursed no one and wronged no one at any time in this kingdom, but we shall be ready to do all these things and more still, if we are called upon to do so for her Royal Highness.[25]

Furthermore, he was terrified that he might find himself dangerously within her reach if the Lancastrians triumphed in battle, because Warwick fully expected him to rejoin the Yorkist army and again to threaten his enemies with excommunication.

Both sides fully appreciated the importance of the Legate's authority. Warwick had been trying to enhance it and had been seeking a cardinalate for his ally since the previous August. The Lancastrians in their turn 'had put about the report that he was not a legate and the Pope had recalled him and was displeased about the things which had happened through his efforts'.[26] In January, after Wakefield, Warwick redoubled his own efforts, writing both to the Pope and to the Duke of Milan and stressing that Coppini's promotion to cardinal was crucial: 'The people will then see that our adversaries . . . daily scorn your authority and the legate's . . . adding marvellous falsehoods to make him unpopular, to the detriment of the Church and the king'.[27] Warwick was working hard to secure what would have been a glorious promotion for Coppini—and he expected something very important from the priest in return.

Coppini was in a singularly unenviable position. His dilemma and his excuses were later succinctly described by Prospero di Camulio, Milan's Ambassador to France, in a letter to his ducal master: 'He [Coppini] promised Warwick to go into the camp and excommunicate the enemy and give the benediction to the followers of Warwick'. But 'seeing the bad weather, and the Queen's power, and not feeling well, he did not go. At this Warwick took offence'.[28] Having angered two extraordinarily powerful and vengeful people, on 10 February Coppini sensibly opted for the lesser risk of crossing the Channel at an extremely hazardous time of year.

Although this deprived Warwick of the immediate spiritual power of the legate, he still had that of the divinely anointed King. When what was now being described as the royal army marched north from London to face the forces of Henry's Queen and Prince, Warwick made sure he took Henry with him.

As in 1455, the strategically placed town of Saint Albans was to provide the point of collision for the two armies. There were a great number of similarities in the way that the two battles of Saint Albans unfolded, including an attack from an unexpected direction, an outflanking manoeuvre down undefended alleyways, and the need to withdraw troops from prepared positions in order to sustain a battle line under severe pressure.

But there were also crucial differences. This was no 'scuffle in the street'; for one thing, the armies were much larger. Also Warwick's troops, of around nine to ten thousand men, this time arrived well before his foes. He, with the Dukes of Norfolk and Suffolk, the Earl of Arundel and a small number of other peers, including Warwick's own brother John—recently ennobled as Lord Montagu—and their uncle Lord Fauconberg, prepared a formidable defensive position in the centre and to the north of the town. Warwick was able to utilize the latest in military hardware, medieval anti-personnel devices such as caltrops: large, spiked metal balls that would be half buried in the ground, ready to impale men's feet or shred the hooves of any horses that rode over them. Another innovation was the pavisse, a large spiked shield that could be dug into the ground, with shooting holes like miniature arrow slits so that the user could continue the assault with greater protection from enemy shot. Then there were spiked nets that could be expanded or contracted and fitted together to give defence against both infantry and cavalry. In addition to these, Warwick had Burgundian hand gunners, who were capable of firing specialized arrows of forty-five inches as well as the usual stone shot.[29]

The chronicler Gregory and Abbot Whethamstede both give accounts of what happened. It seems that on this occasion, both were eyewitnesses. Gregory places himself more specifically, with his dismissive comments on horsemen and by writing that 'in the footmen is all the trust'.[30] It is from these two accounts that one is able to bring together the different elements of a confused and confusing picture.

Warwick, who had been such a dashing and decisive attacking com-mander in 1455, now proved himself to be an indecisive and uncertain defensive general. Having created such a strong position, he decided, on the basis of one report that the northern army was still nine miles away to the north-east, to move to a new position in that direction, covering both the Luton and Wheathampstead roads, whilst preserving a force of archers near the abbey. However the intelligence was false. The Lancas-trians had already diverted westwards to Dunstable to attack and smash through a Yorkist forward post; and, astonishingly, were well advanced on the near-thirteen mile advance to Saint Albans before Warwick real-ized the true situation.

The Lancastrian army of around twelve thousand men, wearing the livery of the Prince of Wales, reached the town and attacked in the early morning of Shrove Tuesday, 17 February. They struck just east of the abbey and against a still well-defended position by the Eleanor Cross, where they were beaten off. But in a mirror image of 1455, Trollope then made a flanking move through 'the backsides' gardens and the alleyways to the west of the market place. This took them to the top end of Saint Peter's Street and round the Yorkist barriers, with the Queen's forces striking the defending archers to the south and rear. Still the Yorkist defenders held and, particularly at the abbey end of the defences, inflicted severe casualties on their opponents.[31]

Warwick could not properly reinforce the archers. His other troops were disadvantaged by the need to reverse their position from facing north-east to south-west and by the need to move their own defensive paraphernalia—the caltrops, pavisses and nets. By noon, it was too late even to contemplate aiding the beleaguered bowmen. They had become completely isolated as the main bulk of the Lancastrian troops attacked Warwick's hastily reorganized vanguard. This held firm, but the archers were wiped out.

Military historians differ as to the reason why Warwick did not reinforce and extricate the archers. Some believe that the raw quality of Warwick's troops meant he could not trust them to make the necessary complicated manoeuvres. Others that he established a solid enough position for fighting a defensive action until nightfall, and thus, at the sacrifice of his archers, enabled the bulk of his forces to get away. It is probable that both armies, composed largely of undisciplined raw troops, were undertaking manoeuvres which only the more professional of the soldiery would have been capable of executing properly. Thus it seems certain that the bulk of soldiers did not actively engage, but of those that did, it was the Lancastrians, both able to move more freely and better marshalled, who were to prove the more effective.

Warwick was also hampered by a turn in the weather, with adverse wind and snow constricting movement and arrow range and rendering the combustible Burgundian guns more of a danger to themselves and to their allies than to the enemy.

One factor did come to Warwick's aid: the shortness of the winter day. With darkness approaching, he and four thousand of his force broke through the Lancastrian lines and headed west. Many of his troops in the

engaged vanguard also managed to escape the battlefield under cover of
darkness, though his brother Lord Montagu did not. Thus, with the exception of the archers in the town, the Yorkist losses in terms of manpower
were far lighter than the strategic defeat might have warranted.

But as a strategic defeat it was momentous. The road to London lay
open, leaving the capital at the mercy of Queen Margaret's unruly and
much-feared army. Furthermore, Warwick had lost more than the battle.
Momentously, in the confusion, he had also lost the King.

In a repeat of 1455, Henry was taken to the abbey. He was there reunited
with his Queen, with his son the Prince and with the Lancastrian lords,
including Somerset, Northumberland and Clifford.

The role of Trollope in this victory and his importance for the Lancastrian cause was recognized when he was the first to be knighted by the
young Prince.[32] He had been wounded by a caltrop, but he had not found
his immobility a problem, as he said to the Prince: 'My lord I have not
deserved it for I slew but fifteen men, for I stood still in one place and they
came unto me, but they bode still with me.'[33]

One of the inner circle of Lancastrian lords was the former Sir Thomas
Courtenay, now Earl of Devon, and it is likely that he, infamous for the
treatment of Nicholas Radford in 1455, took on a persuasive role in what
happened next.

The duties during the battle of Lord Bonville and Sir Thomas Kyriell, veteran of the French Wars, had been to ensure that the King was
kept safe and to protect him from any possible harm, but their role as non-
combatants counted for nothing in the face of Devon finding himself with
the opportunity to dispose of Bonville, his family's long-term hated rival.[34]

In such circumstances, it seems odd that the lives of Lord Montagu and
of Lord Berners, who was captured with him, were spared. Yet there was
a very good reason: their survival gave Somerset surety for the life of his
younger brother, a prisoner of the Yorkists in the Tower of London.

London, meanwhile, was in a state of panic. With Warwick having fed the
citizens with tales of Lancastrian troops leaving a trail of destruction in
their wake, Londoners were convinced that a terrible fate awaited them.

After all, the Queen's soldiers would, for the most part, have no sense of connection with the capital and no compunction in sacking it.

Yet the Queen held back. Was this because she was worried that London would be sacked, or was she swayed by the pleas of the dowager Duchesses of Bedford and Buckingham on behalf of the city authorities? It seems highly unlikely. If London was concerned about Margaret, then she, in her turn, had concerns about London. After all, five years earlier she had taken the decision to leave the city and move the court to the Midlands. The great palaces in and around London had since then received only the occasional visit from the King, until he fell into the Yorkists' clutches after the Battle of Northampton. Even the Palace of Westminster itself, the centre of government since Edward III, had been completely neglected between the middle of August 1456 and September 1457 and, after that, had been used very sporadically and just for a few days at a time. This abandonment would have hurt London's pride, but more importantly it would have hit the pockets of those citizens, be they rich merchants or poor artisans, who supplied the provisions and luxury goods that all but the personally austere King seemed to require.

So far as the common people were concerned, Margaret was the French queen who had brought no dowry but who, through her plotting on behalf of Charles VII, had been responsible for the shameful end of the French Wars. It was not true; but it was what they believed that mattered. In contrast, York had been the popular 'heir' of Gloucester, while Warwick had been hailed as the charismatic Captain of Calais, his successes at sea at last restoring some national pride. Thus when the cautious city authorities agreed to supply victuals to Margaret's army, it was the common citizenry that first held the provisions back and then distributed them amongst themselves.[35]

Even as four aldermen of London negotiated with four 'cavaliers' of the Queen's party as to when and with how many troops the victorious Lancastrians would enter the city, all waited for news from the west. On 20 February, three days after Saint Albans, negotiations broke down and the Queen, who had advanced to Barnet, withdrew back to Dunstable.

Whether additional talks would have brought a resolution cannot be known, as later that same day came the news that the youthful Earl of

March had won a spectacular victory in the West at Mortimer's Cross and his army had closed much of the distance that separated the Welsh Borders from London.

The dynamic for Margaret immediately changed. It was possible that her northern levies might just have held together for an occupation of London, but there was the danger that they would break ranks and disperse in an orgy of looting and pillage. If they did, the Earl of March—with fresher troops and reinforced with Warwick's regrouped forces—would have been able to retake a devastated city. Another option would have been to head off March's forces, but to achieve that Margaret would need reinforcements from the Earl of Pembroke in the West. And even if those reinforcements arrived, there was a risk that her own troops, denied the plundering of London, would disintegrate in battle and desert for home. The safest option seemed to be to withdraw to Lancastrian heartlands in the Midlands and the North. There, with Henry back at her side, she would be able to recruit reinforcements in the name of the anointed King, while the Yorkists would be placed at the additional disadvantage of having to march towards her. An action they would need to take in order to secure their very survival.

Taking a fundamental decision, the martial Queen Margaret opted to turn back towards the North.

Had Margaret been able to occupy London and establish order over the city and the neighbouring areas of the South East, then the Yorkists would have been vanquished. If the threat of March to the West had abated, then Margaret would have been able to re-order and bring greater discipline to her forces. An accommodation between her and the London Court of Common Council would then have been inevitable. And they in turn would have helped to enforce the acceptance of what would have been an increasingly quiescent citizenry. Margaret would thus have secured her place as Regent for the next decade, until such time as her talented young son could take over the practice of government.

It is in this context that the strategic importance of the young Earl of March's victory at Mortimer's Cross in Herefordshire was out of all proportion to the numbers involved—with just a few thousand on each side.

*   *   *

Modern readers might wonder that the eighteen-year-old Edward, Earl of March, did not simply crumble on the news of his father's death. But eighteen was not so young at a time when sixteen-year-olds were expected to fight. Henry II and Edward III, both great imposing Plantagenet kings, had fought battles and managed the affairs of state at a similar age.

Moreover, March was no ordinary eighteen-year-old, being an imposing giant of six foot three and a half inches, blessed with inordinate vitality, physical and sexual, both of which he put to good use. As one of the Calais earls, he had been happy to be led by Warwick, but now he was operating independently. He was also, of course, independent of the Duke of York, his late father, who had been an aloof man and a very different character to his son. Where York was 'proud and reserved', Edward of March was noted for his 'charm and affability'.[36] So different was March from his father (not to mention his much smaller younger brothers, George and Richard) that it was later alleged he was not a son of York at all, but that of an archer named Blaybourne, having been conceived during one of the Duke's absences from Rouen. This can be dismissed for a number of reasons: it wasn't raised until much later and then for political reasons; it wasn't believed overseas;[37] and it certainly did not accord with the pious nature of Duchess Cecily.[38]

Edward was as remorseless as his father had been when it came to the pursuit of his own interests, but unlike his father, he was possessed of a personal magnetism that claimed the support of others. His charm was liable, however, to vanish in an instant—particularly when he came under threat. Those who actively opposed him were to find that he was capable of a brutality even surpassing that of his cousin Warwick.

In the aftermath of Wakefield, March nursed an intense hatred for those who had been responsible for the killing of his father and, perhaps even more on account of his younger brother Edmund, Earl of Rutland. The two had been extremely close; only a year apart in age, from the time they were six and seven they had shared a household separate from their parents.[39] And now Rutland was dead, killed by Clifford in what March knew to have been particularly hideous circumstances.

The death of his father had left March himself under immediate threat. His only hope had been to manoeuvre his own troops strategically to intercept those of Jasper Tudor—the Earl of Pembroke and King Henry's half-brother—before they could reinforce Margaret in her move on London. This he successfully achieved at Mortimer's Cross. Like Blore Heath, it is not a well-documented battle. That said, it is possible to reconstruct what happened.[40]

Since the battle was fought in the Duchy of York's own heartlands and on the estates of their staunch associate Sir Richard Croft, it is likely that the Yorkist core would have been March's own retainers and those of his close allies. With no prospect of an ordered retreat, March had to make full use of his positional advantage, so Croft's local knowledge would have been invaluable, particularly in winter, with the river swollen and the ground boggy. He would most likely have opted to block Pembroke's route so that the bridge over the twenty-foot-wide River Lugg was directly at his back.

Pembroke had his own inner core of troops, made up of Welshmen like himself. He also had Irish, Breton and French mercenaries under the command of Wiltshire the 'flying earl'. The third Lancastrian battlefield commander was Pembroke's own father, Owen Tudor, who so many decades before had married Henry V's widowed queen.

As the troops on both sides prepared to face death on that dark February day, they witnessed a great feat of nature: in the sky above them they saw not one pale sun, but three. This phenomenon is understood today as a parhelion: when the sun shining through ice crystals creates the effect of a mirror and those below see the sun twice reflected. In that pre-scientific age, however, March could interpret it as a sign from God. March took it to signify two things: firstly, a blessing from the Father, the Son and the Holy Ghost; and secondly, that the intended recipients were another trinity, the surviving three Yorkist brothers, March himself and his two younger brothers, George and Richard. This he powerfully communicated to his troops, now an inspired force.

March's battle tactics were risky. He aimed to hold Pembroke's centre in check, but to let the Lancastrian wings move forward into marshy pockets near the river where they would be picked off by archers as they made for obvious crossing points. In this way he would take advantage of any lack of cohesion of movement in the enemy troops. His own soldiers would have to hold firm.

This was exactly how the battle proceeded: Pembroke's centre weakened through its need to aid the wings who had become sitting targets in the boggy ground. It weakened and then broke. Fleeing through their opponents' heartlands, the chances for escape for the common soldiery would have been greatly reduced. There were better opportunities for those who could escape on horseback, including Pembroke himself. Not, of course, before Wiltshire added spectacularly to his reputation as the flying earl, again escaping in disguise, but this time at the battle's very outset.[41]

One man who did not escape was Pembroke's father, Owen Tudor. With other important captives he was taken to Hereford and summarily beheaded. The confused old man did not understand the temper of the times; even when faced with the axe and the block, he was still expecting a pardon. It was not until the collar of his red velvet doublet was ripped off to ease the passage of the coming blow that he grasped his fate. His head was taken and placed on the market cross, where it was later tended by a mad woman. After washing the blood from his face and combing his hair, she placed a hundred burning candles around the severed head.[42] This act, tender, even pious in its intent, but gruesome in its context, served to mirror the distortions of a troubled age.

March did not delay long after the battle but started towards London. At Chipping Norton he rendezvoused with Warwick's re-assembled forces. It is very possible that Warwick excused his own defeat to his young cousin by putting the blame then, as he was later to do, on the betrayal of a Kentish captain called Lovelace. On 27 February, accompanied by 'a great power of men, but few of name' March and Warwick entered the city of London.[43]

Once there, the full meaning of the 1460 Act of Accord and the oaths for its acceptance became clear. Henry having broken the conditions he had been given, March now stood to inherit more than his father's dukedom.

Two days after his arrival in London, Edward of March was acclaimed by Londoners as well as Yorkist troops—a gathering of up to four thousand—at Saint John's Fields in Clerkenwell and his title to the throne was outlined by George Neville, the Lord Chancellor.[44]

On 3 March, at Baynard's Castle, just east of modern Blackfriars, the available Yorkist lords together with the Archbishop of Canterbury and the Bishops of Salisbury and Exeter took a momentous if inevitable decision. The next day, in Westminster Hall, March was proclaimed Edward

IV, the new King of England. For full propaganda effect, the ceremony needed to be magnificent. And, particularly considering the speed at which it was arranged, it was. There was even a version, revived after a century of neglect, of the *Laudes Regiae*, the ritual adoration of the ruler.[45]

Prospero di Camulio learned from his London correspondents that 'his lordship accepted his royal sceptre and staff and all the other ceremonies except the unction and the crown, which they postponed until he has annihilated the other king and reduced the island and the realm to a stable peace and, among other things, exacted vengeance for the slaughter of his father'.[46] Di Camulio was in no doubt about the importance of these developments:

> Those who support the claims of Edward and Warwick say that the chances in favour of Edward are great, both on account of the great lordship which he has in the island and in Ireland, and owing to the cruel wrongs done to him by the Queen's side, as well as through Warwick and London which is entirely inclined to side with the new king and Warwick, and as it is very rich and the most wealthy city of Christendom, this enormously increases the chances of the side that it favours.[47]

London was indeed with the Yorkists. The physical support of the mass of Londoners for Warwick, then York, now Edward had been well noted in the collective mind of the city's government. The commercial links between London and a Calais secured for York by Warwick were strong. Finally, once the Calais earls had been admitted to London after their 1460 invasion, the capital had lived with the fear of a Lancastrian reconquest and a possible sack that could have far outstripped the excesses of 1450. As a result, London's commercial interests had provided massive financial support to the Yorkists—to the tune of at least £13,000—between July 1460 and the early months of 1461.[48] This in itself would have been enough to pay 26,000 archers for twenty days' service.

London's support had enabled the Yorkists to survive the defeats at Wakefield and Saint Albans. Yet they were still opposed by an anointed King, a uniquely powerful Queen consort, the bulk of the nobility and a large part of the country. Certainly Edward had been acclaimed by some lords and some clergy. But it was not enough. He had to appeal to the widest possible audience and in terms that spoke not just of potential triumph, but of the necessity of victory for survival against a savage foe. He did so in a series of proclamations. The example quoted below was addressed to the sheriffs of London, but very similar versions would have been replicated across his new kingdom.[49] Just two days into his 'reign', it combines the language of royal command with the language of the common weal, that of the Cade petitioners of 1450 and that used by Warwick in 1460. A model of black propaganda, it has the mark of Warwick himself. Most importantly, the articulate language of protest of 1450, the rallying cry of Warwick to consolidate his collection of interests in 1460, is here used in an attempt to reconnect king and people:[50]

> To the sheriffs of London
> . . . Cause proclamation to be made of the accession of King Edward. Reciting that:
> - he is born the true inheritor of the crowns of England and France and the lordship of Ireland.
> - the lamentable state of this realm
> - the loss of France and duchies of Guyenne and Normandy, and of Anjou and Maine
> - the oppression of the people and decay of commerce
> - justice having been exiled through the negligence of the rulers
> - promising that the said realms shall be restored to fame, honour and prosperity
> - charging all men to take him each for his sovereign lord

It continues Warwick's language of the 'Great Fear', previously focused on the march south of Margaret's army. But it is aimed more directly against their noble Lancastrian opponents, dressing up their 'crimes' in terms that would most appal the Proclamation's target audience:

> Forasmuch as it is notorious that Henry duke of Exeter, Henry duke of Somerset, Thomas earl of Devonshire, Henry earl of Northumberland, Thomas de Roos knight, John Clifford, Leo of Wells and John Neville, knights, with many accomplices with a great number of rebels in war-

like guise have ridden in divers places committing treasons, robberies etc. And of oppressing wives, widows, maidens and women of religion, slaying and maiming liegemen, in such cruelness as has not been heard done among Saracens or Turks to christian men. And he that calls himself Henry VI, contrary to his promise made to such lords as went with him to the field [at the 2nd Battle of St Albans] suffered certain of them to be murdered and destroyed . . .

Charging none of the liege people upon pain of forfeiture and death to give any of those persons or the king's said adversary, or his party, help or favour with men, money etc. for victuals, horses, harness etc. But to withstand them, nor to obey commandments or proclamations made by the adversary . . .

Finally there is the appeal to national pride, or rather the pride of one part of the nation. Edward and Warwick continued to play on the fear that had helped to close the gates of London to Margaret's army. This conflict was presented as a war between the South and the rebellious part of the country north of the Trent, the latter being identified with the country's greatest enemies:

No man without special license shall pass over the water of Trent towards the said adversary. And forasmuch as the earls of Pembroke and Wiltshire, adherents to the said adversary, have brought into this land both Frenchmen and Scots, and now busy themselves in bringing a great multitude of the said enemies . . .

There then followed a list of captains whose demise would bring a reward of the enormous sum of £100—four thousand times the daily pay of an archer. At the head of the list of those whom the Yorkists sought to '*effectually destroy and bring out of life*' was Andrew Trollope, even above the Bastard of Exeter who had been personally responsible for the death of Warwick's father.

The rough and ready acclamation of his troops and assembled Londoners on 1 March, his 'election' by some peers and higher clergy on 3 March and the more formal ceremony in Westminster Hall on 4 March had all been cobbled together in an attempt to create a form of compact—of oath and acclamation—similar to that of a coronation.[51] But Edward did not have time, nor indeed the authority for a coronation. He had to assert his legitimacy in the most primal way of all: through the annihilation of his enemies in battle. His proclamation was backed by the second greatest mobilization of men during the entire Wars of the Roses. The greatest being that of their Lancastrian opponents at the very same time.

Nine

A COUNTRY AT WAR— NORTH VS SOUTH

THE MARCH NORTH TO TOWTON
March 1461

During February and March 1417, life for geese in twenty southern English counties suddenly got colder.[1] By command of the Crown, three primary feathers from both wings of every goose were to be plucked and sent to the Tower of London.[2] In theory at least, using feathers from the same goose would help balance the arrow in flight. This was not a one-off command: it was one that was regularly issued in times of war. Indeed, at the end of the following year, sheriffs were expected to supply a further 1,190,000 goose feathers by Michaelmas.[3] Why goose? Because in the words of the sixteenth-century author Roger Ascham, 'the goose is the best fether [sic] for the best shooter', a feather that 'hath all commodities in it'.[4] The reason for this intensity of effort was that the longbow was devastatingly effective, having been chiefly responsible for England's great fourteenth-century victories in the Hundred Years War at Crécy and Poitiers and its fifteenth-century triumphs at Agincourt and Verneuil. An insistence on quality did not just extend to the flights, but to the arrow shafts made from the finest possible ash and poplar and to the bowstaves made of yew. Not English yew, but that of continental Europe, which was denser and grew straighter. As for the bow strings, these had to be made from finest cannabis sativa. All these elements together made an extremely powerful weapon.

Just how powerful has been underlined by the research on bows recovered from the wreck of the *Mary Rose*, now encapsulated in *The Great War Bow* by Professor Matthew Strickland and Robert Hardy, the actor and world authority on the medieval longbow.[5] Though millions of bows were created, scarcely any have survived. The study of longbows produced less than a hundred years later than Towton and with no major change of design shows a weapon of devastating power at 100 yards, an effective range of 200 yards and an extreme range of 300.[6] To reach these upper distances a pulling power of at least 100 pounds, perhaps reaching up to 150 pounds, would be required. To attain that strength in adulthood, archers would have started building up their technique from childhood. On reaching the age of sixteen, the common man was expected, by decree of successive kings, to practise every Sunday and feast day until the age of sixty. The strength of the average archer was prodigious, it came from a body that had been shaped, in fact distorted, by the repeated effort required; this can be seen in the skeletons found at Towton. It made the Anglo-Welsh archer devastatingly effective, forcing the French to adopt the counter-measures and organisation which would at length win them the Hundred Years War.

During the Wars of the Roses, archers were to be employed, for the first time in two generations, by Englishmen against Englishmen in battles on English soil. They had shown their power at the beginning of the Wars when, from close range, they rained their steel-tipped projectiles down on the market place of Saint Albans. Again at Towton they were to prove deadly against any combatant, and especially against the vast majority, who lacked the protection necessary to resist their arrows.

These razor-sharp, four-ounce projectiles rotated through the air at around a hundred miles an hour.[7] When one of these missiles struck, the energy retained in the wood of the arrow from the enormous compressive force of its launch would be released on impact, not just once but repeatedly, with the percussive power of a hammer drill. Aside from the obvious more general threat of death from all types of arrow, as they struck organ, artery, an unprotected neck or head, different effects were obtained from the various arrowhead designs: the broadhead would slice through flesh, while the bodkin was capable of piercing all but the best armour plate over a short distance. There was also a dual purpose, with elements of both,[8] and the arrows might also be barbed.

The initial threat of being injured on impact, with many thousands of archers shooting arrows at a rate of around twelve per minute per archer, was bad enough. Injuries could be compounded by the burning power of copper sulphate, a compound used to help firm the glue used on the flights, which often leaked down the shaft and on to the arrowhead itself. Beyond that was the more insidious danger of tetanus. As can be imagined, archers would be interested in keeping their arrowheads sharp, but they would have no particular interest in keeping them clean. The French, naturally, claimed that English archers deliberately sought to introduce the disease.[9] However, it is probable that the reason an archer might take his arrows from his quiver before a battle and push them head-first into the ground would be to make them easier to retrieve and thus speed the rate of shot. Whatever the reasoning, untreated tetanus is horrific. After an incubation period of anything from four to twenty-one days, symptoms include muscle spasms such as lockjaw, with death occurring due to septicaemia, asphyxiation, cardiac arrest or kidney failure.[10]

Last, but not least, there was the possibility of gangrene.

Those who could not afford protection, 'the naked men' of the muster with little or no equipment, were exceptionally vulnerable and thus ineffective. Hence, if a large number of troops was not required, these were the men who would be left behind. (They were not left behind before Towton: every vaguely viable man was needed.)

Of course, the most effective defence against an archer was the attacking prowess of another archer, but there were also means of deflecting or even absorbing an arrow's impact.

For absorption there was the 'jack', a padded jacket shaped like a jerkin. Despite the fact that it gave no protection to the arms and legs, it was described approvingly in the 1480s by Dominic Mancini, a visiting Italian cleric: 'Only the wealthy wear metal armour; ordinary soldiers prefer comfortable tunics (stuffed with tow) which reach down to their thigh. They say that the softer they are the better they withstand blows; besides which in summer they are lighter and in winter more useful than iron'.[11] Iron perhaps, but not tempered steel. That said, these jackets, which as well as having the tow—rough flax—would have layer upon layer of wool or linen material which, packed tightly together, could prove effective both against arrows shot from a distance and against some blows from hand weapons close up. But not against arrows from close up: from one hundred yards or so there was nothing a jack could do. Moreover, as happened at Northampton, when faced with retreat through deep water, the wearer of a jack faced an unenviable choice: strip it off and be completely vulnerable to arrows, or keep it on and feel the materials become saturated with water rendering death by drowning almost inevitable.

On their heads, both archers and soldiers wore the sallet or helmet. Some preferred to forgo head protection, particularly some of the archers themselves, for a helmet would interfere with their ability to get the hand which drew the bowstring closer to the eye, and thus hinder their accuracy. For others, the decision not to wear one was a matter of finance: a sallet or helmet would cost the equivalent of many days' wages. Of course, a victorious army would have access to many newly available ones in the aftermath of a battle.

The position of the wealthy aristocracy was altogether different. The greatest artillery threat to the medieval knight on the field of battle had been the longbow. But by the 1460s, full armour had evolved to defend against it. At first glance, this armour gives the impression that every possible surface is covered. Almost as if it is a self-standing, fully enclosed ceremonial suit. In fact it was composed of many different pieces, all with their own individual names, mostly of French derivation. The interconnecting plates of the best armour, measured exactly to the requirements of its wearer, moved smoothly together. They were attached to a quilted doublet underneath with 'arming points' or laces. There might be an upper and lower breast plate, a separate plate for the back, a skirt, different sections to enable the flexing of limbs with reinforcement over knees and elbows and specific pieces for the feet. The head was protected by a sallet with a visor and with a bevor for the lower part of the face and a gorget for the neck. Or instead of having sallet and bevor, the knight—for it is likely that he would be at least a knight or an esquire—might have an all-in-one bassinet. Whatever the headwear, when the visor was closed there would be holes at eye level to provide a limited degree of vision.

The armed man had to have the ability to move, and if his armour fitted well and the weight was properly distributed, he could do so, even though the armour weighed anything between fifty to seventy pounds. Areas such as the inner arm, the inner leg, the armpit and the groin were covered by

the less protective but more flexible mail, which allowed running, jump-
ing and, most importantly, riding a horse. But even these more vulnerable
mailed areas might have additional protection such as the besagews (discs
overlapping the armpits), with the left-handed—the one thought more
likely to be facing an opponent—often being larger in continental armours,
though English-made armour tended to more symmetrical.

Some of the elements of armour might seem to be merely decorative—
none were. For instance, the little wing of metal attached to the poleyn,
which protected the knee, might look like an adornment, but it was essential in preventing an opponent from slashing the vulnerable back of the leg
with an angled weapon. Similarly, lines of fluting were not there to create a
pleasing pattern but to deflect arrow tips and blades.

All this protection came with some disadvantages: vision and hearing
were impaired and full armour made the wearer extremely hot. It would
also be advisable for its owner to keep to a reasonably constant weight.
Some adjustment, through the laces, was possible, but there was only a
small degree of tolerance. If the pieces did not fit smoothly together, the
wearer's movement, as well as his protection, would be compromised.

The very best armour at this time was thought to come from Italy,
particularly Milan, and from Germany. But English armour was also well
established[12] and the bulk of the armour in use on England's battlefields
was English made.

As for cost, armour was extremely expensive. An account bill for a Sir
John de Cressy, a commander in the Hundred Years War, survives from
1441. He ordered three suits, the most expensive for himself and two others
for members of his retinue, at a total cost of over £20, or more than 800
times the day rate of an archer.[13]

Depending on their position or military expertise, a noble's own household retainers would have anything from full armour down to just necessary elements of it: for instance a mounted man-at-arms might compromise
on protection to give him the advantage of speed. Further down the social
chain, the ordinary billman would wear whatever he could grab or afford.
Helmets and pieces of armour were a precious commodity and were end-
lessly recycled to their eventual destruction. Some protective equipment
was still being used in the Civil War, two centuries later. Mark Taylor,
Chairman of the Towton Battlefield Society, identified one such helmet

on display with a skull at Jedburgh Castle Museum. The fate of its last user could be deduced by the hole made by a seventeenth-century musket ball and confirmed by a matching piece of sallet metal embedded in the skull.[14] Military technology had moved on.

The very best archers were greatly prized. A noble house who had such a man in its service would take pains to ensure his loyalty. He would have been very well fed and rewarded with presents. The Duke of Norfolk handed down one of his own second-best coats to such a man.[15] This was no small prize at a time when the wealthiest would have replaced rather than washed clothes that were dyed with non-colour-fast natural dyes, so this coat would have been of high quality and in good condition.[16]

However, exceptional cases apart, most of the military members of a noble's household would have been men-at-arms, the men who fought in a group around their lord on the battlefield. As these were the men on whom the lord would depend for his life, his bodyguard in fact, they were highly trained. They would be noticeable for the badges they would wear on behalf of their lord, but also for their height. Like professional boxers today, those who most effectively used weapons in medieval hand-to-hand combat needed 'reach' as well as strength and dexterity.[17] Should the lord require it, these men were always to hand; most would have been well used to accompanying their lords in London during the uncertain periods of the 1450s. It was assumed by some doom-laden Victorian historians[18] that the country was impoverished by the great magnates permanently employing many hundreds or indeed many thousands in this way. In fact, these men should be numbered in some dozens per household rather than many hundreds. It is likely that the average size of an earl's household in the 1450s would have run to about two hundred,[19] and although it would have been almost exclusively made up of men,[20] they would not all have been military men.

However, the magnates were able to call upon many hundreds of reinforcements at speed in time of need. The Black Death may have ended pre-existing forms of economic feudal obligation, but it had not done away with social and military obligation. The men who ate at the great lord's table—gentry, esquires, even lesser lords—together with the yeomen and husbandmen who rented the lord's land, were all expected to come to his aid in time of trouble. In return, he was expected to come to theirs. This process could be informal or formal. For the lord's own household there was no need for a formal arrangement; with those less attached, it could be under terms of indenture, whereby the indentured man would contract for a fixed time and an agreed sum to be of service: the indenture referring to the contract being torn in two, with half being given to each party. With no tear being exactly the same, the two pieces could, if required, be exactly matched.[21]

How Bastard Feudalism worked in practice can be extrapolated from the records on the 710 indictments brought by the Nevilles against the Percy adherents after the confrontation at Heworth in 1453. Of the Percy followers who can be identified, 6 were knights, 32 esquires, 26 gentlemen and 24 clerks (including parish priests); with the majority consisting of 330 yeomen and 44 husbandmen, all of whom would have been Percy tenants.[22] There were also about 100 from the city of York, demonstrating the ability of the local magnate to dominate neighbouring towns and cities as well as the countryside.[23] These retainers could be supplemented by short-term measures to bring in hired mercenaries—professional soldiers with the requisite skills—as Sir John Fastolf did to protect his London house against Cade's mob in 1450.

Bastard Feudalism was a highly effective means of raising men, but as its name implies, it was a distortion. The raising of large numbers of troops for service through livery and maintenance—the wearing of a lord's colours and badges, and being maintained in cash or kind by him—had, by the 1450s, been diverted from the intended purpose of military recruitment for the monarch. Livery and maintenance was intended to provide protection for the king against rebellion and with troops for foreign wars. Through the formal process of Commissions of Array, this had been the means by which a nation of around three million had, from the time of Edward III onwards, been able to go to war against the French—with a population upwards of seven and a half million—and to do so without the expense of a standing army. It was not intended for other purposes.

But at this juncture massive recruitment served faction rather than repressed it. At the local level, force or the threat of force had replaced the King's justice as the means of a nobleman advancing his cause. In the 1440s, Suffolk had maintained a semblance of order with a policy of seeking to support the stronger of two parties in a dispute. By the 1450s there were two centres of national authority: one based on Queen Margaret, acting in the name of King Henry and Prince Edward; and one on the House of York and their allies. To gain predominance or indeed satisfaction against a local rival, landed men who were not already tied into the system of mutual obligation would look to the principle of 'The Lord who is the enemy of the Lord of my enemy, should be my Lord'. National authority, under a strong king, was designed to resolve disputes. But with two factions of comparable strength themselves competing for national authority, combatants would look to the leadership of their faction for support. It also meant that these same combatants would be ready to flock to the banner of their leader in time of emergency. By this means, landed society could be split from top to bottom.

In March 1461, the final layer of bastardization was added. After the acclamation of Edward IV, there were now two kings of England issuing Commissions of Array against rebellious subjects. To refuse such a commission was treason. In any event it was difficult to avoid. The apparatus of enforcement was policed by the great magnates themselves,[24] who directed the lower level of royal officials, be they sheriffs, mayors, bailiffs or village constables to muster all sound men between the ages of sixteen and sixty. They used royal command to bring to their forces those who were not already part of their 'affinity'. The distortion was complete: two kings were using the accepted forms of military recruitment at time of national emergency to suppress a rebel. But which was the true king and which was the rebel?

The means that had served England in war against its great neighbour France and its lesser neighbour Scotland had become warped to become the means of mobilizing the fighting nation for Civil War. It helps to explain the enormous numbers at the battle of Towton.

From the age of seven, a medieval boy of noble birth would be sent away from home and brought up for some years in the household of a great man, perhaps even the superior lord of his father. Here the boy would be taught good manners: the conventions of etiquette, how to carve and serve at table, together with the arts of music and dancing. He would receive scholastic tuition in Latin and grammar and learn the practicalities of estate management and law.[25] He would also receive professional instruction from an experienced soldier, on fighting and on the rules of strategy and command; there were, in the age just before printing, widely circulated manuscripts on both. One of the most respected commentaries on strategy was written by a Roman of the fourth century called Vegetius.[26] The fact that it was over a thousand years old at this time was of no account, because many of his strictures on campaigning were still valid, in fact they were acted out over the winter of 1460–61. Vegetius's *Epitoma Rei Militari* contains a series of aphorisms, one that is striking when applied to that winter is 'the single most effective weapon is that food should be sufficient for you while dearth should break the enemy . . . for armies are more often destroyed by starvation than battle, and hunger is more savage than the sword'.[27]

As well as those of Vegetius, the words of other great ancients were included in *The Book of Feats of Arms and of Chivalry*, together with its author's own more contemporary wisdom.[28] The author was an Italian-born noblewoman, Christine de Pisan, who, unusually for the time, had received a quality of education normally reserved for boys.[29] The deaths of her father and husband in the 1380s, both formerly well connected at the French court, forced her to make her living by her pen and she was extremely successful, with a range of ballads and religious poems to her name, as well as the *Feats of Arms* and a final 'Ditié', a paean of praise to Joan of Arc, written just before De Pisan's own death in 1430.[30] Manuscripts containing *Feats of Arms* were greatly prized, with Margaret of Anjou being presented with one by Talbot, England's great warrior, as a wedding gift; and there was also a later magnificent Yorkist copy. But however fabulous their decoration, these books were valued for their words. And sensibly so, for what De Pisan described as the three most important elements of securing the 'advantage of the field' all played a role at Towton.[31]

She quoted Vegetius directly on food supplies. Though the competing armies had not exactly suffered famine, they had certainly paid the price for being found wanting in terms of provisions. Their shortage had led to the pillaging carried out by Margaret's army on the march south, which, amplified by Warwick's propaganda, had ensured the gates of London would be shut against her. Prospero di Camulio, writing just after the collapse of Warwick's army at the Second Battle of Saint Albans, described how desertions 'for lack of victuals'[32] had contributed to defeat. Finally, Margaret's army had been forced to abandon London and turn back north for a secure supply base.

What seems surprising is that the army should have retreated so far north. Passing through the Leicestershire heartlands of the Duchy of Lancaster, centred around Kenilworth, which Margaret had made her centre of power in the 1450s, the Lancastrians finally based themselves just north of the Trent. There, in the totally friendly territories of the Percys, they had access to provisions and to possible French and Scottish reinforcements through the port of Hull. They also had York, the second most populous city of the kingdom. Micklegate Bar still held the heads of the fathers and a brother of both Edward IV and of Warwick, as testament to the disastrous foray north of less than three months before; and the Lancastrians knew that this would serve as a spur rather than a deterrent to the two Yorkist cousins. Even more importantly, they knew that Edward would be forced to follow his father's example and march north in order to assert his authority. Strategically, Edward would have to bring Margaret's forces to the battlefield and tactically he would try to do so by threatening their centre of operations at York. They knew that geography would dictate the route he would take and when and where he would be most vulnerable, constrained by the needs of a huge army making its way up the country.

Edward may have been acclaimed king, but he had not been anointed and crowned. He may have won his army's confident loyalty through a gift of providence in the form of the parhelion and subsequent victory at Mortimer's Cross, but he would need confirmation of his royal legitimacy through ultimate victory in battle. This was where Edward departed from the advice of Vegetius to do everything to avoid the hazard of battle. Just as the Lancastrians knew he would. For, as the diplomat Philippe de Commynes later commented: 'Of all the people in the world [the English are] the most inclined to give battle'.[33]

The mechanisms of Commissions of Array might enable the extremely rapid recruitment of men, but they also required that the men be speedily deployed and then disbanded, because English troops expected to be properly provisioned and paid. The challenge to Edward, as described in *Knyghthode and Bataile*, a contemporary poetic translation of Vegetius, was to 'have purveyance of forage and victual for man and horse; for iron smiteth not so sore as hunger doth if food fail',[34] particularly bearing in mind that the last sixty miles or so would be in enemy territory. This was a test indeed for the teenage King.

Two days into his reign, Edward's denunciation of his enemies was accompanied by his issuing Commissions of Array for thirty-two counties—only one of which, surprisingly Northumberland, the Percy heartland, was north of the Trent. For the first time in nearly forty years, an army of England, or part of it at least, was being personally commanded by someone with the title of King.

It was not until the Victorian era that the *Wars of the Roses* became established as the generally accepted, all-encompassing name for the series of English battles that took place between 1455 and 1487.[35] During the wars themselves, the red rose and white rose badges were amongst a great number employed by the two sides. Edward IV's own favourite badge, in honour of the parhelion at Mortimer's Cross, was the 'Sun in Splendour'; that of the Beaufort Dukes of Somerset was the Yale, a mythical beast rather like a ferocious-looking tusked antelope;[36] that worn by the adherents of the young Prince of Wales was a white swan. That said, the two roses were being singled out as badges and conjoined for propaganda purposes, both in writing and in pageantry, within a few months[37] of Henry VII's 1485 victory at Bosworth.[38]

The first major association of Edward IV himself with the rose as a badge was in the context of the Towton campaign, and in the verse and song that also commemorated his birthplace. This was the 'Rose of Rouen'.[39] Running to fifteen verses with a chorus, it is obviously far more complex than the battlefield chants of 'A Warwick' or 'A Harry' and, indeed, the football and rugby songs of today which are its distant successors. Taken as a whole, it might be tedious to the modern ear, but it is a valuable resource in as much as it establishes, through the images of badges, the peerage and important gentry that came to Edward's support and the cities that were major centres of supply for the Yorkists.

It is also at one with the proclamations to the sheriffs. The Yorkists were promoting this as a war of South against North: as captured in the following, non-consecutive, verses:

The northern men made their boast when they had done that deed,
Between Christmas and Candlemas[40] a little before lent,
all the lords of the North they wrought by one assent.
For to destroy the south country they did all have intent.
Had not the Rose of Rouen been, all England had been shent.

and

The northern men made their boast when they had done that deed,
The northern men made their boast when they had done that deed,
'we will dwell in the south country and take all that we need.
These wives and their daughters our purpose they shall see . . .'

The areas that were first singled out for praise were the core areas that had supported the 1460 invasion and continued to do so:

Had not the Rose of Rouen been, all England had been shent.
For to save all England the rose was intent.
With Calais and with lone London with Essex and Kent
and all the South of England up to the River Trent . . .

The Yorkist leaders such as Warwick, Norfolk, Fauconberg, Lords Grey of Ruthin, Scrope of Bolton and Viscount Bourchier were all identified by their badges, as were major cities. One can also detect separate routes: Canterbury, Windsor, Salisbury, Bristol, Gloucester and Worcester; and Northampton, Coventry, Leicester, Nottingham. To that can be added another route, that of the Duke of Norfolk and, most likely, the young Duke of Suffolk too, through their East Anglian territories.

The challenge of Queen Margaret and the Lancastrians was to draw Edward and his allies into what was becoming increasingly perceived as alien territory. Bearing in mind how many troops Edward would need to bring with him and the mammoth task of provisioning them, the Lancastrians sought to force their opponents into battle on vastly unequal terms, with regard to the crucial elements of numbers, provisions and morale. In line with the principles of Vegetius, these were textbook tactics.

*   *   *

In order to have any chance of victory, Edward would have to mobilize all the resources of his new half-kingdom. Though, like the rest of Europe, England might suffer financial crises, it was in essence a wealthy country.[41] Rich enough that thirty years of intermittent fighting over the course of the Wars of the Roses did not destroy its economy. In fact, the country was to be rarely despoiled. Yet, had there been other months like the one between Edward's acclamation as king and the battle at Towton, it might have been a different story.

That brief period was unique in terms of the number of nobles involved. Through a complete vacuum of authority, three-quarters of the peerage had become ensnared in disputes that were now national as well as local. And their only hope of resolution seemed to be by victory in battle. Thus, for the first time, England saw mass recruitment on behalf of two kings as, using the effective mechanisms established by Bastard Feudalism, the nobles assembled vast retinues to join them in battle. In this urgent activity they were spurred on by the knowledge that defeat would in all likelihood mean death in battle or execution for themselves and disinheritance for their families. Never again would the number of nobles embroiled in the conflict reach such a level—the traumatic outcome of the Battle of Towton saw to that.

With the bulk of the peerage still loyal to Henry and the House of Lancaster, the numbers were in the Lancastrians' favour. And even though Margaret's army had needed to march north, it had benefited from more time to prepare and provision while based in friendly territory.

The Yorkists realized that they had been saved from losing London—and most likely the war—through portraying Margaret's army as pillagers. They would not make the same mistake themselves. Instead, they followed the approach which would, a few years later, be set out in *De laudibus legum Angliae*, Sir John Fortescue's book of instruction for Edward, Prince of Wales:

> The king, by his purveyors, may take for his own use necessaries for his household, at a reasonable price, to be assessed at the discretion of the constables of the place, whether the owners will or not: but the king is obliged by the laws to make present payment, or at a day to be fixed by

the great officers of the king's household. The king cannot despoil the subject without making ample satisfaction for the same.[42]

With funds advanced from London and Calais, the Yorkists acted swiftly. Norfolk left London for East Anglia on 5 March. Warwick, just two days later, with a large body of troops, headed for the West and the Midlands, where he raised very many more. On 11 March, Fauconberg set out with the advanced guard of the main army. Edward himself followed on 13 March with a great train of supply wagons.[43] Ahead of them, both before departure and on the march, went hordes of messengers on horseback, taking demands to supporters and potential supporters in the towns and the country ahead, helping to stimulate recruitment and arranging the provisions necessary to satisfy an army on the march. Professional soldiers such as the Kentish captain Robert Horne were there to organize, assemble and guarantee payment.[44] With the ability of horsemen to ride great distances, captains could very quickly activate subordinates in an ever-increasing network of engagement of troops.

Not all went smoothly. John Paston III tells us in the Paston letters that: 'Most people of this country (district) have taken wages saying they will go up to London; but they have no captain, nor ruler assigned by their commissioners to await upon, and so they straggle about by themselves, and likeliness are not like to come to London half of them'.[45]

The 'Rose of Rouen' gives hints to Edward's progress—but there are more substantive sightings too. We know that Edward proceeded by way of Saint Albans—there was to be no third battle there—and by the seventeenth he was already in Cambridge. Here he was met by Sir John Howard, who brought the extremely large and welcome sum of £100 from the abbot and convent of Bury Saint Edmunds.[46] There would be a lot of contact with monasteries on this journey; they could be exceedingly wealthy institutions and were great producers of ale—so necessary for armies on the march.

As well as those horsemen who would ride ahead to give warning of the requirements for the coming troops, there were others, known as scourers, who would advance in great numbers to secure the supplies for men and for horses. William Gregory of *Gregory's Chronicle* had a typical infantryman's low opinion of these cavalry troops: 'As for spearmen they be good to ride before the footmen and eat and drink up their victuals and many more such pretty things they do . . . For in the footmen is all the trust'.[47] This view was not shared by commanders, because these horsemen, also called aforeriders, were paid 12 pence per day, twice the pay of archers. They were seen as essential, most of all as procurers, which role might even eclipse their use on the battlefield.

When one sees the amount of food and fodder they were expected to secure, their importance is unquestionable. Napoleon's dictum 'an army marches on its stomach' was as true in 1461 as it was at the time of Austerlitz. The fare on offer was not of the standardised nature of the seventeenth-century English Civil War, where the staple was cheese and biscuits—or rather a crumbly weevil-infested Cheshire-type cheese with hard tack. For a short campaign, it would have been whatever could be gathered, with the difficulties of provisioning highlighted by its unseasonal nature. Military campaigns were supposed to take place in the summer months, when food was being produced; not at the very end of winter when stores of preserved supplies would be severely depleted.

For the ordinary soldier, the lack of fresh fruit and vegetables would not have been a problem. They would have been naturally suspicious of anything that absorbed water, as contamination of water and waterborne diseases were rightly feared, even on such a short campaign. What they looked to for their staple was bread—made, of course, with well-boiled water. The bread would most likely have become coarser as they travelled further north, thanks to the use of wheat substitutes such as maslin (a wheat and rye mix) or mixtil (wheat and winter barley). Finally, with supplies diminishing, any fresh bread would probably have been made of plain barley or oats. The quality, as with all war supplies, would have been distinctly variable: some poorer quality bread would contain very fine grit from the miller's wheel, which grinds down the teeth. One of the Towton victims shows just such a pattern of wear.

As for sources of protein: it must be remembered that it was now Lent. The devout man was supposed to abjure meat. It is likely, however, that Yorkist priests would have given absolution to men of troubled conscience unable to get the meat of water animals that were classified as fish. For the absolved meat eaters, much of what they obtained at this time of year would have been dried or cured, such as bacon, but there would also have been some fresh mutton or even beef on the hoof. In these circumstances, nothing would have been wasted: for instance, a horse that broke its leg would be rapidly killed and butchered. Fish would have been dried and or salted, including cod, skate, eels, pilchards and herring—the latter possibly pickled. Eggs and cheese would also provide protein and were acceptable on fish days.

One cannot know how much the Yorkists were able to find to eat on the march—probably far less than their Lancastrian counterparts. It is possible that, on occasion, the men marching from the south and west would have been forced to return to the diet of their more impoverished forefathers from that time before the Black Death had thinned out the population. This would have consisted of bread made from the poorest quality cereals and from dried beans and peas. In such cases also, these peas and beans would have been boiled up in clean water with oatmeal and scraps of bacon to make the earlier medieval staple of pottage.

A supply of clean water would have presented the biggest challenge: it much needed to be boiled for greater safety. But the soldiers would not have been expected to drink this: for liquid intake they would have been looking for water which had been purified through being brewed with malt to form ale.

The exertions of the march would have expended far more energy than that required by a static force. The rate of progress at the end of winter was staggering. To arrive close to the Towton battlefield by the night of the twenty-eighth, Edward's main force would have to have travelled 180 or so miles in sixteen days: it is likely that there would have been rest days for re-provisioning, perhaps at Cambridge and certainly at Nottingham, a perfect supply base, with its castle and large walled and fortified outer bailey. Assuming the army left on the twenty-third, that would have meant travelling the best part of twelve miles per day, which, encumbered with supply wagons, was at breakneck speed, even approaching that of Edward III's famous advance towards the Somme in 1346.[48] Much of the last part of the march was through what could be considered to be enemy territory. On the twenty-seventh the Yorkist main army had reached Pontefract, dominated by its castle, the place of imprisonment and slow death of Richard II. But an advance guard under Lord Fitzwalter was well ahead, for it was absolutely essential to secure a river crossing over the River Aire, either the bridge at Ferrybridge or the ford at Castleford, three miles upstream.

The army had grown steadily en route as allied lords joined with their retainers and the Commissions of Array did their work. The main army under Edward, including Fauconberg's advance guard, had been joined by Warwick. The last part, under John Mowbray, Duke of Norfolk, was, it was thought, just a short distance behind. Even without Norfolk it was a vast force of twenty thousand or more. Norfolk himself had in the region of five thousand men. Yet it did not compare with the greater forces that the Lancastrians were able to bring to bear: their own Commissions of Array, their magnates and their affinities, had collected a force closer to thirty thousand, possibly well on the far side of it.[49] It must be remembered that the vast majority of the peerage, who acted as the fulcrum of the entire recruitment process, were involved in fighting in 1459–61. Of the total 68 members of the peerage, 53—or perhaps 54, according to some sources—fought. Of these, a clear majority of 31, which included most of the higher ranks from viscount upwards, fought for the Lancastrians.[50] Absence, it seems, could only be excused on grounds of old age, infirmity, idiocy or being abroad.

The Lancastrian plan was to hold the Yorkist army at the River Aire for as long as possible, in the hope that the difficulty of finding provisions in enemy territory would induce the Yorkist troops to start melting away. Edward would be short of food for men and horses. It was hoped that he would be forced into a retreat, where his disordered army would soon become a rabble and, as at 2nd Saint Albans, would begin to break up. He, Warwick and all of the Yorkist leadership would have to flee. Except, unlike at 2nd Saint Albans and, indeed, Ludford Bridge, this time they would be in enemy territory. But the plan may have had an additional dimension: it may have factored in the possibility that the Yorkists would be able to fight their way across the Aire through the shallow waters of the ford after which Castleford was named and then continue their march towards York.[51] Or, alternatively, it may have been to hold the Yorkists with dismounted troops before withdrawing these at nightfall and allowing the enemy across. It may have been a complicated feint. It would have drawn the Yorkists towards the battlefield at Towton, because the Saxton–Towton plateau blocked the only obvious route to the target of the Yorkist advance: the city of York, which commanded the North of England, and was effectively its capital.

Perhaps it was a complicated plan for the time, but Somerset and Edward were of a new young generation of commanders, uncluttered by the memories of the Hundred Years War. Somerset had Sir Andrew Trollope as his military adviser, whose name was the very first on the Yorkist proscription list issued in London. It was for good reason that the Burgundian near-contemporary Jean de Waurin was to describe Trollope as a '*tres soubtil home de guerre*'.[52]

For a complicated plan to succeed, all its elements have to come together in the right order. The Lancastrian commanders were surprised in one crucial respect: the speed with which the Yorkist advance guard under Fitzwalter arrived at Ferrybridge. Sources differ at this point, but working with the new thesis of battlefield archaeologist Tim Sutherland, the following seems likely, and it includes elements of the accounts of both the chroniclers Jean de Waurin and Edward Hall.[53]

Fitzwalter arrived late on 27 March, probably in the dark, and found the bridge partially destroyed, perhaps even in the actual but dilatory process of being dismantled. If so, this would explain the presence of a small number of Lancastrian troops on the southern bank. There was a very short engagement, but with insufficient troops to hold the south bank, the remaining Lancastrians attempted to flee back across the bridge. Some of them were picked off by Yorkist archers; some made it back to the north bank, from where they fled on horseback to make contact with their commander Lord Clifford, who was just a few miles away. At this point Fitzwalter ordered a picket to patrol the north bank and sent back messengers to the Yorkist main army for reinforcements. But the Lancastrian army was much closer to Ferrybridge than the Yorkist one, so it was Clifford with at least five hundred mounted men who got to the bridge first, swiftly overcame the picket and caught Fitzwalter—not in his night shirt, as has been supposed, but certainly unarmoured and off-guard. Both Fitzwalter and Warwick's half-brother, the Bastard of Salisbury, were killed and the bridge retaken.

It may have been when Fitzwalter's initial messengers arrived at Edward's camp, or more probably when men fled there after Clifford's attack, that the decision was taken by the Yorkist leadership to risk splitting their forces.

Fauconberg was sent with mounted troops to the secondary crossing at Castleford in order to seize it at daybreak from any Lancastrian defenders, while Warwick set off for Ferrybridge.

One can assume that, with Ferrybridge and Castleford just three miles apart, the two mounted Yorkist forces would have attacked around the same time. But inexplicably Castleford was undefended, and this is where Tim Sutherland's thesis is compelling.[54] He believes that when Waurin wrote 'the [Percy] Earl of Northumberland . . . failed to attack soon enough', he was referring to Castleford rather than Towton. And this would indeed have been staggering because these were mainly Percy-dominated lands, like the battlefield at Towton itself. It seems impossible that the Lancastrians, when we see the care they took to select what might have been the secondary point of conflict at Towton, would neglect to defend one of the primary points of entry to north of the Aire—the crossing at Castleford. We can only speculate on the reasons for Northumberland's delay, but for Clifford they were catastrophic.

The action at Ferrybridge began successfully for Clifford. The narrow defile of the partially repaired bridge meant Yorkists trying to cross could be picked off with ease by archers using the longbow or, particularly useful for close sniper work—the crossbow. The Yorkists were at bay. Gregory tells us that Warwick was himself wounded in the leg by an arrow.[55] Yet without the protection to his flank that would have been provided by Northumberland holding Castleford, Clifford was completely vulnerable. Perhaps Fauconberg sent a horseman back to Ferrybridge to check the position, or perhaps, due to the close proximity of the two crossings, Fauconberg rode to Ferrybridge to confer with his nephew, Warwick. Whichever, the result was that Fauconberg felt able to risk a charge along the north bank of the river with fast mounted troops, to attack Clifford and trap him. Clifford and his mounted horsemen, the 'Flower of Craven' were soon in full flight north, with Fauconberg's own aforeriders in hot pursuit.

What would have made strategic sense for Fauconberg, of course, would have been to make Clifford not just the potential prey of one group of horsemen, but of two. The first to flush out Clifford; the second, with a head start, to charge along the old Roman ridge road four miles to the west of the established main road north, with directions to strike east across the moor, back on to the main route, there to cut off Clifford's forces. A risky strategy if there were signs of the Lancastrian army moving into position. But there were no such signs. Clifford's forces were blocked and engaged by the forward group. Caught by the second of the pursuing forces and encircled, Clifford, either through heat or exhaustion, removed his helmet and was killed by an arrow—possibly a ricochet, as this was an arrow that had lost its head.

Common sense, even custom, dictated that when the lord was killed, his affinity might be allowed to disengage. This practice suited both defenders and attackers: the leaderless and no doubt unpaid troops of the dead man could seek greater safety: and the victors could, unmolested, strip the dead lord of anything of value. A case of 'spare the commons'. But this was a different type of war. The Flower of Craven were annihilated. This happened, at Dintingdale, to the east of the village of Saxton and just to the south of the Towton battlefield plateau itself.

Clifford's death was a further act in the cycle of killing and revenge that began at 1st Saint Albans. In terms of the fate of his troops, it was to presage what was to come the following day.

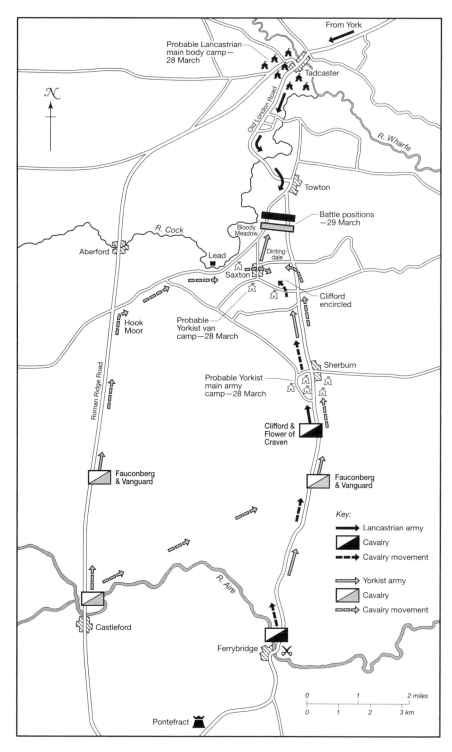

The pursuit of Clifford and area map for 27–29 March 1461

Ten

—◆◇◆◇◆—

TOWTON—PALM SUNDAY 1461

THE MOST BRUTAL DAY IN ENGLISH HISTORY

It is just possible that the main Lancastrian army had already arrived on the battlefield while Clifford's debacle unfolded out of sight from them. If the wind was blowing in the other direction they might have heard nothing. Even so, it is scarcely credible that they would have missed all signs of a melee involving two large detachments of horsemen. Given any indication at all, Somerset would have risked sending forward reinforcements from the main army to investigate; but there is absolutely no indication that he did so. One explanation put forward is that there was jealousy amongst the commanders and the remainder were happy enough for Clifford and the Flower of Craven to be killed to a man by their Yorkist opponents.[1] This seems inconceivable. A far better explanation is provided by Andrew Boardman, the first Chairman of the Towton Battlefield Society, who believes that the Lancastrian army were at the town of Tadcaster, two miles to the north, and only came to the battlefield early on the day of the battle itself.[2] And that was most likely just the main part of it. With the city of York only a few miles further away, the substantial extra billeting there would also have been used.

Anyone visiting the battlefield can see immediately why it is so implausible that the Lancastrian army would have wanted to be in position the night before the battle. The reason lies in geography and topography. The villages of Saxton and Towton stand about a mile and three-quarters away from each other, broadly on a north–south axis. There has been some recent building development, but not a great deal. They remain small villages. Between them lies a plateau on top of rising ground. This was to be the scene of the battle. In spite of its protection on one side by areas of woodland, likely to have been rather greater in 1461 than now, it would have been a very exposed, windswept place in which to spend the night. Whereas, in contrast, Tadcaster and York had superior billeting for the Lancastrian leaders.

From Tadcaster the Lancastrians could not have seen Clifford's desperate retreat. What is more, they would not have perceived a need to be in position, as they had no expectation that the Yorkists would be in the vicinity so quickly. Certainly they would not have anticipated Fauconberg's crossing the river so soon. All the indications are that the Lancastrian plan was to block, weaken and demoralize the Yorkist army, which they expected to be low on supplies. It was in the Lancastrians' interest to keep their opponents south of the Aire for as long as possible. That the position of the battlefield adjacent to the main route north and the nature of its terrain made it the most suitable place for a massive confrontation cannot be doubted; but this would have been one of several possible alternatives.

As for the Yorkists on the night before the battle, according to Waurin they were indeed low on supplies.[3] It is likely that the main army had not been fully re-provisioned after they left Nottingham, almost a week before. Individual soldiers carried food in bags they attached to themselves, but probably only had enough for a few days at a time. When it came to billeting for the night, the Yorkists would have established themselves at the larger settlement of Sherburn in Elmet, three miles from the battlefield. Although they surmised that the main Lancastrian force was near, they did not know its exact whereabouts. Another reason for deciding on Sherburn is that Edward's main army was well behind Fauconberg and that distance, six miles from Ferrybridge, would have represented a stiff enough march, complete with baggage. It is possible that, as with the Lancastrians and the city of York, some with the advantage of horsepower would have stayed in the more comfortable conditions of Pontefract, just south of the newly consolidated bridgehead over the Aire.

Warwick's whereabouts that night are also uncertain, but we have a tantalizing clue. A short distance to the west of Saxton on the B1217 is a pub named The Crooked Billet: an exact synonym for Warwick's Ragged

Staff emblem. Research by Graham Darbyshire, a local historian and the Secretary of the Towton Battlefield Society, has revealed that this was for centuries the site of a farmstead and brewhouse and was probably one as far back as 1461. That would have made it an attractive spot for positioning troops. In any event, even if Edward and the main force were not yet in the vicinity of Saxton, Warwick's uncle Fauconberg was already there, following his defeat of Clifford.

Regardless of their exact whereabouts on the night of the twenty-eighth, the commanders of the two sides anticipated a major battle on the morrow. Successive engagements having been fought during the day, each side knew that the other was close. It was probably at this point that the Lancastrian commanders under the leadership of Somerset decided to break the bridge over the River Wharfe at Tadcaster, in order to protect themselves against the same type of night attack that had been perpetrated so successfully by Clifford the night before.

In the expectation of further fighting, the camps of both sides were a hive of activity.[4] Armourers would have been busily preparing the armour of their masters and principal retainers. This was an intensive job. In order to provide the maximum possible protection, the plates of armour had to move smoothly together. One factor inhibiting this was, as has been said, changes in the weight of the wearer. Another crucial factor was the weather. These suits of armour were made of tempered steel. Kept inside in careful storage they needed little maintenance. However, worn outside in damp conditions they rusted quickly. They needed to be treated with a mixture of sand and vinegar, and depending on the conditions this might need to be done on a daily basis. Once the coating of rust was removed, the armour would be rubbed with olive oil. This intensity of preparation was, of course, the preserve of the very wealthy and those they chose for special treatment. The others did as much or as little as they saw fit.

Weapons would be sharpened. Nobles and men-at-arms carried two major weapons and a dagger. Defensively, good armour made a shield unnecessary. Armour's hardness and weight also gave its wearer a tremendous potential forward momentum as well as protection, transforming him into a one-man medieval tank. Considered in these terms, it is less surprising that Edmund of Somerset killed four men at 1st Saint Albans before he himself was taken down. It also gives complete credibility to Trollope's boast that he was able to dispatch fifteen men at 2nd Saint Albans, even when wounded by a caltrop.

The extra protection of the vulnerable armpit area, introduced by the middle of the century, gave the armoured man the opportunity to exploit the full potential of the most powerful hand-weapon on the battlefield: the poleaxe, rightfully described as 'the preferred staff weapon of the knightly classes'.[5] This was five weapons in one and would have made short work of an unarmoured man. Its different elements were mounted on a solid wooden shaft, made even sturdier by metal reinforcers called langets, running down from the head. Generally around five feet long, the poleaxe had a sharpened point at each end. The top point formed part of the head, which might have an axe on one side and a hammer head like a sledgehammer across from it, though there was no uniformity as these weapons were customized to the owner's requirements. The head might also have three spikes of different shapes, with one on each side of the pole at right-angles to the axe and the hammer, with a third beak-like recurved spike mounted on the hammer itself. Some had a hand guard, but many did not, depending on whether the knight preferred to rely on his gauntlets to protect him as he slid his fingers up and down the shaft, shifting his grip to adapt its workable length and to change the type of blow and its force. Specifically weighted in order to maximize impact, in powerful hands with a full swing, the poleaxe delivered a blow that could decapitate an unprotected neck with ease.[6]

A poleaxe used against armour was more of an equal competition. The ridges that deflected arrows were also designed to turn a lethal blow into a glancing one. Even a full-on strike would not cut through well-cared-for metal. That said, a particularly well-timed and heavy blow could send shock waves through the body, with a force to break bones on top of its impact in buckling and distorting the plates. Once in that state, further pound-ing blows with axe or beaked hammer would cause additional damage, through the blows themselves and through pushing the warped plates on to the body underneath it. Even though a padded jacket was worn between armour and body, such blows would create much more than superficial bruising. An assault of this type could result in massive organ damage, or deliver further shocks to the victim so great that they could trigger a heart attack or stroke, or, potentially as deadly in a battle situation, a fatal loss of consciousness. With the victim on the ground, an assailant could finish off his victim with a dagger thrust through an unopened visor, or prise it open and stab him through the eye and straight into the brain.

Of course, a wise knight would not finish off a seemingly grievously injured man himself—he would get his men to do it. A man on the ground might be badly wounded or he might just be temporarily unconscious. Someone leaning over to inflict the death blow would himself be vulnerable, offering the completely unprotected area of his groin to his grounded knightly opponent, who, if he was able to gather his wits, could stab upwards—or his own men would attempt to strike in another area dangerously left open by the raising of arms and leaning forward: the inner arms and armpits.

If, however, the victim of the initial hammer blows was, miraculously, still on his feet, using his own poleaxe to defend himself, what then? Where would the assailant look to strike and which of the deadly poleaxe components would he use? Success usually depended on spotting a gap between the different pieces of armour, which the knight would then attempt to widen by smashing it with the spikes. As soon as the opening was wide enough, he would finish off his opponent with a fatal thrust of the topmost spear point—or look to his men to move in for the kill. There would be danger all the while from the defender's men-at-arms, who would not be standing idly by if they saw their man in trouble, but would try to interpose themselves and enable him to be pulled away.

As for the knight's second weapon, this would most likely be a sword. In the struggle for supremacy between the defence provided by armour and the offensive weapons designed to penetrate it, the shape of the sword and its use had changed. The ability of the large two-handed broadsword, with both edges sharpened, to smash and slash through mail had been negated by the end of the fourteenth century through the development of plate. Thus the shape of the blade changed to take this into account. No longer of uniform width down its length, the blade now tapered to a sharp point. No longer so broad, the sword was consequently lighter, which accounts for the sword's name: the 'hand-and-a-half'. Both edges were still sharp and held in both hands and used in a stabbing action, the sword could probe for vulnerabilities in the same way as the end point of the poleaxe, rather like a long two-handed bayonet. Alternatively it could be used with one hand in sword play.

The protection of hands by steel gauntlets also enabled the sword to be employed in a rather unexpected manner. As we can see from illustrations in the Fight Books,[7] it could be grasped at the blade end, with the pommel, the weighted end of the hilt, effectively serving as the end of a club. This could be brought down with impressive force on an opponent. Evidence of its effectiveness remains in the verb still in use today: to pummel.

The knight's third weapon was his dagger. He would have used the rondel, named after the rounded disc which served as a guard for the hilt, and which was designed specifically for military use. Yet daggers were scarcely the preserve of the knightly class. Everybody had a dagger. They were an essential everyday tool, used for cutting up food and for the myriad other tasks that required a sharp blade. They were worn attached to the belt and being on show, some had highly ornamented hilts, to demonstrate the wealth and social position of their owners. The most common type was the ballock, its name deriving from a resemblance between the shape of the hilt and male genitalia. The use of a dagger in battle was straightforward: grasped in the fist and brought down with force, it was ideal for finishing off an opponent. The blade was reinforced so that it would not break off when hitting metal or bone.

If all else failed, and the knight was completely disarmed, he had one last weapon: his armoured body. Not just his gauntleted fists, but every hard surface and every edge of the metal that encased him.

Archers, the type of men who had used the dagger so effectively at Agincourt, were lightly clad. They had another means of defence in hand-to-hand combat. This was the buckler, a light circular shield of beaten iron plate or of leather stretched over wood. An archer's main side-arm was a sword, slightly shorter than the hand-and-a-half. This made him quick and nimble in close fighting, but a sensible archer would remain on the periphery of the separate skirmishes of battle. He would have spent the night before Towton waxing and polishing his bow and waxing and oiling his bowstring. It was essential that both were maintained so that the bow did not dry out and crack and the string could withstand difficult weather conditions.[8]

Swords and poleaxes were the weapons of the professionals. Those who were mustered from their traditional peacetime roles in town or country brought an array of pole-mounted weapons, which were used to slash and stab. Most common was the bill hook, an agricultural tool designed for chopping hedges and brushwood, which, with small adaptations for military use, became a weapon resembling the continental halberd in appearance. Its hook could be used to reach around the back of the opponent's leg and then be pulled back. If the sharp blade hit largely unprotected flesh, it could cut through the tendons. If it hit an area that was padded, the force of the pulling motion could be enough to knock the man off balance. In addition, the bill had a stabbing spike like a bayonet on its top end and a shorter spike on the reverse of the head. The latter might be recurved for pushing into gaps between plates of armour, or when shaped like a lozenge tapered to a point, it might even punch through poorer quality plate.

Another weapon was the glaive, effectively a sharp knife mounted on a pole: this was primarily used for slashing, though some also had a back spike for stabbing. There were spears, cheap to produce, simple to construct, and of course axes: brought by woodsmen who only needed to change the shaft length of the tool to transform it from wood axe to battle axe.

Also there was the mace: this, like all battlefield weapons, was massively varied in form. It could be mounted on a shaft of any length, but it was probably most effectively used as a one-handed club, tightly gripped within the fist with the aid of a leather strap. With its lead-weighted and spiked or multi-bladed head it would have distorted overlapping plates of armour and caused horrific injuries on the unprotected.[9] The higher quality maces used by nobles were composed of broad-bladed segments, or flanges, designed to administer maximum force but not to stick into the victim; these could be deployed in a frenzy of repeated sharp percussive blows.

And there were also hand gunners. Discoveries in 2010 proved for the first time that mobile field artillery was in use at the Battle of Bosworth, fewer than twenty-five years after Towton. No shot from field artillery—as opposed to hand cannon—has, as yet, been found at Towton. If, as seems likely, field artillery did not feature at the battle, this may have been for one of two reasons: firstly, that the speed of the Yorkist advance and their crossing of the Aire at Castleford did not give the Lancastrians time to prepare the necessary fixed positions. Secondly, that the commanders had learned from experience. After all, during the previous battles of the war, field artillery had proved at best ineffective, at worst counter-productive. At Ludford Bridge, it was used only to fire warning shots. It slowed the Duke of York's march north in 1460 and was sent back to London. At Northampton, the guns in the Lancastrian emplacements had become waterlogged and unusable. At 2nd Saint Albans, the disorder of the artillery redeployment was one of the factors that created the chaos leading to Warwick's defeat. Perhaps its use by the Austin Friar after Blore Heath was its only positive contribution.

This is not to say that artillery was ineffective per se. It had been usefully deployed for decades; cannons could fire cannonballs of prodigious size with impressive effect. When Henry IV besieged Berwick in 1405, such was the effect on the town walls of one shot from his cannon, that the town surrendered immediately.[10] Its effects could be very gruesome indeed. The last Montagu Earl of Salisbury—the Kingmaker's maternal grandfather—was one of the earliest high-ranking casualties of artillery fire: at the siege of Orleans, a ricocheting stone ball embedded an iron bar from a window frame in his face. The gentleman who was killed by the stone ball with its next bounce was fortunate in comparison; the poor earl lingered in agony for eight days.[11] Effective cannon could indeed be decisive in a war of sieges: as Charles VII showed when reducing the towns of English Normandy.

But the Wars of the Roses were wars fought through battles, not sieges. This was partly cause and effect. England's towns were either not fortified or their fortifications were neglected, making sieges and the use of siege cannon unnecessary. England may have been long at war with the French, but there had been no real fear of invasion until the 1450s. The earlier use of guns, at Northampton and 2nd Saint Albans, consisted of an attempt to re-create the fixed positions of siege warfare within the context of a battlefield by building fortified earthworks and firing guns from them. The fiasco for Warwick at 2nd Saint Albans was partly due to his being caught between one such position and another. By Towton, it seems that lessons had been learned on both sides.

In any case, practical considerations dictated that the English should ignore the cautionary words of Vegetius and of Christine de Pisan 'not to risk all in battle'.[12] The dynamic of having large armies of paid troops in a civil war meant that campaigns had to be extremely swift. For although punishment for deserters could be brutal, the worry of desertion by unpaid and unfed troops was a real one for a commander.

Some gunnery artefacts have, however, been discovered at Towton and they are remarkable. The hand cannons fired by individual gunners were long tubes designed to project an explosive force from the far end. It is amazing that these were able to fire at all at Towton, given the conditions on the battlefield. But European specialists did so for both sides. Yet for all the sound and fury, it is extremely unlikely that many of the opposition were killed. The greatest effect would have been in the noise and smoke, which would have impressed one's own troops rather than the enemy's. And not necessarily positively: the barrel itself could explode—as shattered fragments from two separate guns found recently at Towton bear witness— and kill the gunner and those around him. These weapons were still at the experimental stage. So was the ammunition they used and an artefact found at Towton is, like the guns themselves, historically important. It is shot of an impressive three centimetres in diameter, not of stone but of iron encased in lead. It is, at the time of writing, the oldest 'composite' lead shot ever found on a European battlefield.

Handguns were partly taking over the role of crossbows on the bat-tlefield; both could be penetrating, but both were very slow to reload in comparison to the longbow. The crossbow was at its most effective when the rate of shot was not so important; they also required less in the way of strength and technique from the user. Women and young boys were known to have used them from continental castle walls to resist sieges. Once the crossbow was loaded, the only skill required was to point and aim. It was the perfect weapon for a sniper: one such had killed Richard the Lionheart, another was to achieve immortality at Towton.

Finally, what of the horsemen and their horses? Far more horsemen trav-elled to the battlefield than fought there. The nobles and their men-at-arms travelled by horse, as did some of the mustered men. Some did, but not all. For one thing, the amount of feed necessary to maintain tens of thousands of horses was prohibitive; for another, the mustered men were expected to bring their own equipment, and horses were expensive. Their use on campaign and in battle had become more restricted with the advent of the longbow, the devastating effect of the latter having drastically changed the nature of warfare. By the time of Towton, horses for the knightly class were often most valued as conveyances to and from the battlefield. As in Shake-speare's *Richard III*, 'My kingdom for a horse', they were essential in dire emergency—the getaway cars of the fifteenth century. With that potential purpose in mind, the role of the groom, who might be little more than a child, was extremely important. He was expected to remain on standby at his post. Any desertion was liable to be severely punished, for instance with the loss of an ear.[13] The phrase a clip around the ear denoted a lasting punishment in that period.

On the march, horsemen, as described earlier, were sent ahead to secure food and supplies. They could be used away from the main army to gather intelligence, though, as we have seen, they were not necessarily effective in that role. They could be deployed—as they were the day before Towton—in cavalry confrontations against enemy horsemen. Chillingly, in set-piece battles, they could be placed at the back of their own lines for potential use against their own troops. In this role, as 'prickers', they would run down and kill anyone trying to desert during the battle; the 'pricking' being accomplished with the aid of the ten-foot lance they carried.

The cavalry were most deadly in pursuit of enemy soldiers fleeing from the field. Frantically tearing off jacks and helmets in an effort to run more quickly, these would be completely vulnerable to horsemen equipped with sword, axe and mace, or the specialist weapon of the horseman's hammer. This last, otherwise known as a warhammer, came with sledgehammer and beaked spike. In this context the horseman took on the role of the hunter.

Returning to the eve of battle and the billeting of troops, it would have been the case that if the commanders of the two armies found themselves sheltered billets of reasonable comfort, the common soldiery would not have done. The medieval man was far hardier, far better able to withstand the rigours of the outdoors than we are today. There was no problem sleeping under the stars in the spring, summer and autumn months—the normal period for military campaigning. But though the calendar showed the first days of spring, the weather itself was decidedly wintry. It would have been an uncomfortable night, sharpened on one side by pangs of hunger; on the other by the fate of Clifford and the Flower of Craven.

At daybreak on Palm Sunday morning, both sides began to prepare for battle. The weather was stormy,[14] but that was not the only reason the day was inauspicious for battle. For medieval man, 'the solemn feast of Palm

Richard, Duke of York

In stained glass—Trinity College, Cambridge

Henry VI and Margaret of Anjou

Being presented with a wedding gift by John Talbot, Earl of Shrewsbury, England's warrior general at the end of the Hundred Years War. The manuscript, in the British Library, contains Christine de Pisan's 'Le Livre des Faits d'Armes et de Chevalerie'.

(opposite page) **Micklegate Bar, York**

The heads of some of the greatest men in the land were impaled on the top of the tower.

Legate Coppini's two Masters:

(left) **Francesco Sforza, Duke of Milan**

(below left) **Pope Pius II**

England was strongly affected by the backwash of Italian power politics.

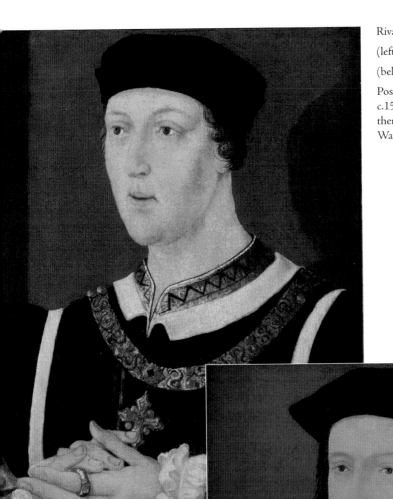

Rival Kings:

(left) **Henry VI**

(below) **Edward IV**

Posthumous portraits produced in c.1540—probably as a pair. Sadly, there are no similar 'likenesses' of Warwick the Kingmaker.

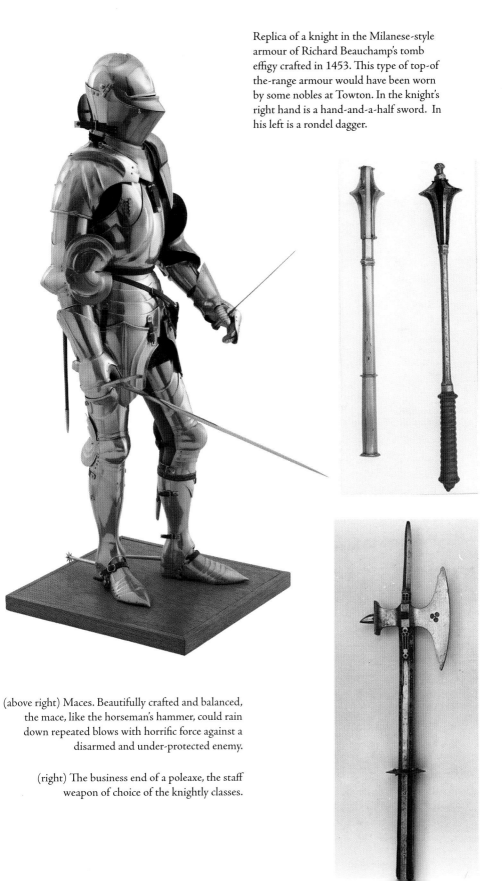

Replica of a knight in the Milanese-style armour of Richard Beauchamp's tomb effigy crafted in 1453. This type of top-of the-range armour would have been worn by some nobles at Towton. In the knight's right hand is a hand-and-a-half sword. In his left is a rondel dagger.

(above right) Maces. Beautifully crafted and balanced, the mace, like the horseman's hammer, could rain down repeated blows with horrific force against a disarmed and under-protected enemy.

(right) The business end of a poleaxe, the staff weapon of choice of the knightly classes.

Towton in a snow storm

The edge of the escarpment dropping down to the valley of Cock Beck below.

Photograph taken from Cock Beck looking upwards to highlight the downward slope off the battlefield for a fleeing army being funnelled down Towton Dale. What it cannot show is the treacherous conditions underfoot of frozen snow and slush for men hurtling towards the swollen icy waters of the medieval River Cock in full spate.

The battlefield at Towton from the Lancastrian lines looking diagonally across towards the Yorkist right.

Three Towton battle victims, excavated in 2005.

Edward IV receiving a dedicated manuscript from Jean de Waurin.

Sunday'[15] signified more than just the beginning of Holy Week; it was a day when peace was particularly venerated. In addition to risking their lives, the men who fought on that day would be jeopardizing their chances in the hereafter. It was therefore considered vital to attend Mass and receive absolution for their sins in preparation for the coming battle. Should they be killed, their best hope of salvation was to be buried on a west–east axis, with head to the west and feet to the east, preferably within a consecrated church and as close to the altar as possible. Thus when the resurrection came, the soul clothed in new flesh would be best placed for the second coming, the new dawn of life. This manner of burial, for the Church of England at least, remains the custom to this day.[16]

In reality, this option would only be available to a few. For the rest, if they were lucky they would be buried in the correct position in consecrated ground. The unlucky would be thrown into a pit in unconsecrated ground, to lie in haphazard fashion with their bones jumbled up with fellow unfortunates; their expectation, at best, would be everlasting purgatory. The position was not irredeemable, however, provided you were disinterred and reburied in the correct manner within consecrated ground. For some at Towton, this occurred as recently as 1996.

Occasionally, consecrated ground could come to you. This happened at the battlefield at Shrewsbury, when the troubled King Henry IV sought to give himself peace of mind by commissioning the beautiful memorial church of Saint Mary Magdalene over the grave pits and having the surrounding ground specially consecrated. It also happened at Towton, where the victor likewise commissioned a memorial chapel, to be completed by Richard III. The Towton Chapel was a victim of the vicissitudes of history. In contrast to Shrewsbury where a Battlefield Church remains to this day, the Towton Chapel all too quickly became a memorial to an event that a new dynasty, the Tudors, wanted to forget. The building materials decayed; they were removed for other purposes. The memorial was lost, though it may now be in the process of being rediscovered.[17]

While accepting that he could not control the treatment of his body after death, there were other ways a soldier could protect his soul in the afterlife and the means were readily available. Pardoners sold indulgences under special licence to reduce the time spent in purgatory,[18] though the nature of the licences and therefore the pardons given could be distinctly dubious. Impoverished men who had been disfigured in warfare did well to approach an army before battle, as an act of charity towards them would figure in the calling of accounts after death and also give the donor some faith that such an act of compassion to the afflicted might forestall a similar fate for him.

There was another potential cause of damnation: that of opposing the rightful king. Henry VI might still be in York with Queen Margaret and Prince Edward but he remained an anointed and crowned king: his Standard would be raised in battle, and to oppose it even in his absence was treason. Few of Henry's men would have met their sovereign and, in view of the King's broken condition, it is probably as well that they had not done so. But they revered him as God's ordained ruler and viewed Edward as a traitorous insurgent.

Edward was not a crowned and anointed king, merely an acclaimed one. He was, however, present on the battlefield.

Henry just may, in his own mind, have once seen himself as the embodiment of the very ancient role of priest as king, but Edward was obviously the incarnation of the warrior lord. The roles that Henry V had been able to combine, through his piety and through his conquest, were now split between the two contenders. The Lancastrians would be reassured by Edward's lack of legitimacy, but his own troops would be inspired by his charisma as they made their final preparations for battle.

Whether the armies were close enough for the heralds to travel to and fro is not known. If they were, it is likely that a 'parlay' was attempted merely for form's sake. Ahead of a battle it was the heralds' role to act as messengers between the two sides to settle the rules of engagement. When it was over, they had the grim task of noting those of quality[19] who had perished, as well as estimating the overall number of dead. At Towton, however, their work would begin at the end of the battle. There was no need to discuss rules of engagement for the attitudes of the nobles on both sides were well known. The Somerset and Northumberland heirs sought revenge for 1st Saint Albans, and the York and Neville heirs looked to avenge Wakefield—these grievances alone would have ensured that there would be no mercy, 'no quarter' for the defeated.

As for the soldiery on each side, there was also a sense of alienation, of an acute antipathy. Only this and the particular strain of the battle can explain the events that followed. For one thing, each regarded the other as being in league with a foreign enemy: the Lancastrians had French and Scottish troops and the Yorkists Burgundians. For another, there was a basic regional difference between the two sides: the Lancastrians were mainly from the North with some from the Midlands; the Yorkists were mainly from the South and West, including Wales, and again with men from the Midlands. The River Trent was the dividing line. Certainly there would have been some Yorkists north of the Trent, for example from the Duke of York's own territories and those of the Nevilles; similarly the Earls of Wiltshire and Devon and others like them would have been able to draw on some of their affinities from further south. But recruitment would have been more difficult. As for the areas in between, they competed under the Commissions of Array, which would have meant that those who, for instance, arrived first in towns were able to recruit 'unattached' townsmen.

The troops of the two sides sounded very different, both in terms of their accents and in their phraseology and use of language. Some, mainly Yorkists, would have been Welsh speakers. Even their bread, the staff of life and a major part of the diet of the common man, was different. Due to the shorter growing season in the North, the bread there was based on rough barley and oats—something that would have caused grumbling amongst the Yorkist troops as they travelled northwards. In the case of the men from Kent, it is likely that their drink of choice was different, as Flemish weavers had brought hops and hence beer to Kent in around 1400. Hops were important as a preservative, beer keeping far longer and far better than the unhopped ale. But it was an acquired taste, one that would have been adopted in Kent, London and other parts of the South East—but certainly not north of the Trent, where the sweeter taste of ale would have still held sway.[20]

There was a definite sense of cultural difference, as reflected by *John Benet's Chronicle*, which noted an Oxford student riot between Northerners and Southerners earlier in Henry VI's reign, leaving many injured; followed the next day by a battle between Northerners and the Welsh.[21] In a riot, such a sense of difference can cause injury; in the extremities of warfare, as the world's experiences of more recent times can testify, it can engender massacres.

Before moving up to the battlefield, ale would have been consumed by both sides, with the nobles probably drinking mulled wine. Because of the numbers involved, preparations began well before dawn. These numbers were huge indeed—as would be the losses. Even if the Towton Battlefield Archaeological Survey were able to excavate every inch of the battlefield, their sterling work would still not give us the exact number of the dead, because huge grave pits were cleared, for extremely strong political reasons, in the 1480s. However, we can attempt to deduce the numbers from other evidence. This we can also do for those who moved into position at the beginning of the battle. Indeed, we come back first to the figure, widely reported immediately afterwards, which placed the number of dead at 28,000. This total may include the figures for the subsidiary battle the day before at Ferrybridge and the pursuit and annihilation of Clifford and the Flower of Craven; it may also need to be reduced slightly for the manner of counting by the heralds. Even so, it is enormous. Even if we go for a lower figure such as 20,000 for the battle and the rout,[22] this is the largest one-day death toll on British soil. That in itself is due to the nature of the battle and the recruitment for it.

As discussed, Commissions of Array, effectively an order to mobilize for the King, were not easily avoided. Even less avoidable were they now when issued by two competing kings and enforced by men such as the Earl of Warwick, with an urgency created by the expectation that this would be one last desperate effort in order to secure their own and their families' survival. As the generators and enforcers of this recruitment the great majority of the active nobility were present; as has been stated above, a greater percentage were at Towton than engaged in any other battle during these wars.[23]

In these circumstances they did not just enrol well-armed and well-protected men between sixteen and sixty. There were many who were less well-suited, particularly in terms of their defensive equipment; men who at any other time would have been disregarded as 'naked men'. From this perspective, figures such as 50,000 seem probable, and even the 75,000 quoted by one military historian, representing 10 per cent of available men, is not impossible.[24]

These figures would also make sense in terms of the terrain. Across a potential battlefront of up to half a mile, it would take these numbers to spread across the ground in significant depth of ranks to prevent the threat of either gaps being punched through the line or of being outflanked. With such numbers, they could stay engaged, as we shall see, for many hours.

In the early morning, the Lancastrians moved into position first and awaited their opponents, a council of war having previously decided their exact positions on the field. Somerset, advised by Trollope, was in command. He was not the most senior Lancastrian—that was Henry, Duke of Exeter—but Somerset had a record of victory at Wakefield and some, if partial, success in Calais. Whereas the kindest word to describe Exeter would be 'reckless',[25] his actions in the 1450s had been a record of desperation and defeat. It seems that Exeter, therefore, commanded the Lancastrian reserve, with Northumberland taking responsibility for the left and Somerset the right.

It was appropriate that the blood feud which began with the skirmish at Saint Albans in 1455 should be settled by the direct heirs of its initial protagonists, Somerset and York. For the Yorkists also looked to the younger man. Edward was no longer in Warwick's shadow as he had been at Northampton. He had been successful in his own independent command at Mortimer's Cross and, more importantly, he had become King— or, at least, *a* king. Warwick, the hero of Calais, had lost both the battle and Henry VI at 2nd Saint Albans. Though he had blamed, caught and executed the errant Kentish captain Lovelace,[26] and though the remainder of his men from Kent still revered him, his authority had dimmed just as that of his young cousin had risen. And there was a further cause for Warwick to be overshadowed at Towton: the arrow wound he had received at Ferrybridge.[27] The third Yorkist commander was Fauconberg, fresh from the destruction of Clifford, with command of the vanguard and responsibility for the archers.[28] Yet the Yorkists had been waiting frantically for a fourth—Norfolk—of whom, and his troops, there was still no sign.

The terrain of the battlefield at Towton in March 1461 is clearly recognizable from the topography today. It is agricultural land, as it was then, and has not been built upon. The nature of the farmland in 1461 was different, some pasture, some arable, some managed woodland. Trees and bushes were probably individually dotted around the plateau, but woods in any profusion were to the west, that is to the right and rear of the Lancastrian position. The Lancastrian position itself was ideal. For though it is accurate to describe the entire area between Towton and Saxton as a plateau, in so far as it was raised above the surrounding countryside—indeed marking the highest point between Ferrybridge and York[29]—the land was not flat. It consisted of undulating ground, the sort of landscape which in other times and other places might be considered for a racecourse, for an Epsom or a Doncaster, and then rejected due to its more extreme features. From the highest point of the northern part of the plateau, the ground slopes down more steeply from north to south for around 400 yards. The top of this incline corresponds to the very point where the Cock Beck, down in the valley below, snakes sharply inwards before snaking out again (*see map, p. 150*). An army on top of the ridge would have a commanding position. In fact its complete protection from flank attack on a narrowed front made it extraordinarily strong. On their right, the land dropped precipitously to the Cock Beck—shallower today but still likely to flood in winter—with the stream arching around to the back of their position. To their left the ground fell away towards marshland. Unable to outflank them, the hungry and numerically inferior Yorkist army would have no alternative but to attack up the rising ground.

There was only one conceivable area of weakness. Should the Yorkists make the same manoeuvre as they did at Castleford and get behind the Lancastrian army, they could strike at the rear. This they could do by crossing the west-to-east stretch of the Cock Beck a mile and a half to the west at Aberford,[30] then cutting across country three and a half miles to the north-east, and recrossing the river at the bridge on the London road between Towton and Tadcaster. However, as at Tadcaster, the Lancastrians could, if necessary, destroy the bridge.

The speed of Edward's advance, the delay of Northumberland in meeting it, and the annihilation of the Flower of Craven was, of course, unexpected. It would have shaken the Lancastrian leadership. That said, the Lancastrians had established what seemed an unassailable position and Edward would have to attack them, both to get to York and to obtain fresh supplies. Battle would be joined, because the Yorkists required it and because the Lancastrians now sought it, having engineered it on terms and territory of their choosing.

For the Lancastrians, Towton was the best ground on the direct route between the River Aire and York. We cannot know whether it was always the Lancastrian commanders' intention to lure a weakened Yorkist army across the River Aire and deeper into alien territory and thus to destruction at Towton, or whether this was a secondary position, based on the assumption that the forces of their 'treasonous upstart' enemy would dissolve at the River Aire just as those of his associate Warwick had done at 2nd Saint Albans. If it was a secondary choice, it was still one chosen with extreme care. And it offered the potential to double the role that might be played by the Aire; for, with the Yorkists broken on the battlefield and in headlong retreat to the south, the river would again become a substantial barrier. This time it would not be used to prevent entry to the North, but to bar escape.

Thus Somerset and his fellow commanders had every reason for confidence as the Lancastrian forces raised their highly coloured and decorated banners: those of Somerset with the quartered arms of England and France within a blue-and-white chequered border; Northumberland's with the blue lion rampant on a yellow background and three lucies (river pike) on bright red.[31] The badges on the surcoats of the men of each affinity matched the banners. There was no uniformity of colour for the contending sides, and no uniform as such. But there was little chance of confusion for an army all facing the same way and organized in blocks of affinity which operated all the way up from the lowliest soldiers to the commanders: Somerset, Northumberland and Exeter. Thus Northumberland's block would naturally contain the northern Lords Dacre, Fitzhugh, Mauley and Lord John Neville; Somerset's would take in Devon, Wiltshire, and the Lords Hungerford, Rivers, Scales, Rougemont-Grey and De La Warre—and of course, to the fore, Sir Andrew Trollope; finally Exeter would naturally have Lords Welles, Willoughby and Grey of Codnor.[32]

All gathered together, they began to move forward—being in position on the ridge by around 9 a.m.

The only thing, of course, for which they could not plan was the weather, which continued cold, blustery and threatening.

When the Yorkists were sighted, a resounding shout went up from both armies, the acclamation of support for their respective kings. As the Lancastrians had the commanding position, Fauconberg was forced to move the Yorkist archers to the foot of the far slope of Towton Dale, giving the advantage of height, thus distance and killing power, to the Lancastrians. But the sixty-year-old, physically unimpressive 'little Fauconberg' was a seasoned soldier of vast experience and he knew how to read the weather.

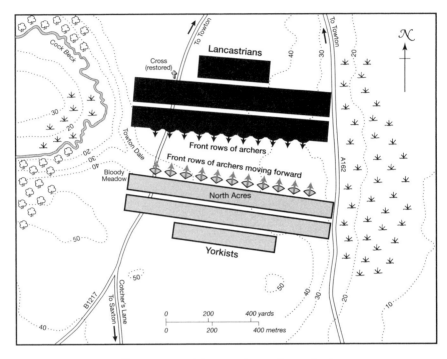

Opening positions—the archery duel

As the archers of the two sides set up position, a storm of biblical pro-
portions broke out.[33] Sleet and snow were to alternate during a day of
appalling conditions. At this critical moment, according to Hall's *Chronicle*, it was sleet.[34] The wind direction was crucial: it came directly from
the south and recent scientific tests on the battlefield in extremely blustery
conditions have shown what a difference this would have made. Heading
into such a wind, the Lancastrian arrows would have lost range; by the
same token, the Yorkist arrows would have gained it. The Yorkists now had
the advantage of distance—probably more than fifty yards—of impact and
of visibility. The Lancastrian archers were blinded by sleet being driven
directly into their faces. They could not see where their arrows were landing and began to shoot volley after volley at an enemy flickering in and out
of vision in the distance, hoping to best their opponents through quantity
of shot—but their arrows were falling short.

Fauconberg knew that his Yorkist archers had to measure the wind, to
gauge its effect on distance and to adjust their shooting angle. This would
not have been a simple matter. Frantic hand signals down the line directed

the men to try one ranging volley. Then they were able to put their experience, based on years of practising on Sundays and festival days, to good use. Unencumbered by the hazard of enemy arrows and with the wind in their favour, the Yorkist arrows began to find their targets with sickening effect. The Lancastrian archers started to fall, pierced in a fusillade lasting perhaps seven or eight minutes and involving hundreds of thousands of arrows, which, even considering the appalling conditions, would have been shot at a rate of around ten per minute.[35] Some Yorkists, their own arrows spent, moved forward and began to pick up the Lancastrians' arrows and shoot them back into the now advancing soldiery. For under such unrelenting arrow attack, the Lancastrian infantry had no alternative but to abandon their strong position and to move forward to halt the Yorkist archers and prevent the annihilation of their own men.

As the enemy closed, the Yorkist bowmen were forced to turn and, facing the storm of sleet, run back to the protection of their lines. Yet the Lancastrian advance would have been unsteady. In poor visibility, tripping over and through the wasted arrows of their own side, they eventually arrived at the flatter ground at the bottom of the slope.[36] The advantage of position had been lost.

In these conditions, it would have been remarkable if Somerset's advancing men had not missed the end of the Yorkist line, possibly overlapping it. Thus with the Yorkists themselves surging forward some yards to resist the momentum of the enemy, and with those on the Lancastrian right engaging more quickly, this in itself would have caused the two lines to start pivoting from facing roughly south/south-west and north/north-east now towards south-east/ north-west, particularly if the reserve of each side was thrown in haphazardly, with the Lancastrian right reinforced. Had this happened, in the chaos of battle, that in itself would have been enough to swing the battle line forty-five degrees.[37]

The skewing of the line so early on would give credence to accounts of Edward's crucial role at this stage of the battle.[38] Under the banner of the arms of the King of England, Edward's own position on the battlefield would have been obvious. At nearly six foot four inches, his height would have made him stand out; so also would his killing potential. As children at Ludlow, he and Rutland had had the best available tuition in combat from the best available fight masters. They had access in manuscript form

to the fight manuals of the day. They would have mastered combat techniques through constant practice. At nearly nineteen, with a good diet and
a body able to burn up calories through rigorous daily exercise on foot or
on horseback, Edward would have been exceptionally fit. His size gave him
that essential advantage for the armoured knight at this period: reach. In
addition, he had exceptional self-confidence; after all, at Mortimer's Cross
he had seemed blessed by providence.

These attributes stood Edward in good stead now, for the still superior
numbers of the Lancastrians, magnified in this part of the line, started to
push him and his men back in the 'press' of the battle. And 'press' was the
word: the space required for the full flourish of poleaxe and sword would
have been denied.

Despite their own hours of fighting practice—training with staves
to deflect the long shafts of their opponents' weapons before following
through with the dagger—the common soldiery, as men with no armour,
would have found the conditions horrendous. Just the act of keeping their
feet must have been difficult: the ground under their loose leather boots
was becoming increasingly slippery, particularly with sleet becoming snow,
with blood and dead bodies underfoot. And with a sudden stumble there
was always the risk of lurching forward and exposing the neck and back to
an opponent's spike.

This was the general manner of battle. It would have been punctuated
along the line by demonstrations of far greater destruction from men who,
better armed and fully armoured, could risk much more. Not that they, in
the front line, would have had the room to swing the full weight of their
poleaxe. Some might have tried the tactic of standing one line behind their
own men to give protection to their inside arms and armpits as they brought
the hammerhead down; this would have been difficult but not impossible
amongst troops fighting as a unit. And each lord's men would have been a
unit, with him as the spearhead, and his trusted personal household men
and closest retainers around him. It was a formation that reflected a relationship of mutual advantage: the lord depended on his men for his life; the
men on their lord for preferment, lifestyle and livelihood.

Writing about 2nd Saint Albans, Gregory had said that the men who
won the day were the officers of the royal and noble households and those
on permanent pay, 'the household men and feed men',[39] and in the close

hand-to-hand fighting of these battles, they were always likely to have a major advantage. In the press of battle, the better fed, the better trained and maintained, the better armed and the better protected were bound to be more effective. Quantity of manpower was important, but so was its quality. The requirement was for men for whom the preparation for war was a matter of honour, opportunity, or just a very good living; men for whom combat was a full-time job.

These were the men that Edward now relied upon as the Lancastrians, having overcome such a disastrous start to the battle, began to claw back the advantage. With their greater destructive power, generated by having more nobles and their attendant professionals and fortified by a higher head count, they began to push the Yorkists in Edward's sector backwards. Under immense pressure the line buckled—but it did not break. This was the second event that could have shifted the battle line on its axis to north-west/south-east.

The third came in early afternoon when Norfolk's forces at last arrived. Rather than coming over the back of the plateau to form a new reserve, as might have been expected, they continued north at the far right of the battlefield and on a lower level along the side of it. This may have been due to the lie of the land and the poor visibility obscuring the true disposition of the troops; the dreadful weather conditions may, if anything, have worsened, and the howling wind could have 'thrown' the sound of battle. But the choice of deployment might, conceivably, have been due to the genius of its commander. It brought Norfolk's troops around the base of the plateau, into the flatter ground known as North Acres, and into the side of the Lancastrian line. Suddenly the pressure was on the Lancastrians.

But it was their turn not to buckle. That the two armies held firm under such pressure was partly due to bravery, leadership and determination. It was also due to the nature of the terrain. The area that saw the bulk of the fighting, that of North Acres and Towton Dale, is lower-lying area ground bordered by slopes. This was the area in which the tens of thousands of troops were jammed.

Towton had become a long battle, a far cry from the short skirmish of 1st Saint Albans. It was kept going through the men's ability, in spite of the restrictions of space, to move from front rank to back. This was vital for the shock troops of the battle, the men in full armour. Fighting in full armour

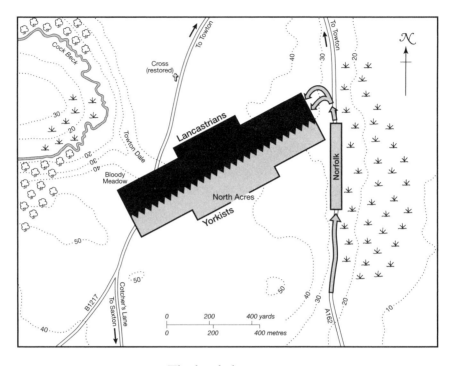

The battle lines turn

was hot and, with visor down, airless. In one sense, the cold of the day at
Towton was helpful, though some parts of the body, those protected only by
mail, would have felt the chill. It was essential to take quick breaks, perhaps
to risk taking off the helmet and, as Clifford had done so fatally the day
before, to remove the gorget that protected the throat, in order to have a sip
of wine. This is exactly what the Lancastrian Lord Dacre of Gilsland did.
Dacre was a soldier experienced in the harsh clashes of raid and counter
raid in the Scottish borders; he had organized the Lancastrian Commission
of Array in Cumbria in 1459 and had probably done so again in 1460–61.[40]
Having pulled back from the front line, he would have felt safe. What happened next was formerly marked by a Bur or Elder Tree, one of many successors on the battlefield, as succeeding human generations have continued
the link with the past stretching back five and half centuries. Legend has
it—and it is a legend—that Dacre was deliberately targeted for assassination
from the original bur tree by a sniper with a crossbow, a young lad who hated
Dacre for treatment his father had received. In reality, as Andrew Boardman
concludes, it is unlikely that someone could have been stalked in this way

on a medieval battlefield, particularly one involving so many thousands of troops in such ghastly conditions.[41] Whatever the motivation and the means, Dacre was struck in the throat or the head with a crossbow bolt or an arrow. His tomb, remarkably for a noble, and due to special circumstances, is not in a church but in the churchyard at nearby Saxton.[42] Many more nobles were to die that day.

At last, in the late afternoon, one of the lines broke. We do not know how and under what circumstances; perhaps a lord was killed, and his men, having lost their paymaster, lost the reason for fighting. Perhaps an outflanking manoeuvre succeeded and allowed the end of the line to be attacked from three sides. In such circumstances, ones and twos making a fateful decision can, in a matter of minutes, even seconds, turn into dozens, then hundreds, until the coherence of the Lancastrian army began to dissolve. This was the moment when the young grooms caring for the horses of the great magnates and their most important men-at-arms held the power of life and death. The higher peerage took flight. Wiltshire, the 'flying earl', was on this occasion joined by Somerset, Exeter and Devon. For some it was to be a brief respite. Northumberland got away, but he was mortally wounded and was to die within hours at York. Of the lesser peerage, Lords Welles, Mauley and Lord John Neville—the betrayer of Richard of York at Wakefield—joined Dacre amongst the Lancastrian dead. So did Andrew Trollope, who this time was overwhelmed on the battlefield. No fewer than forty-two captured Lancastrian knights were summarily executed on Edward's orders.[43]

This, in comparison to the previous battles, was a staggering number of lords and knights. But they formed a mere fraction of the overall death toll. The appalling weather that continued all day, the treacherous conditions underfoot, the lie of the land, all combined to engender a disaster. The forty-five-degree turn of the armies, combined with the necessity of the Lancastrian advance, had transformed their seemingly insuperable battle position into a death trap. The fleeing troops had two main escape routes from the battlefield. If they were on the left of the line, they could try to climb back up the slippery slope and make their way on to the northern part of the plateau. But this brought them into open country—cavalry country. And their immediate exit route away from the cavalry was to the right, down a vertiginous slope to the sodden ground leading to the icy waters of the overflowing Cock Beck below. The other alternative for the soldiers was to join, in individual panic, their thousands of slipping and sliding brothers-in-arms who were being funnelled down from the flat ground of the battlefield, down into the area of Towton Dale, down into what opened out to become the wider open space of what would become known as Bloody Meadow and then down further towards the Cock Beck. Many must have died in the tripping, trampling crush. And as the Lancastrians struggled, they were being targeted.

In later years and quieter times, Edward IV told Philippe de Commynes that: 'In all the battles he had won, as soon as he sensed victory, he mounted his horse and shouted to his men that they must spare the common soldiers and kill the lords, of whom few or none escaped'.[44] This statement befitted a man of imperious charm that could turn to sudden violence within the flicker of an eye:[45] a man who, with every justification, felt blessed by providence and whose reality could, to a great extent, be what he wanted it to be. The latter part of his statement to Commynes was only partially true. The first part was a blatant lie. It is doubtful that Edward could have reined in his exhausted but vengeful army, even if he had wanted to do so. He did not. Edward had been in the Yorkist camp at 1st Saint Albans, six years before;[46] though too young to fight, he had seen the complete lack of mercy of those who did. The chronicler Edward Hall was in no doubt of Edward's planned intention, that 'he made proclamation that no prisoner should be taken, nor one enemy saved'.[47] His army, primed to expect and to give no quarter, was surging forward with the adrenaline levels produced by victory and pursuit.

Some of the fleeing Lancastrians desperately pulled off clothing, including jacks, to speed their attempted escape. Others sacrificed speed for protection. All were at the mercy of Yorkist pursuit troops on horseback. Some of these may have been mounted archers, but most would have been mounted men-at-arms, including the prickers. Cavalry, so vulnerable facing the longbow, was brutally effective in its use of the horseman's hammer on the heads and backs of men running away.

Some of the 'Northern men' nevertheless managed to reach the swift deep waters of Cock Beck, perhaps trying to make for the bridge across it—not knowing that it had already been destroyed. What then? The answer lies at the far end of Bloody Meadow as it bends around the side of the

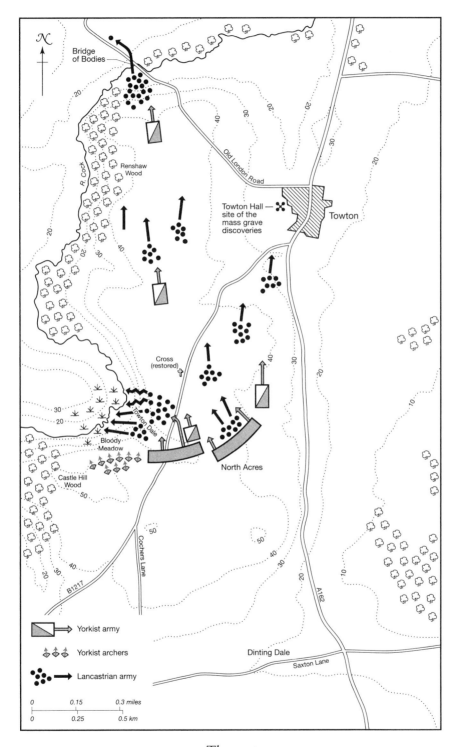

The rout

northern plateau and as Cock Beck itself snakes to the east. Today it is secluded, tree-lined and shaded, but in the late afternoon gloom of Palm Sunday 1461, it bore a very different aspect. In place of the bridge that the Lancastrians, to protect the rear of their position, had themselves destroyed before the battle—just as they had at Tadcaster—another one began to rise from the depths to the top of the waters. This was a bridge formed by men who had been dragged under the surface, whether by the press of their comrades or because their multi-layered jacks continued absorbing water until they became as heavy, perhaps heavier than the armour of the horse-less, stranded men-at-arms flailing through the water. It was also partly formed by others, who, slowed to a standstill in the crush of crossing, had proved easy targets for arrow or hammer. It now became a horrific lifeline as the men struggled over their dead comrades. Its name survives to this day: the Bridge of Bodies.

The pursuit was relentless. Some Lancastrians who fled due north and over the back of the escarpment then crossed Cock Beck further to the east and succeeded in reaching Tadcaster. Here they faced the fate intended by their own commanders for the enemy. Instead of the Yorkists being caught and slaughtered at the broken bridge over the River Aire at Ferrybridge, many Lancastrians died on the banks of the River Wharfe or drowned trying to cross it. The scale of the killing is captured in Lord Chancellor George Neville's letter to Coppini, written just days after the battle, in which he reports that so many were slain 'dead bodies were seen as to cover an area six miles long by three broad and about four furlongs'.[48]

The chase did not stop at Tadcaster, it continued into the night and on another ten miles to York itself. The soldiers hunted down en route were 'small change' in comparison to the big prizes of the 'ex-royals', Henry, Margaret and young Prince Edward, but hunted down they were.

Somerset reached York before the pursuers and he, with Henry and his family, 'with such small company as they had',[49] desperately fled northwards.

That night Edward stayed close to the battlefield. A field of war where only the wealthiest of the wounded could have any chance of being tended, only the more illustrious of the dead any hope of being buried in conse-crated ground. The heralds began their duty of counting and the victorious troops the work of stripping corpses. Reusable armour and weapons were recycled. The dead were relieved of valuables and money that they would have taken into action as an emergency fund, perhaps to enable instant hire of new bodyguards or a horse. The strings that attached purses to belts were cut, fingers with stubborn rings cut off to remove them. The following day Edward moved to York. The Earl of Devon was captured. He had got to York but was, it seems, too badly injured to go any further.[50] He was executed and his severed head joined those of the other Lancastrian lords on Micklegate Bar, as rapid replacements for those of York, Salisbury and their sons. As for Wiltshire, he got away yet again. But the wings of the 'flying earl' were to be clipped at last: he was eventually captured at Cockermouth, taken to Newcastle and decapitated in front of King Edward on 1 May, with his head being sent south to decorate London Bridge.[51]

With a battle of such size, such duration and so momentous an outcome, ensuring the destruction of a dynasty, it would have been surprising if a myriad of myths and legends had *not* grown up around the events of Palm Sunday 1461.[52] Was the whisper of massacres just another of these? Was the recorded volume of deaths merely the result of the sudden collapse of one army in circumstances that left it little room for escape and trapped it on the battlefield? Or was there something more sinister: the killing of disarmed men who were not allowed to surrender? Without evidence, this idea would remain a myth. Then, in recent times, some disturbing evidence came to light.

Builders working on an extension at Towton Hall in 1996 unearthed a mass grave to the north-east of the battlefield. Within it were packed the skeletal remains of thirty-eight people.[53] Some were buried west to east, as if care had been taken to prepare them for the next world, though some of these were, unusually, face down; but others, on top of them, lay packed together in the opposite direction. The only consideration had been to fill the grave with as many bodies as possible before covering them with earth.[54] However, it was only when the skeletons were professionally and reverentially removed by a specialist team of archaeologists from Bradford University that the horrific nature of this find began to emerge.[55]

There was no doubt that these were soldiers from the battle. They were men between the ages of seventeen and fifty,[56] all of whom had died violent deaths; and the date of the bones tied the event to 1461. From the geographical location and the nature of their burial, these were obviously Lancastrian troops. Some of the remains bore signs of single massive injuries that were commensurate with death on the battlefield. The marks on others were far more sinister. Trauma on the arms showed that they had been raised to protect the head from repeated blows delivered by sharp, heavy objects. Injuries to the skulls were also significant: they bore the signs of blows, some obviously administered from behind, that would have killed. There were not one or two, but many. Some skulls had sustained so many injuries that they had become distorted. Here were men, who just possibly might have begun the encounter with weapons, but certainly ended it weaponless and unprotected. They had been dealt a multitude of blows, and this was made clear through the forensic skills of the archaeologists.[57] How many of these blows were delivered before and how many after death we cannot know, but either way the implications are horrendous. These were Englishmen—we can be almost certain that these were Englishmen from the nature of the bones themselves[58]—who had been treated without any trace of humanity at all. If the blows had been administered before death, then they were delivered in a frenzy, making sickening sport of unarmed men. If afterwards, then, according to the beliefs of the time, it was with the intention of obliterating the identity of the men in order to deny them the afterlife.

The massacre of unarmed Frenchmen by Englishmen at Agincourt and that of unarmed Englishmen by Frenchmen at Formigny were atrocities of war, though the first at least had the shred of justification of dire military necessity. But this, at Towton, was something of a different order, both in its nature and in its participants. These were Englishmen treating fellow Englishmen, albeit from a different part of the country, as alien and dehumanized. Of course, one cannot specifically lay the blame for this on Warwick and on Edward. Yet in order to secure their own survival, they had amplified the regional nature of the conflict; Warwick had stressed the uncivilised nature of the men coming down from the north before 2nd Saint Albans, and he had made himself the 'captain' of his own ruthless men from Kent. This demonization was the final element towards making this the most brutal as well as the bloodiest day in English history. A low point of barbarity had been reached.

As for the long-term causes of Towton, these did not stretch back to the deposition of Richard II in favour of Henry IV, as Shakespeare and even some twentieth-century historians have surmised.[59] The shadow of that event had been lifted within one generation by Henry V. The removal of kings, or their restraint just short of removal, had happened often enough before. Rulers who had alienated and tried to outmuscle significant sections of the nobility, including those close to them, had often paid that price. The problem darkening the reign of Henry VI was Henry VI himself, and it was a problem of a completely novel nature. This was not a strong king but an irrevocably weak one; a monarch who, at a time when England operated as a personal monarchy, would not personally rule. A united nobility could replace an 'overmighty' capricious king, as they had shown with Richard II. Yet it showed no desire to remove a distinctly 'undermighty' one. Then cracks in the cohesion of the nobility appeared after 1450 with the ramifications of the loss of France and the fears produced by Cade—cracks but not a break. To the bulk of the nobility, the nature of York's personality was thought to be even more troubling than Henry's lack of one. In consequence, had the rebellious Yorkists not diverted the financial resources of the Merchants of London and the Staplers of Calais from the Crown to themselves, they would not have survived. It was the same desperate aim that led Warwick, having stirred the forces of popular revolt, to set one region against the other—South versus North—with horrific consequences at the point of victory and afterwards.

In the modern-day world, where something has to be the biggest, longest, even bloodiest, in order to be remarkable, then Towton has many claims to be that singular event on English soil. Yet it is its brutality, its final casual indifference to the rules of war and of humanity that should mark it out.

Edward stayed in the North until June, when he was to return to the capital. On 28 June, King Edward IV was anointed and crowned at Westminster with all the pomp and ceremony of his predecessor, the boy king Henry VI, over thirty years before. Yet the perception of the monarch and of the monarchy itself had now changed for ever.

IN MEMORIAM

1461–2011

It was through an ill wind that the Lancastrians lost Towton. Without it they would almost inevitably have won. Sound strategy, as described by Christine de Pisan and Vegetius,[1] dictated that they take up the best ground with a larger force and secure themselves against flank attack. This they did. Without the blizzard, they would, from their superior position, have rained down their arrows on the Yorkists at the bottom of the slope. The Yorkists would have been forced to leave their position and, at most medieval battles, as at Towton, it was the side that first abandoned their starting position that lost.

One could understand it if the Yorkists were somewhat conflicted as to how they might present their victory. On the one hand a true account of their good fortune could be represented, just as with the parhelion at Mortimer's Cross, as having derived from the benevolence of God acting on their behalf; on the other, their victory might be seen as a fluke.

Legate Coppini, safe in Flanders after his difficult voyage, received letters from at least three different sources that were written within days of the battle. In the Milanese state archives are letters from Chancellor Bishop George Neville; from Richard Beauchamp, Bishop of Salisbury; and from Nicholas O'Flanagan, Bishop of Elphin in Ireland. All three stressed the difficulty of the battle; Beauchamp referred to the result being 'doubtful the whole day, until at length victory declared itself on his [King Edward's] side, at a moment when those present declared that almost all on our side despaired of it, so great was the strength and dash of our adversaries'.[2] All agreed on the figure of 28,000 killed—in the words of Beauchamp, 'a number unheard of in our realm for almost a thousand years',[3] though he did then embroider by saying that these did not include those 'wounded and drowned'. The trio of Bishops either gave absurdly low figures for the Yorkist dead or did not differentiate. However Prospero di Camulio, Milanese Ambassador to France, offered different details when writing to his Duke on 12 April, giving the figures for the fallen, on what was interestingly still referred to as 'Warwick's side' as 8,000, compared with 20,000 on 'King Henry's side'.[4] He wrote from Bruges in Burgundian Flanders, where he and Coppini would have conferred. Di Camulio went on to confirm these figures in a further letter to Duke Francesco on the eighteenth, with the addition of the telling phrase 'all counted by heralds after the battle'.[5] His letter crossed with one written to him by Duke Francesco: 'Letters have arrived to-day from Bruges of the 10th inst., stating how the new King of England and the Earl of Warwick have routed the Queen's army, and doubtless the new king will obtain the state. That being the case, we desire you to take leave of the dauphin [who was at loggerheads with his father Charles VII and thus at Bruges] and go to the said king, offering your services and commending yourself to him as you think most fitting, consulting my lord, the Legate [Coppini], and informing yourself fully of all the affairs of those parts, sending us a full account of everything immediately, and you shall return to us as soon as possible'.[6] Duke Francesco Sforza was in no doubt that it had been Margaret who was the prime enemy; matters in England were of very great interest—but most particularly for their impact on France.

If these figures seem to be suspiciously consistent, with the exception that, depending on audience, the 8,000 Yorkist casualties might shrink to 800, then we have one additional source. King Edward may later have had a well-deserved reputation for mendacity, but if there was one person to whom the eighteen-year-old King was unlikely to write a lie at this stage, it was the redoubtable Duchess Cecily of York. That we know of the King's letter to his mother, written immediately after the battle, is due to the *Paston Letters*. Better than that, in this particular case we have a first-hand witness as to its contents. The excitement of William Paston writing to his elder brother John on 4 April leaps off the page:

Please you to know and have wisdom of such news as my Lady of York
has by a letter of authority, under the sign manual of our Sovereign
Lord King Edward, which letter came to our said Lady this very day at
11 o'clock and was seen and read by me, William Paston.

In it we have the figures for the Lancastrians:

Is dead Lord Clifford, Lord Neville, Lord Welles, Lord Willoughby,
Anthony Lord Scales [though that was mistaken—he later became
the King's brother-in-law], Lord Harry [Stafford], and by supposi-
tion the Earl of Northumberland [who died of his wounds in York],
Andrew Trollope, with many others, gentle and commons, to the
number of 20,000.[7]

However, with so many dead, why is there no absolutely conclusive archaeological evidence? The answer for that is simple and the reason was highly
political. As shown in the final Dramatis Personae (see page 185), Edward
IV died in 1483, when the succession was again usurped. His sons Edward
V and Richard, Duke of York, best known to history as the Princes in the
Tower, were probably killed in the same year by order of Edward's younger
brother Richard, Duke of Gloucester, crowned as Richard III.[8] From 1471
onwards, Richard had been an authoritative and successful ruler of the
North on behalf of his brother; after his usurpation, the area north of
the Trent was his power base. But there was a problem that needed to
be resolved and that was Towton. Edward IV never returned to Towton,
nor did he show any great verve in following the example of Henry IV
and creating a memorial chapel. Plans for converting an existing chapel
were drawn up, but were not taken forward. This was something Richard
sought to remedy. He also dealt with the unconsecrated grave pits. Cavern-
ous and filled with methane gas, they were a reminder of the genesis of
Yorkist rule; of the defeat of a large army of the North by an 'invader' from
the South. Richard was keen to present Towton as finished business and,
to the satisfaction of the landholders who would have undertaken the bulk
of the work, returned to farmland. Richard's action was prescient, because
after his usurpation the pattern of power was reversed; it was from the
South and Wales that the threat of Henry Tudor would come; it was on

the North that Richard relied. The consequence of what may have become an urgent process of exhumation and reburial is that we do not know with what degree of care the exhumed bodies were treated or exactly where they were all reburied. It is certain that this action removed much of the archaeological evidence that is one important source for uncovering the detail of a battle.[9]

Thus, with this resource depleted, it is even more imperative to protect today's battlefield from the depredations of night hawkers. When material is arbitrarily removed from a battlefield, important evidence is lost. Recent excavations by Tim Sutherland and the Towton Battlefield Archaeological Survey, with their discovery of lines of arrow heads, have completely changed the accepted opening position of the Yorkist battle lines. More excavations are planned, once funding is gained, but the artefacts have in the interim to be safeguarded from being removed under non-archaeological conditions and that has to be strongly sanctioned by law. The Towton Battlefield Society and the Battlefields Trust, working with local landowners, the police and other agencies have themselves led the way in 2010 with the country's first accreditation scheme for metal detectorists on an historic battlefield. It is hoped that this type of initiative will extend around the country and become statutory.

Fortunately the fifteenth century can no longer be described as it once was by McFarlane, one of its greatest historians, as 'the Cinderella Century'.[10] McFarlane himself was one of the first to undertake detailed research of records and this has been followed and built upon by what is now many successive generations of academic historians. Their recovery of detail has served to sharpen the importance of personality and most importantly of all in a personal monarchy, the personality of the King.

One cannot make the claim that Henry VI was the last medieval king. David Starkey has, with supreme authority, shown that this role belongs to Henry VIII, placing him at the pivotal point of English history as both the last medieval king and the first modern one.[11] However the life and reign of Henry VI does see the beginnings of significant change: he was the last English king, in fact if not in aspiration, who had an Anglo-French empire. He was the last monarch whose personal rule was so completely dependent on the sanctity of his position as the anointed and crowned king that, even as a cipher, no government could operate without him. In the absence of any personal direction from him and with the collapse of substitutes for his authority, other forces bubbled to the surface, those that spoke of the rights of the 'commons of England' including the right to complain against injustice and to petition the King in defence of the common weal; forces that were exploited by Warwick the Kingmaker, whether cynically or not, with a genius for propaganda and a political organization that seem chillingly modern.

There was to be a future point when events were to echo back to 1450, that crucial year of Henry's reign, and it was through attempts to sanction arguably the most dramatic event in English history—the trial of Charles I. King Charles, from his coronation onwards, tried to dress himself with the semi-divine status of a medieval king; in their turn, the Rump House of Commons of 1649, denied the traditional authority of the monarch himself, needed a new one with which to try him. The phrase they used was *'An Act of the Commons of England Assembled in Parliament, for Erecting of a High Court of Justice, for the Trying and Judging of Charles Stuart, King of England'*.[12] It was the final, logical extension of the language of the first, non-violent, part of Cade's rebellion.

As for King Henry VI himself, his life was brutally ended during the night of 21–22 May 1471—very probably by a mace in the hands of Richard of Gloucester—when praying at the tiny oratory at Wakefield Tower within the Tower of London. Every year on 21 May, there is a moving and dignified private service in the Presence Chamber of the Plantagenet Kings, which houses the Oratory. There the Provosts of Henry's two great foundations, Eton College and King's College Cambridge, lay flowers on the spot where he was killed. The service is called the Ceremony of Lilies and Roses after the flowers used, which are those respectively in the arms of the two foundations. The lilies in Eton's arms are white. So, ironically, are the roses of King's.

DRAMATIS PERSONAE AND DECISIVE SEQUENCE OF EVENTS: AFTER TOWTON

Henry VI: after Towton, the Lancastrian royal party reached Scotland and the protection of Mary of Guelders, the Queen Regent. From there border raids were mounted in support of the great Northumbrian fortresses still in Lancastrian hands. But these never threatened the new Yorkist regime. And in 1463, Edward's truce with Louis XI, the new King of France, meant that Scotland, France's perennial ally, would no longer shelter Henry and he became a fugitive in the North of England, passed from house to house until captured and taken to the Tower of London. Here he spent five years in reasonably treated confinement until his 'Readeption', more puppet king than ever, between September 1470 and April 1471. With Edward IV back in control, Henry was swiftly back in the Tower. This time, as we have seen, not for long.

Edward IV and Warwick the Kingmaker: in the early years of his reign, Edward was happy for Warwick to act as his chief minister. Relations between the cousins were good until 1464 and Edward's secret marriage to Elizabeth Woodville, a poor Lancastrian widow, on May Day. It remained a secret until the summer, when Warwick's negotiations for a royal French marriage for Edward were so far advanced that Edward had to reveal his true marital state. This was a humiliation for Warwick in the eyes of Europe and though, on the surface, it seemed that relations were repaired, in truth 'never was there amity between them again'. By 1469 the two were leading the opposite sides in a Yorkist civil war. As before Towton, there was an astonishing series of switches of fortune, until, in one of the greatest changes of allegiance in English history, Warwick made his peace with Margaret of Anjou, Edward was forced into exile and Warwick 'readepted' Henry VI. Warwick deserved the title of Kingmaker for his exploits in 1460–61, but even more for those of 1470–71. But Edward was not finished: in March 1471 he landed, just as Henry IV had done, at Ravenspur in Yorkshire; and, just like Henry IV, he claimed not the kingdom, but his Duchy. Through a combination of guts, charisma and luck, Edward expanded his forces until, on 14 April, Easter Sunday, he defeated Warwick at Barnet. Warwick was killed, so was his brother John, Marquess Montagu. George Neville, now Archbishop of York, was disgraced. With Fauconberg having died in 1463, the power of the Nevilles was at an end.

Margaret of Anjou: in 1463 Margaret and Prince Edward went into exile, shuttling between France and Burgundy before living in some poverty on a pension provided by her father. But by 1468 the situation had changed. The marriage of King Edward's sister, Margaret of York to Charles, Duke of Burgundy sealed an anti-French alliance. King Louis, fittingly nicknamed 'the spider', now had a use for Margaret again. He brought Warwick and Margaret together politically, but not militarily. Margaret's largely French army did not land until the very day of the Battle of Barnet. Once again Edward IV marched to prevent Margaret's forces joining up with Jasper Tudor's Welsh recruits; he achieved this at Tewkesbury on 4 May. This was the battle that secured Edward's throne for twelve years, before he died prematurely due to his excessive lifestyle. The Lancastrian Edward Prince of Wales, now seventeen, was killed at Tewkesbury, either in the rout or, more darkly, after being captured, roughly handled by King Edward and passed to his younger brothers to be butchered in cold blood. Margaret was captured and imprisoned in the Tower. After the deaths of her husband and her son, she was no longer of any threat or any value to Edward IV; in 1475 she was sent back to France, neglected by both her father and then Louis. She died in 1482.

Henry Beaufort, Duke of Somerset: Somerset remained Margaret's general. He coordinated the Lancastrian resistance from the Northumbrian castles. However, he surrendered Bamburgh on Christmas Eve 1462 and came to terms with Edward. They even shared a bed. But in November 1463 he rejoined Henry VI in Northumberland and sought to establish a foothold in the Far North of England. It was short-lived. He was defeated by Warwick's brother John, Lord Montagu, at Hexham in May 1464 and summarily executed.

Henry Holland, Duke of Exeter: Exeter went into exile with Margaret. After defeat at Barnet, he was imprisoned in the Tower. His poor state of health and marriage to the King's sister probably saved his life, but he lost everything else. He was divorced and divested. That he was allowed to join Edward's expedition to France in 1475 is probably more surprising than his fate on the return sea voyage. He drowned. Foul play seems a certainty.

The Papal Legate—Francesco Coppini, Bishop of Terni: Coppini never became a cardinal. Pius II, for short-term political considerations, accused Coppini of having exceeded his authority and dismissed him from his Bishopric in 1462. Pope Pius completed the job for posterity, by blackening Coppini's name in his memoirs.

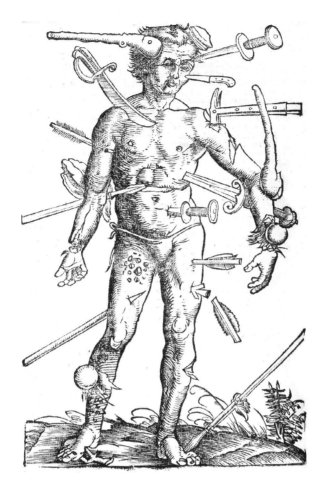

THE WOUND MAN

From late medieval times, surgeons used 'Wound Men' illustrations to indicate the types of battle injury they would need to treat. The sophistication of the armour of the time is a tribute to the power of the weaponry it was designed to deflect. The Wound Man graphically shows the impact against unprotected areas. The so-called 'naked men', those with inadequate protection, would have been very quickly dispatched during a rout on a battlefield where surrender was not sanctioned and escape was difficult.

This 'Wound Man' is from Gerssdorff 's *Feldbuch der Wundartzney* (1517).
Photograph: Dr Jeremy Burgess / Science Photo Library

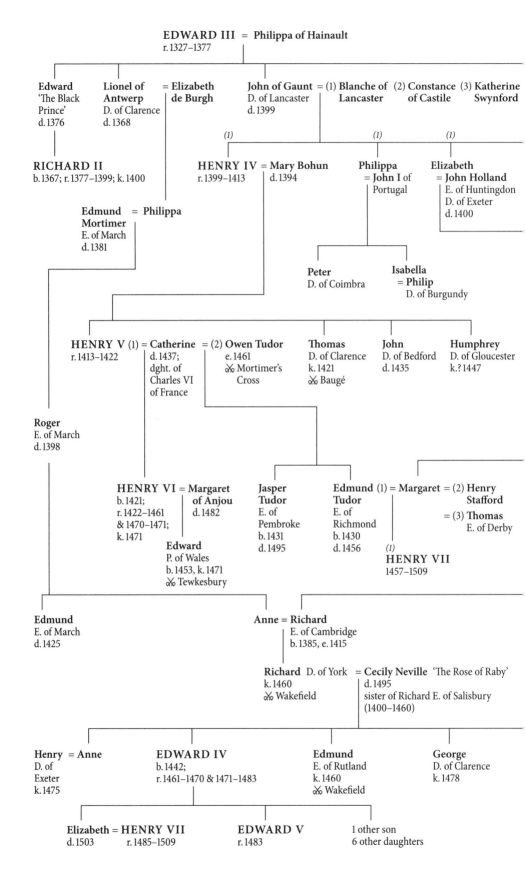

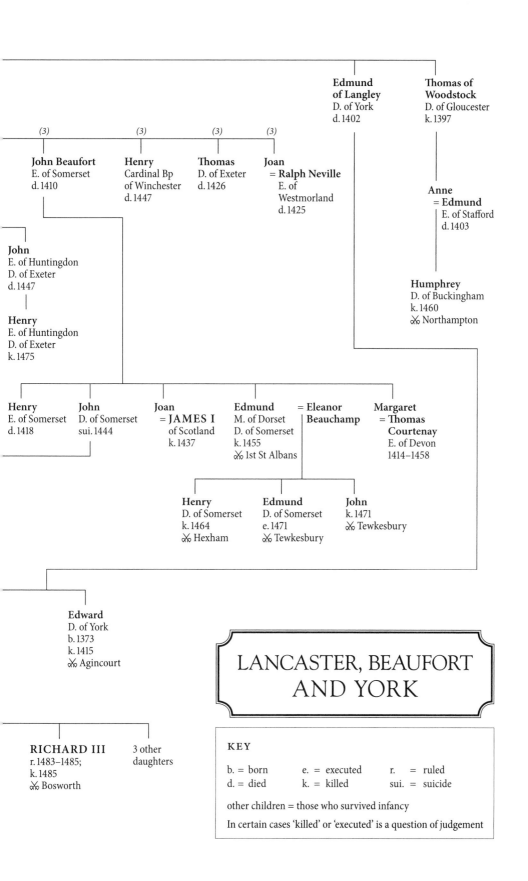

Edmund
of Langley
D. of York
d. 1402

Thomas of
Woodstock
D. of Gloucester
k. 1397

(3)
John Beaufort
E. of Somerset
d. 1410

(3)
Henry
Cardinal Bp
of Winchester
d. 1447

(3)
Thomas
D. of Exeter
d. 1426

(3)
Joan
= Ralph Neville
E. of
Westmorland
d. 1425

Anne
= Edmund
E. of Stafford
d. 1403

John
E. of Huntingdon
D. of Exeter
d. 1447

Humphrey
D. of Buckingham
k. 1460
⚔ Northampton

Henry
E. of Huntingdon
D. of Exeter
k. 1475

Henry
E. of Somerset
d. 1418

John
D. of Somerset
sui. 1444

Joan
= JAMES I
of Scotland
k. 1437

Edmund
M. of Dorset
D. of Somerset
k. 1455
⚔ 1st St Albans

= Eleanor
Beauchamp

Margaret
= Thomas
Courtenay
E. of Devon
1414–1458

Henry
D. of Somerset
k. 1464
⚔ Hexham

Edmund
D. of Somerset
e. 1471
⚔ Tewkesbury

John
k. 1471
⚔ Tewkesbury

Edward
D. of York
b. 1373
k. 1415
⚔ Agincourt

**LANCASTER, BEAUFORT
AND YORK**

RICHARD III
r. 1483–1485;
k. 1485
⚔ Bosworth

3 other
daughters

KEY

b. = born   e. = executed   r. = ruled
d. = died   k. = killed   sui. = suicide

other children = those who survived infancy

In certain cases 'killed' or 'executed' is a question of judgement

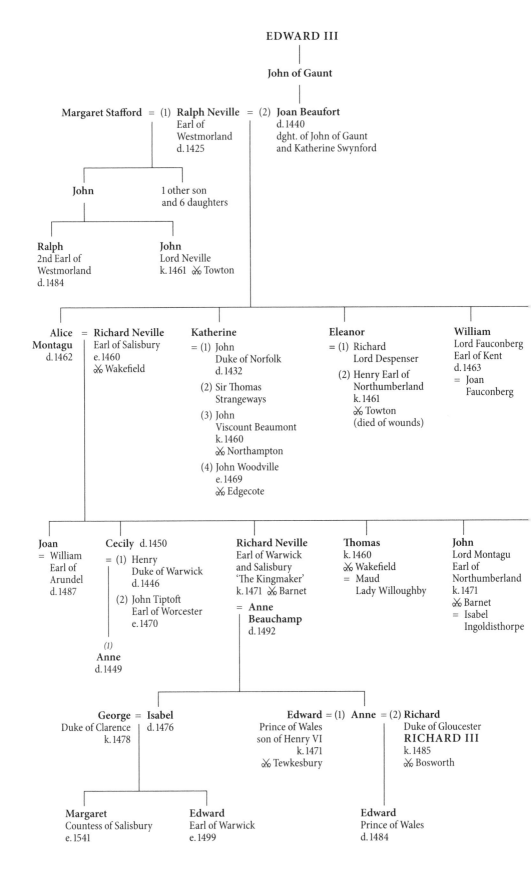

EDWARD III
|
John of Gaunt
|

Margaret Stafford = (1) **Ralph Neville** = (2) **Joan Beaufort**
　　　　　　　　　　　Earl of　　　　　　d.1440
　　　　　　　　　　　Westmorland　　　dght. of John of Gaunt
　　　　　　　　　　　d.1425　　　　　　and Katherine Swynford

John　　　　　1 other son
　　　　　　　　and 6 daughters

Ralph　　　　　　　**John**
2nd Earl of　　　　　Lord Neville
Westmorland　　　　k.1461 ✕ Towton
d.1484

Alice = **Richard Neville**　　**Katherine**　　　　　　**Eleanor**　　　　　　**William**
Montagu　Earl of Salisbury　= (1) John　　　　　= (1) Richard　　　　Lord Fauconberg
d.1462　　e.1460　　　　　　　Duke of Norfolk　　　Lord Despenser　　Earl of Kent
　　　　　✕ Wakefield　　　　d.1432　　　　　(2) Henry Earl of　　d.1463
　　　　　　　　　　　　　(2) Sir Thomas　　　　　Northumberland　　= Joan
　　　　　　　　　　　　　　Strangeways　　　　　k.1461　　　　　　Fauconberg
　　　　　　　　　　　　　(3) John　　　　　　　✕ Towton
　　　　　　　　　　　　　　Viscount Beaumont　(died of wounds)
　　　　　　　　　　　　　　k.1460
　　　　　　　　　　　　　　✕ Northampton
　　　　　　　　　　　　　(4) John Woodville
　　　　　　　　　　　　　　e.1469
　　　　　　　　　　　　　　✕ Edgecote

Joan　　　　**Cecily** d.1450　　**Richard Neville**　　**Thomas**　　　　**John**
= William　　= (1) Henry　　　　Earl of Warwick　　k.1460　　　　Lord Montagu
Earl of　　　　　Duke of Warwick　and Salisbury　　✕ Wakefield　　Earl of
Arundel　　　　d.1446　　　　　'The Kingmaker'　= Maud　　　　　Northumberland
d.1487　　　(2) John Tiptoft　　k.1471 ✕ Barnet　　Lady Willoughby　k.1471
　　　　　　　Earl of Worcester　= **Anne**　　　　　　　　　　　　✕ Barnet
　　　　　　　e.1470　　　　　　**Beauchamp**　　　　　　　　　　= Isabel
　　　　　　　　　　　　　　　d.1492　　　　　　　　　　　　　Ingoldisthorpe
　　　　　(1)
　　　　Anne
　　　　d.1449

George = **Isabel**　　　　　**Edward** = (1) **Anne** = (2) **Richard**
Duke of Clarence | d.1476　　　Prince of Wales　　　　　Duke of Gloucester
k.1478　　　　　　　　　　　son of Henry VI　　　　**RICHARD III**
　　　　　　　　　　　　　　k.1471　　　　　　　　k.1485
　　　　　　　　　　　　　　✕ Tewkesbury　　　　　✕ Bosworth

Margaret　　　　　**Edward**　　　　　**Edward**
Countess of Salisbury　Earl of Warwick　　Prince of Wales
e.1541　　　　　　　e.1499　　　　　　d.1484

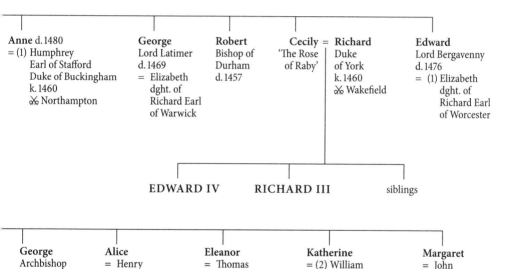

THE NEVILLES
Their path to the centre of the Lancastrian and Yorkist establishments

Anne d. 1480
= (1) Humphrey
Earl of Stafford
Duke of Buckingham
k. 1460
⚔ Northampton

George
Lord Latimer
d. 1469
= Elizabeth
dght. of
Richard Earl
of Warwick

Robert
Bishop of
Durham
d. 1457

Cecily =
'The Rose
of Raby'

Richard
Duke
of York
k. 1460
⚔ Wakefield

Edward
Lord Bergavenny
d. 1476
= (1) Elizabeth
dght. of
Richard Earl
of Worcester

EDWARD IV   **RICHARD III**   siblings

George
Archbishop
of York
d. 1476

Alice
= Henry
Lord Fitzhugh
d. 1472

Eleanor
= Thomas
Lord Stanley
d. 1504

Katherine
= (2) William
Lord Hastings
e. 1483

Margaret
= John
Earl of Oxford
d. 1513

KEY

b. = born   e. = executed
d. = died   k. = killed

other children = those who survived infancy

In certain cases 'killed' or 'executed' is a question of judgement

NOTES

A number of the primary sources quoted here are also available through British History Online at www.british-history.ac.uk. It has been created by the Institute of Historical Research and the History of Parliament Trust, with the aim of supporting academic and personal users around the world in their learning, teaching and research. It is a tremendous resource—see ◊ in the Select Bibliography for online availability.

INTRODUCTION

1. T. Smith, *De Republica Anglorum*, ed. M. Dewar (Cambridge, 1982), p. 88.
2. D. Starkey, 'Henry VI's Old Blue Gown', *The Court Historian* 4 (1999), pp. 1–28.
3. Reproduced, for example, in D. Starkey, *Crown and Country* (2010).
4. What follows is a summary of the argument of *Crown and Country*.
5. R. L. Storey, *The End of the House of Lancaster* (1966), p. 6; E. Hall, *The Union of the Two Noble and Illustr[ious] Families of Lancaster and York* (1809) and Scolar Press reprint of edition of 1550 (1970).
6. M. P. Siddons, *Heraldic Badges in England and Wales*, 3 vols. (Woodbridge, 2009) II i, pp. 211–26; N. Pronay and J. Cox, eds., *The Crowland Chronicle Continuations, 1459–1486* (1986), p. 185.
7. W. Campbell, ed., *Materials for a History of the Reign of Henry VII*, 2 vols., Rolls Series 60 (1873) Vol. I., pp. 392–8; P. L. Hughes and J. E. Larkin, eds., *Tudor Royal Proclamations*, 3 vols. (New Haven and London, 1964–9) Vol. I, pp. 6–7.
8. C. G. Bayne and W. H. Dunham, eds., *Select Cases in the Council of Henry VII*, Selden Society 75 (1958), p. 8; A. B. Emden, ed., *A Biographical Register of the University of Oxford to A.D. 1500*, 3 vols. (Oxford, 1959) Vol. III, 1609–11.
9. What follows is a summary of the argument about the relationship of bastard feudalism and politics that first developed in 'The Age of the Household' in S. Medcalf, ed., *The Later Middle Ages* (1981), pp. 26–86.
10. *ODNB sub* 'Fortescue' and 'Morton'. The radical changes brought about by Henry VII in the last decade or so of his reign are well discussed in M. R. Horowitz, ed., 'Who was Henry VII?', *Historical Research* 217.

PROLOGUE

1. Ross, *The Wars of the Roses* (1976), p. 138.
2. Though Henry VII's victory at the Battle of Bosworth in 1485 put him on the throne, it was his victory at the Battle of Stoke Field in 1487 that secured it and brought the Third War of the Roses to an end.
3. Ross, *The Wars of the Roses*, p. 136 and p. 138. This figure is extrapolated from his estimation on p. 136 that 25 per cent of the population would have been of fighting age, and from the 75,000 figure on p. 138. With an estimate of 3 million for the overall population, 750,000 would have been males of fighting age. 75,000 at the battle = 10% of the 16–60 yrs population.
4. Mortimer, *The Perfect King: The Life of Edward III, Father of the English Nation* (2006), p. 392.
5. Both kings were displayed after their deaths and it was important that there should be no visible mark of violence on them. This was achieved, so it is thought, in the case of Edward II, by a red-hot poker thrust into his anus; and in that of Richard II through slow starvation.
6. See Starkey, Introduction to this work, p. xxiii.

1. A STEP TOO FAR

1. John Milton, 'On his Blindness'.
2. Armstrong, 'Politics and the Battle of St Albans, 1455', *BIHR* 33 (1960), p. 23. Here referred to as a town as it did not become a city until the Royal Charter of 1877 as per 'The city of St Albans: The borough', *A History of the County of Hertford: Volume 2* (1908), pp. 477–83. www.british-history.ac.uk.
3. Gairdner (ed.), *Paston Letters* (1910), No. 238, p. 325.
4. Ibid., p. 326.
5. Ibid., No. 239, pp. 328–9.
6. Armstrong, *BIHR* 33, p. 26, n. 6.
7. Cornwell, *Harlequin* (2000), 'Historical Note', p. 484. Bernard Cornwell cites Benjamin Franklin, the US Founding Father and inventor of genius, as one such: Franklin believed that the American Colonists would have won the war far more speedily had they been practised longbowmen. Cornwell himself, who, through his rigorous research for his novels on the medieval and Napoleonic periods is in an excellent position to compare and judge, is in no doubt, believing 'it is quite certain that a battalion of archers could have outshot and beaten, easily, a battalion of Wellington's veterans armed with smoothbore muskets'.
8. See Chapter 9, note 7.
9. Courtesy of the Saint Albans tourist office.
10. *Gregory's Chronicle: The Historical Collections of a Citizen of London in the fifteenth century*, ed. Gairdner (1876). The author of the *Chronicle* was one Gregory Skinner (meaning William Gregory of the Skinners' Company) who was Mayor of London in 1451. The *Chronicle* begins with the accession of Richard the Lionheart in 1189 and ends in 1469, with the last two or so years covered by a 'continuer' as Gregory himself died in 1466 or 1467. It is a remarkable

document for the years where Gregory was a contemporary witness, including the Battles of Saint Albans and Cade's rebellion in 1450 (when Gregory would already have been a senior figure in the City of London). Often sparkling with wit, it also gives a serious insight into the attitudes of London's mercantile elite. *Gregory's Chronicle* is also available on British History Online, www .british-history.ac.uk.

11. *Gregory's Chronicle, 1451–60*, pp. 196–210.
12. Gairdner, *Paston Letters*, Vol. I, No. 239, p. 331.
13. Armstrong, *BIHR 33*, p. 46, and Dijon Relation infra p. 64.
14. Ibid., pp. 49–50.
15. Myers, *English Historical Documents* (1969), p. 277 ('The Dijon Relation', Dijon, Archives de la Côte-d'Or, B.11942, No. 258, French, printed by Armstrong, *BIHR 33*, pp. 63–5).
16. Maurer, *Margaret of Anjou* (2003), p. 91, n. 67.
17. C. Oman, *The Political History of England 1377–1485* (1920), p. 367, also quoted in Lander, *The Wars of the Roses* (1990), p. 9.
18. Armstrong, *BIHR 33*, p 7.

2. A GREAT MAN'S LEGACY—MINORITY

1. Barker, *Agincourt* (2006), p. 301.
2. Barker, *Conquest* (2009), p. 8 and p. 39.
3. ODNB, C. T. Allmand, 'Henry V (1386/7–1422)'—doi:10.1093/ref: odnb/12952.
4. Ibid.
5. Quoted by Malcolm Vale, BBC Radio 4, ' "In Our Time"—The Siege of Orleans' (broadcast on 24 May 2007).
6. Barker, *Conquest*, pp. 28–9.
7. This includes William II, Richard I, Edward II—all of whom had violent deaths—and Richard II, who also had an untimely one. Exclude them and the average goes up to almost 60.
8. ODNB, C. T. Allmand, 'Henry V (1386/7–1422)'—doi:10.1093/ref: odnb/12952.
9. ODNB, Jenny Stratford, 'John, duke of Bedford (1389–1435)'—doi:10.1093/ ref:odnb/14844.
10. Wolffe, *Henry VI* (2001), p. 53.
11. Fabyan, *Great Chronicle of London* (1938), ed. Thomas and Thornley, p. 137.
12. Ibid., p. 138.
13. *Gregory's Chronicle, 1420–26*, pp. 128–61.
14. Fabyan, *Great Chronicle of London*, p. 139.
15. Ibid.
16. Nicolas (ed.), *Proceedings of the Privy Council (PPC)*, III (1834), p. 238.
17. Mortimer, *The Time Traveller's Guide to Medieval England* (2009), p. 21. Westminster Abbey is arguably still 'unfinished' and there are plans to give it a more complete architectural harmony, as per Westminster Abbey's A Strategy for 2020 and Beyond; see www.westminster-abbey.org.
18. www.westminster-abbey.org/our-history/royals/coronations/guide-to-the-coronation-service.

19. Strong, *Coronation* (2006), p. 141.
20. 'A History of Legal Dress in Europe' by W. N. Hargreaves-Mawdsley (Oxford: Clarendon Press, 1963, pp. xii, 116) for statement that judicial scarlet probably derives from the livery of the House of Lancaster.
21. Strong, *Coronation*, p. 84. The day before the coronation as per item 4 of the *Liber Regalis*.
22. Editions Magnificat, *Lives of the Saints*, www.magnificat.ca/cal/engl/11–06.htm.
23. *Gregory's Chronicle*, 1427–34, pp. 161–77.
24. Ibid.
25. Ibid.
26. Wolffe, *Henry VI*, p. 59, n. 38 (citing M. R. Powicke, 'Lancastrian Captains' in *Essays in Medieval History presented to Bertie Wilkinson* [1969], pp. 371–82).
27. ODNB, Christine Carpenter, 'Beauchamp, Richard, thirteenth earl of Warwick (1382–1439)'—doi:10.1093/ref:odnb/1838.
28. *PPC*, III, pp. 296–300.
29. Hallam, *The Chronicles of the Wars of the Roses* (1988), p. 174, trans. of *Journal d'un bourgeois de Paris sous le règne de Charles VII*.
30. Ibid., p. 173, from Waurin, *Recueil Des Croniques*, eds. W. E. Hardy and E. Hardy (1864), Vol. V, Book. 4, p. 240.
31. Barker, *Conquest*, pp. 107–9.
32. Barker, *Conquest*, p. 125, n. 1 (p. 419 citing *PPC*, III, pp. 330–8).
33. Beauchamp, a key figure in the plays of Shakespeare and Shaw, was not involved at all in Joan's trial.
34. See note 26 immediately above.
35. Barker, *Conquest*, p. 150 and n. 24 (p. 421 citing Curry, 'The "Coronation Expedition"', pp. 36–8 and pp. 40–1 in *The Lancastrian Court*, ed. Jenny Stratford (2003).
36. ODNB, Jenny Stratford, 'John, duke of Bedford (1389–1435)'—doi:10.1093/ref:odnb/14844.
37. Barker, *Conquest*, p. 176.

3. AN ABSENCE OF KINGSHIP—MAJORITY

1. *PPC*, IV, p. xlv and p. 134.
2. Watts, *Henry VI and the Politics of Kingship* (1999), pp. 119–20.
3. Ibid., p. 121.
4. Wolffe, *Henry VI*, p. 87.
5. Kingsford, *English Historical Literature in the Fifteenth Century* (1913), p. 147.
6. ODNB, G. L. Harriss, 'Beaufort, Henry (1375?–1447)'—doi:10.1093/ ref:odnb /1859. ODNB, G. L. Harriss, 'Humphrey, duke of Gloucester (1390–1447)' —doi:10.1093/ref:odnb/14155.
7. Harriss, *Cardinal Beaufort* (1988), p. 309.
8. ODNB, E. B. Fryde, 'Pole, Sir William de la (d. 1366)'—doi:10.1093/ ref:odnb/ 22460.
9. Barker, *Conquest*, p. 121.
10. ODNB, John Watts, 'Pole, William de la, first duke of Suffolk (1396–1450)' —doi:10.1093/ref:odnb/22461.

11. ODNB, G. L. Harriss, 'Humphrey, duke of Gloucester (1390–1447)'—doi:10.1093/ref:odnb/14155. Wolffe, *Henry VI*, pp. 126–8. Davies, *An English Chronicle* (1856), pp. 57–8.

12. Ross, *The Wars of the Roses*, p. 26.

13. Within a few years, see later in this chapter, he was to be accused—somewhat fantastically—of trying to put himself closer to the English throne than René was to the French one.

14. J. Chartier, *Chronique française du roi de France Charles VII*, ed. Vallet de Viriville, II, 1858, p. 235, French. See Myers Eng. Hist. Docs., p. 262.

15. Davies, *An English Chronicle*, p. 63.

16. ODNB, G. L. Harriss, 'Humphrey, duke of Gloucester (1390–1447)'—doi:10.1093/ref:odnb/14155.

17. Fabyan, *Great Chronicle of London*, p. 179.

18. Barker, *Conquest*, pp. 395–6.

19. Virgoe, 'The Death of William de la Pole, Duke of Suffolk' in *Bulletin of the John Rylands Library*, Vol. 47 (1965), pp. 489–502 and espec. pp. 499–502.

20. Gairdner, *Paston Letters*, Vol. I, No. 93, p. 125.

21. Castor, *Blood & Roses* (2005), p. 58.

22. 'The Later Middle Ages: Economy and Industrial Prosperity', in *A History of the County of York: the City of York* (1961), pp. 84–91. www.british-history.ac.uk/report.aspx?compid=36333&strquery=population.

23. Barron, 'London and the Crown 1451–61', in Highfield and Jeffs (eds.), *The Crown and Local Communities: In England and France in the Fifteenth Century* (1981), p. 89.

24. Kaufman, *The Historical Literature of the Jack Cade Rebellion* (2009), pp. 98–9, citing Hutton, *The Rise and Fall of Merry England: The Ritual Year 1400–1700*, p. 89.

25. Wolffe, *Henry VI*, p. 220.

26. ODNB, Joseph A. Nigota, 'Fiennes, James, first Baron Saye and Sele (c. 1390–1450)'—doi:10.1093/ref:odnb/9411.

27. A. J. Pollard, *Warwick the Kingmaker* (2007), p. 154.

28. 'Stow's Memorandum' in Gairdner (ed.), *Three Fifteenth Century Chronicles* (1880). Also quoted in Dockray, *Henry VI, Margaret of Anjou and the Wars of the Roses—A Source Book* (2000), pp. 48–50.

29. Gillingham, *The Wars of the Roses* (2001), p. 63.

30. In *Summer of Blood* (2009), the dramatic new book on the Peasants Revolt, its author Dan Jones points out the greater political coherence of the stated initial principles of Cade's rebellion (see p. 208).

31. Hinde, *England's Population*, p. 26.

32. Dyer, *Making a Living in the Middle Ages: The People of Britain 850–1520* (2009), p. 276.

33. Anderson, *British Population History: From the Black Death to the Present Day* (1996), p. 23.

34. See Gummer, *The Scourging Angel: The Black Death in the British Isles* (2009), Appendix 1, 'The Epidemiology of the Black Death: An Overview', pp. 417–20, for an excellent summary of the debate.

35. Some authors have even higher percentage figures for mortality rates for bubonic and pneumonic plague; e.g. Ziegler, *The Black Death* (1969), pp. 27–8, has 60–90

per cent for bubonic plague; Gottfried, *The Black Death: Natural and Human Disaster in Medieval Europe* (1983), p. 2, has 95–100 per cent for pneumonic plague.

36. Dyer, *Making a Living in the Middle Ages*, p. 272.
37. Gillingham, *The Wars of the Roses*, p. 8.
38. Dyer, *Making a Living in the Middle Ages*, Chapter 10, pp. 330–62.
39. Ibid.
40. ODNB, I. M. W. Harvey, 'Cade, John (d. 1450)'—doi:10.1093/ref:odnb/4292.
41. Griffiths, *The Reign of King Henry VI* (1998), p. 644.
42. Davies, *An English Chronicle* (1856), p. 64.
43. *Benet's Chronicle*, Camden Miscellany 24 (1972), p. 164.
44. ODNB, Joseph A. Nigota, 'Fiennes, James, first Baron Saye and Sele (c.1390–1450)'—doi:10.1093/ref:odnb/9411.
45. *Benet's Chronicle*, Camden Miscellany 24, p. 165.
46. Gairdner (ed.), 'Short English Chronicle' in *Three Fifteenth-Century Chronicles* (1880), pp. 58–78.
47. *Gregory's Chronicle, 1451–1460*, pp. 196–210.

4. AN ABSENT-MINDED KING

1. Wolffe, *Henry VI*, pp. 14–15 (citing BL, Cotton MS, Cleopatra A xiii reprinted by Jean-Philippe Genet in *Four English Political Tracts of the Later Middle Ages*, Camden Soc., 1977).
2. Capgrave, *The Book of the Illustrious Henries* (1858). See also Wolffe, *Henry VI*, pp. 15–16 and n. 18.
3. Wolffe, *Henry VI*, pp. 138–9.
4. Watts, *Henry VI*, p. 169 and n. 187.
5. John Ayto (ed.), *Brewer's Dictionary of Phrase & Fable* (2005), p. 405.
6. Wolffe, *Henry VI*, p. 145.
7. Strong, *Coronation*, p. 169.
8. Modern historians do see similarities between the two rulers, for instance, Henry VI is described as 'the greatest single disaster in saintly royalty since Edward the Confessor' in J. W. McKenna, 'Piety and Propaganda: the Cult of Henry VI' in *Chaucer and Middle English Studies in Honor of R. H. Robbins* (Ohio: Kent State University Press, 1974), p. 79, quoted in Keith Dockray, *Henry VI—A Source Book*, pp. xxv and xliii.
9. Curry (contrib. ed.), Given-Wilson (gen. ed.), *The Parliament Rolls of Medieval England (PROME)* (2005), 'Henry VI: November 1450', Introduction.
10. Wolffe, *Henry VI*, p. 138.
11. A slight paraphrase of his statements summarizing Henry VI's capabilities e.g.: 'a baby who grew up an imbecile' (McFarlane, *England in the Fifteenth Century*, 1981, p. 42); 'inanity' (ibid., p. 240); and 'second childhood succeeded first without the usual interval' (quoted in Dockray, *Henry VI—A Source Book*, p. xxv, attrib. to McFarlane in 1938).
12. Griffiths, *Henry VI*, p. 241. Wolffe, *Henry VI*, p. 21.
13. Watts, *Henry VI and the Politics of Kingship*, throughout.

14. 'Schizophrenia as a Permanent Problem: Some Aspects of Historical Evidence', *History of Psychiatry*, 3, no. 12 (Dec. 1992): pp. 413–29.

15. 'Did Schizophrenia Change the Course of English History? The Mental Illness of Henry VI', *Medical Hypotheses*, 59, no. 4 (2002): pp. 416–21.

16. Whethamstede (ed. Riley), *Registrum* (1872) I, p. 163, cited by Wolffe, *Henry VI*, p. 272.

17. Curry (contrib. ed.), Given-Wilson (gen. ed.), *PROME*, 'Henry VI: March 1453', section 32.

18. Findings of a study based on three UK birth cohorts—1946, 1958 and 1970—with, to date, detailed examination of the first two. See, firstly: P. Jones, B. Rodgers, R. Murray, M. Marmot, 'Child Development Risk Factors for Adult Schizophrenia in the British 1946 Birth Cohort', *Lancet*, 344, no. 8934 (1994): pp. 1398–1402. See, additionally, Peter Jones and D. John Done, 'From Birth to Onset: A Developmental Perspective of Schizophrenia in Two National Birth Cohorts', pp. 119–36, in Matcheri S. Keshavan and Robin Murray (eds.), *Neurodevelopment & Adult Psychopathology* (1997). And also D. J. Done, T. J. Crow, E. C. Johnstone and A. Sacker, 'Childhood Antecedents of Schizophrenia and Affective Illness: Social Adjustment at Ages 7 and 11', *British Medical Journal*, 309 (1994): pp. 699–703.

19. E. Walker and R. J. Lewine, 'Prediction of Adult-Onset Schizophrenia from Childhood Home Movies of the Patients', *American Journal of Psychiatry*, 147 (1990): pp. 1052–56.

20. The word 'mania' used to have a specific psychiatric meaning, but this has been eroded through general use. With thanks to Dr Trevor Turner for this clarification.

21. Blacman, *Henry VI*, ed. M. R. James (1919).

22. ODNB, Jonathan Hughes, 'Blacman, John (1407/8–1485?)'—doi:10.1093/ref:odnb/2599.

23. Ibid.

24. Lovatt, 'A Collector of Apocryphal Anecdotes: John Blacman Revisited', in *Property and Politics: Essays in Later Medieval English History*, ed. A. J. Pollard (1984), p. 173.

25. ODNB, Jonathan Hughes, 'Rolle, Richard (1305x10–1349)'—doi:10.1093/ref:odnb/24024.

26. See E. H. Allen, *Writings Ascribed to Richard Rolle* (1927); and especially Rolle, *The Melos Amoris*, ed. E. J. F. Arnould (1957), pp. 144–5 cited by Jonathan Hughes above.

27. Rolle, op. cit. pp. 44–5 cited by Hughes.

28. Blacman, *Henry VI*, p. 38.

29. Watts, *Henry VI*, p. 104 and n. 13.

30. Griffiths, *Henry VI*, p. 254.

31. Blacman, *Henry VI*, p. 26.

32. Ibid., p. 42.

33. Ibid., p. 35.

34. Ibid., p. 36.

35. Ibid., p. 27.

36. Wolffe, *Henry VI*, pp. 370–1, as per Itinerary of Henry's movements. The last time Henry VI was at Eltham before his breakdown was in early February 1453. He did not return there, and then only briefly until 1460 (long after Blacman's retreat into monasticism).

37. Blacman, *Henry VI*, pp. 37–8.

38. Ibid., p. 42.

39. Griffiths, *Henry VI*, p. 242, quoting Whethamstede, *Registrum I*, pp. 248–61.

40. Whethamstede *Registrum I*, p. 415, cited by Wolffe, *Henry VI*, p. 19.

41. Storey, *The End of the House of Lancaster* (1999), p. 35, citing KB.9.260, no. 40a—from the Public Record Office, now the National Archives.

42. Wolffe, *Henry VI*, p. 17.

5. A QUESTION OF HONOUR

1. ODNB, John Watts, 'Richard of York, third duke of York (1411–1460)' —doi:10.1093/ref:odnb/23503.

2. Ross, *The Wars of the Roses*, p. 31.

3. See Chapter 2, for Gloucester's denunciations of Beaufort stretching back to the reign of Henry IV.

4. Maurer, *Margaret of Anjou*, p. 41, n. 21.

5. ODNB on Catherine de Valois: Michael Jones, 'Catherine (1401–1437)'— doi:10.1093/ref:odnb/4890.

6. ODNB, Colin Richmond, 'Beaufort, Edmund, first duke of Somerset (c.1406–1455)'— doi:10.1093/ref:odnb/1855.

7. ODNB, John Watts, 'Richard of York, third duke of York (1411–1460)'— doi:10.1093/ref:odnb/23503.

8. ODNB, G. L. Harriss, 'Beaufort, John, duke of Somerset (1404–1444)'— doi:10.1093/ref:odnb/1862.

9. ODNB, Colin Richmond, 'Beaufort, Edmund, first duke of Somerset (c.1406–1455)'— doi:10.1093/ref:odnb/1855.

10. Ibid.

11. As witnessed by York's attitude to Somerset.

12. Men from the West of Kent are traditionally referred to as Kentish Men. Those from the East are called Men of Kent. As those resisting Fiennes and later supporting Warwick were from both parts, it was decided, for local harmony, to use the neutral, if still descriptive 'Men from Kent'.

13. M. K. Jones, 'Somerset, York and the Wars of the Roses', *English Historical Review* 104, no. 411 (1989): pp. 285–307.

14. This was an extraordinary promotion for someone without royal blood.

15. McFarlane, 'The Wars of the Roses', Raleigh Lecture on History, *Proceedings of the British Academy*, L (1964), reprinted in *England in the Fifteenth Century*, pp. 238–40, cited by Keith Dockray in 'The Origins of the Wars of the Roses', p. 75, in A. J. Pollard (ed.), *The Wars of the Roses* (1995).

16. Excellently demonstrated by the English Heritage information boards. Ref: www .english-heritage.org.uk/daysout/properties/middleham-castle.

17. Keen, *English Society in the Later Middle Ages, 1348–1500* (1990), p. 160.

18. Dyer, *Making a Living in the Middle Ages*, p. 322.
19. Woolgar, 'Meat and Dairy Products in Late Medieval England', eds. Woolgar, Serjeantson and Waldron, *Food in Medieval England: Diet and Nutrition* (2006), pp. 99–100.
20. Dyer, 'Seasonal Patterns in Food Consumption in the Later Middle Ages', p. 203, and Woolgar, 'Group Diets in Late Medieval England', p. 197 and p. 200, in ibid.
21. Woolgar, 'Meat and Dairy Products in Late Medieval England', pp. 91–2, in ibid. Woolgar, 'Fast and Feast: Conspicuous Consumption and the Diet of the Nobility in the Fifteenth Century' in *Revolution and Consumption in Late Medieval England* (2001), ed. Hicks, pp. 15–17.
22. Dyer, 'Changes in Diet in the Late Middle Ages: The Case of Harvest Workers' in *Everyday Life in Medieval England* (1994), pp. 77–101.
23. Woolgar, 'Group Diets in Late Medieval England', *Food in Medieval England: Diet and Nutrition*, p. 199, citing Prestwich, *Armies and Warfare in the Middle Ages*, pp. 247–8.
24. ODNB, Michael Hicks, 'Holland, Henry, second duke of Exeter (1430–1475)' —doi:10.1093/ref:odnb/54462.
25. Storey, *The End of the House of Lancaster*, p. 25.
26. ODNB on Grey of Ruthin, Rosemary Horrox, 'Grey, Edmund, first earl of Kent (1416–1490)'—doi:10.1093/ref:odnb/11529.
27. Castor, *Blood & Roses*, throughout.
28. Fabyan, *Great Chronicle of London*, ed. Thomas and Thornley, p. 207.
29. ODNB, R. G. Davies, 'Kemp, John (1380/81–1454)'—doi:10.1093/ ref:odnb/15328.
30. Barker, *Conquest*, pp. 343–4.
31. Watts, *Henry VI*, p. 274.
32. Ibid., p. 272.
33. Ellis (ed.), *Original letters, Illustrative of English History* (1824), Series I, Vol. I, letter VI, pp. 11–13.
34. Griffiths, *Henry VI*, p. 697.
35. Johnson, *Duke Richard of York, 1411–1460* (1988), p. 119.
36. Griffiths, *Henry VI*, p. 698.
37. Clifton-Taylor, *Six More English Towns* (1981), p. 30.
38. Jenkins, *England's Thousand Best Churches* (2000), p. 713.
39. ODNB, Christine Carpenter, 'Beauchamp, Richard, thirteenth earl of Warwick (1382–1439)'—doi:10.1093/ref:odnb/1838.
40. Pollard, *Warwick the Kingmaker*, pp. 17–23.
41. Hicks, *Warwick the Kingmaker* (1998), pp. 84–5.
42. Pollard, *Warwick*, p. 25.
43. The short-lived Henry, Richard Beauchamp's son and immediate heir, was made a duke by his childhood friend the King. On his death, the dukedom became extinct but his baby daughter inherited the earldom and was thus styled 15th Countess of Warwick. The Kingmaker, inheriting by right of his wife, thus became the 16th Earl.
44. ODNB, A. J. Pollard, 'Neville, William, earl of Kent (1401?–1463)'—doi:10.1093/ ref:odnb/19967.

45. Castor, *Blood & Roses*, p. 97.
46. ODNB, R. A. Griffiths, 'Percy, Thomas, first Baron Egremont (1422–1460)' —doi:10.1093/ref:odnb/50235.
47. Pollard, *Warwick the Kingmaker*, pp. 26–7.

6. A QUEEN TRANSFORMED

1. 1 marc was equal to £2/3 (13s 4d).
2. From *Transactions of the Devonshire Association*, xxxv (1903), modern translation Arthur Goodwin.
3. Ref. ibid.
4. Maurer, *Margaret of Anjou*, pp. 136–7.
5. Hallam (ed.), *The Chronicles of the Wars of the Roses*, p. 216 citing *Hardyng's Chronicle*. See *The Chronicle of John Hardyng* (1812).
6. On Malory: Hardyment, *Malory* (2005), p. 315; Ross, *The Wars of the Roses*, pp. 164–5; & ODNB, P. J. C. Field, 'Malory, Sir Thomas (1415x18–1471)'—doi:10.1093/ref:odnb/17899. And, for lawyers, Keen, *English Society in the Later Middle Ages*, pp. 145–6.
7. McGlynn, *By Sword and Fire* (2008), p. 75.
8. Keen, *Chivalry* (1984), p. 239.
9. John Gillingham, *The English in the 12th Century* (2000), pp. 209–10, quoted in McGlynn, *By Sword and Fire*, p. 75.
10. *Popular Astronomy*, June/July 1908.
11. Pollard, *Warwick the Kingmaker*, p. 1, citing Gairdner (ed.), *Paston Letters*, Vol. III, No. 322, pp. 73–5 (6 Vols. 1904 edition). Unless stated, other citations are from 4-volume edition (1910).
12. Horrox (contrib. ed.), Given-Wilson (gen. ed.), *PROME* (2005), 'Henry VI: July 1455', Introduction.
13. Watts, *Henry VI*, p. 322 and p. 333.
14. Ibid., p. 335.
15. As a starting point for this discussion, see Watts, *Henry VI*, p. 266, n. 15.
16. Wolffe, *Henry VI*, p. 306.
17. Exter Cathedral, MS. 3498/223. See Myers (ed.), *English Political Documents*, p. 280.
18. ODNB, Virginia Davis, 'Waynflete, William (c.1400–1486)'—doi:10.1093/ref:odnb/28907.
19. ODNB, Michael K. Jones, 'Beaufort, Henry, second duke of Somerset (1436–1464)'—doi:10.1093/ref:odnb/1860.
20. Griffiths, *Henry VI*, pp. 806–7.
21. Pollard, *Warwick*, p. 35.
22. Ibid., pp. 37–8. Fabyan, *Great Chronicle of London*, p. 190.
23. Griffiths, *Henry VI*, p. 807.
24. *Gregory's Chronicle, 1451–1460*, pp. 196–210.
25. Ibid.
26. Davies, *An English Chronicle*, p. 83.
27. *Gregory's Chronicle, 1451–1460*, pp. 196–210. In Gregory's words, Duchess Cecily 'was kept fulle strayte and many a grete rebuke'.

7. 'A WARWICK'

1. Pollard, *Warwick*, pp. 127–8.
2. The finest of all came from the March of Shropshire and Leominster, very much the area of the Duke of York's power. See Hallam (ed.), *The Chronicles of the Wars of the Roses*, pp. 202–3.
3. Harriss, 'The Struggle for Calais: An Aspect of the Rivalry between Lancaster and York', *English Historical Review*, 75, no. 294, pp. 45–6.
4. Fabyan, *The New Chronicles of England and France*, ed. Ellis (1811), p. 635, cited in Kendall, *Warwick the Kingmaker* (2002), p. 62.
5. Armstrong, *BIHR 33*, p. 30.
6. Harriss, 'The Struggle for Calais' (op. cit.), pp. 30–53.
7. Ross, *Edward IV* (1974), p. 86, for general characterizations of his licentiousness.
8. Goodman, *The Wars of the Roses: The Soldiers' Experience* (2005), p. 198.
9. See Lander, *The Wars of the Roses*, p. 12, for a pithy explanation of how the 'insincerity, chicanery and ruthlessness' of the diplomacy of the French- and Italian-speaking states would make such an extraordinary new alliance a feasibility and thus something to be planned against.
10. Pius II later repudiated Coppini, saying he had proceeded without authority. This seems unlikely (see Richard G. Davies, 'The Church and the Wars of the Roses', in Pollard (ed.), *The Wars of the Roses*, pp. 157–9.
11. Davies, *An English Chronicle*, pp. 91–4.
12. Gillingham, *Wars of the Roses*, p. 111.
13. Ibid., p. 112.
14. Pollard, *Warwick*, pp. 151–2.
15. Hicks, *Warwick*, p. 191.
16. *Gregory's Chronicle, 1451–1460*, pp. 196–210.
17. Pollard, *Warwick*, p. 156.
18. Dyer, 'The political life of the fifteenth-century English village', in Carpenter and Clark (eds.), *Political Culture in Late Medieval Britain*, pp. 148–57.
19. Pollard, *Warwick*, p. 158.
20. Davies, *An English Chronicle*, pp. 86–90. See Dockray, *Henry VI Source Book*, pp. 35–6.
21. Davies, op cit., p. 89.
22. Kendall, *Warwick*, p. 71.
23. Hinds, *CSP Milan*, 1460, item 37.
24. Warner, *British Battlefields* (2002), p. 81.
25. *Gregory's Chronicle, 1451–1460*, pp. 196–210.
26. Davies, *An English Chronicle*, p. 97.
27. *Gregory's Chronicle, 1451–1460*, pp. 196–210.
28. Gillingham, *Wars of the Roses*, p. 113. And ODNB, Rosemary Horrox, 'Grey, Edmund, first earl of Kent (1416–1490)'—doi:10.1093/ref:odnb/11529.
29. Gillingham, *Wars of the Roses*, p. 115.
30. Davies, *An English Chronicle*, p. 98.
31. Whethamstede (ed. Riley), *Registrum I*, pp. 376–8.
32. See Watts, *Henry VI*, p. 358, n. 413.

33. Griffiths, *Henry VI*, p. 868.
34. Wolffe, *Henry VI*, p. 20.
35. Ibid., p. 324.
36. Horrox (contrib. ed.), Given-Wilson (gen. ed.), *PROME*, 'Henry VI: October 1460', section 16.
37. Wolffe, *Henry VI*, p. 21. See Constance Head, *Archivum Historiae Pontificae VIII* (1970), citing Florence Alden Gragg (trans.), *The Commentaries of Pius II* (1937–57).
38. Hinds, *CSP Milan*, 1461, item 78.
39. Horrox (contrib. ed.), Given-Wilson (gen. ed.), *PROME*, 'Henry VI: October 1460', section 29.

8. THE SUN IN SPLENDOUR

1. Wolffe, *Henry VI*, pp. 20–1, citing Constance Head, op. cit.
2. Dockray, *Henry VI Source Book*, p. xxviii.
3. British Library: ref. BL. Harleian MS 543, fol. 147. See Crawford, *The Letters of the Queens of England, 1066–1547* (1994), p. 129.
4. Horrox (contrib. ed.), Given-Wilson (gen. ed.), *PROME*, 'Henry VI: October 1460', section 32.
5. Goodman, *The Wars of the Roses: Military Activity and English Society, 1452–97* (1981), p. 42.
6. Boardman, *Towton* (2009), p. 25.
7. Cox, *The Battle of Wakefield Revisited* (2010), pp. 48–52.
8. Pollard, *Warwick the Kingmaker*, p. 43.
9. See Haigh, *From Wakefield to Towton* (2002), pp. 29–30.
10. Hinds, *CSP Milan*, 1461, no. 52, cited by Goodman, *The Wars of the Roses*, p. 43.
11. Surely it cannot be for the crass reason that Abbot Whethamstede ascribed to him, that he sought better lodgings for Christmas: ref. Whethamstede, *Registrum I*, p. 381.
12. Goodman, *The Wars of the Roses: Military Activity*, p. 52.
13. Ibid.
14. Ibid., p. 43.
15. Ibid.
16. Maurer, *Margaret of Anjou*, p. 191.
17. Haigh, *From Wakefield to Towton*, p. 37. Cox, *The Battle of Wakefield Revisited*, p. 61.
18. Davies, *An English Chronicle*, p. 106. Haigh, *From Wakefield to Towton*, p. 33.
19. Cox, *The Battle of Wakefield Revisited*, pp. 83–6.
20. Davies, *An English Chronicle*, p. 107.
21. Stevenson (ed.), 'Annales Rerum Anglicarum', in *Letters and Papers Illustrative of the Wars of the English in France During the Reign of Henry the Sixth, King of England* (1861–64), Vol. II, part ii, p. 775.
22. Gairdner, *Paston Letters*, Vol. II, No. 384, pp. 3–4.
23. H. T. Riley (ed.), *Crowland Chronicle* (1854), p. 531.
24. Gairdner, *Paston Letters*, Vol. I, No. 367, p. 541.

25. Hinds, *CSP Milan*, 1461, no. 52.
26. Ibid., no. 54.
27. Ibid., no. 56.
28. Ibid., no. 76. See Goodman, *The Wars of the Roses: The Soldiers' Experience*, pp. 198–200.
29. *Gregory's Chronicle, 1461–1469*, pp. 210–39.
30. Ibid.
31. Whethamstede (ed. Riley), *Registra*, pp. 388–92.
32. *Gregory's Chronicle, 1461–1469*, pp. 210–39.
33. Ibid.
34. Davies, *An English Chronicle*, p. 108.
35. Stevenson (ed.), *Annales Rerum Anglicarum*, Vol. II, part ii, p. 777.
36. Ross, *Edward IV*, p. 13.
37. Kleineke, *Edward IV* (2009), p. 29. Charles VII during the protracted and ill-fated peace negotiations was more than happy for the infant Prince Edward to be betrothed to one of this daughters. This would not have happened if there had been any shadow of illegitimacy.
38. ODNB, Christopher Harper-Bill, 'Cecily, duchess of York (1415–1495)'—doi:10.1093/ref:odnb/50231.
39. Kleineke, *Edward IV*, p. 30.
40. Warner, *British Battlefields*, pp. 89–94.
41. ODNB, John Watts, 'Butler, James, first earl of Wiltshire and fifth earl of Ormond (1420–1461)'—doi:10.1093/ref:odnb/4188.
42. *Gregory's Chronicle, 1461–1469*, pp. 210–39.
43. Fabyan, *Great Chronicle of London*, p. 195.
44. Stevenson (ed.), *Annales Rerum Anglicarum*, Vol. II, part ii, p. 777.
45. Strong, *Coronation*, p. 131.
46. Hinds, *CSP Milan*, 1461, no. 76.
47. Ibid.
48. Barron, 'London and the Crown 1451–61' in Highfield and Jeffs (eds.), *The Crown and Local Communities*, p. 97.
49. Bird and Ledward (eds.), *Calendar of the Close Rolls, 1461–8* (1949), pp. 50–8. Offered online as part of the subscription to *PROME* (see Introduction to these notes).
50. The words themselves are in modern English from its 1940s translation by Messrs. W. H. B. Bird and K. H. Ledward.
51. Stevenson (ed.), *Annales Rerum Anglicarum*, Vol. II, part ii, p. 777.

9. A COUNTRY AT WAR—NORTH VS SOUTH

1. Hardy, *Longbow* (1992), p. 83.
2. Strickland and Hardy, *The Great Warbow* (2005), p. 42.
3. Hardy, *Longbow*, p. 83.
4. Strickland and Hardy, *The Great Warbow*, p. 42, quoting Ascham, *Toxophilus*, ed. J. E. B. Mayor (1863).
5. Strickland and Hardy, *The Great Warbow*, p. 26.

6. The author is extremely grateful for the great assistance given by Stuart Ivinson of the Royal Armouries in terms of the nature and performance of arms and armour—please see Acknowledgements.

7. Tests conducted by the Royal Armouries Museum in 1998 (written up in Royal Armouries Museum Yearbook 3, 1998) on a replica *Mary Rose*–type longbow of 90 lbs draw weight, shooting a bodkin arrow, gave an average velocity of 97.45 miles per hour (or 43.47 metres per second), and a maximum velocity of 44.30 metres per second. With thanks to Stuart Ivinson of the Royal Armouries Museum for this information.

8. Waller (contrib.), 'Archery', in Fiorato, Boylston and Knüsel (eds.), *Blood Red Roses: The Archaeology of a Mass Grave from the Battle of Towton AD 1461* (2007), p. 133, fig. 11.3.

9. Strickland and Hardy, *The Great Warbow*, p. 286.

10. www.nhs.uk/Conditions/Tetanus/Pages/Symptoms.aspx.

11. Gillingham, *Wars of the Roses*, pp. 35–6.

12. English armour was well established in 1461 and the Livery Company that represented Armourers remains to this day: 'The Armourers' Company was founded in 1322 and has occupied the same site in the City of London since 1346. The Company is now one of the leading charities in the UK supporting metallurgy and materials science education from primary school to postgraduate levels'. (From www.armourersandbrasiers.co.uk, the official website of The Worshipful Company of Armourers and Brasiers.)

13. Sir John Savile's Household (Members of the Wars of the Roses Federation) www.savilehousehold.co.uk/html/the_savile_s.html.

14. See p. 221 for further details of the Towton Battlefield Society.

15. John Howard, the slightly later Duke of Norfolk who may have led the Mowbray Duke of Norfolk's troops at Towton, as per Anne Crawford, 'Howard, John, first duke of Norfolk' (d. 1485)—doi:10.1093/ref:odnb/13921.

16. Re the Archer's coat, see *The Household Books of John Howard, Duke of Norfolk, 1462–1471, 1481–1483* (1992), Introd. Anne Crawford.

17. See David Santiuste's *Edward IV and the Wars of the Roses* (2010), pp. 2–3, for an extremely concise and clear explanation of recruitment based on the works of: Anthony Goodman, *The Wars of the Roses: Military Activity*, pp. 119–52; Goodman, *The Wars of the Roses: The Soldiers' Experience*, pp. 78–125; Michael Hicks, 'Bastard Feudalism, Overmighty Subjects and Idols of the Multitude during the Wars of the Roses', *History*, 85 (2000), esp. pp. 389–91; and Rosemary Horrox, 'Service', in *Fifteenth-Century Attitudes: Perception of Society in Late Medieval England* (1994), pp. 61–78.

18. E.g., Charles Plummer in his Introduction to Sir John Fortescue's *The Governance of England* (1885) and William Denton, author of *England in the Fifteenth Century* (1888), cited by A. J. Pollard in his *Wars of the Roses* (2001), in the 'British History in Perspective' series.

19. K. Mertes, *The English Noble's Household, 1250–1600* (1988) quoted in Maurice Keen, *English Society in the Later Middle Ages*, p. 166.

20. As Michael Hicks in *The Wars of the Roses* (2010) describes it: 'all, but the indispensable laundress, male'.

21. Boardman, *The Medieval Soldier in the Wars of the Roses* (1998), p. 64.
22. Gillingham, *Wars of the Roses*, p. 33.
23. Ibid.
24. Boardman, *The Medieval Soldier in the Wars of the Roses*, p. 78.
25. Keen, *English Society in the Later Middle Ages*, p. 227; Kleineke, *Edward IV*, p. 31.
26. Gillingham, *The Wars of the Roses*, p. 49.
27. Vegetius, *Epitome of Military Science* (1993), ed. N. P. Milner, p. 65.
28. De Pisan, *The Book of Fayttes of Arms and of Chivalry* (1932), ed. Byles.
29. Ibid., p. xi.
30. Ibid., pp. xi–xiii.
31. Ibid., p. 79. Those advantages being 'high ground, sun and wind'.
32. Hinds, *CSP Milan*, 1461, no. 71.
33. Quoted in Gillingham, *Wars of the Roses*, p. 28.
34. Vegetius, *Knyghthode and Bataile* (1935), ed. Dyboski and Arend, p. 41. Quoted in Goodman, *The Wars of the Roses: Military Activity*, p. 154.
35. The all-encompassing name is generally accepted and the number of Wars— three—by historians. But within that there is disagreement: for instance Pollard dates the 'First War of the Roses' from 1459–1464, with it ending with the capture of the northern fortresses (see his *Wars of the Roses: Problems in Focus*, p. 2); whilst Hicks states 1459–1461, i.e. from Blore Heath to the 'annihilation' at Towton (his *Wars of the Roses*, p. 5). This author agrees with Hicks on the end date, but believes that the significance of 1st Saint Albans and the divisions that followed should not be underestimated, so that he would date it 1455–1461.
36. As one of the Queen's Beasts, it can be seen, in stone form in Kew Gardens.
37. See Ross, *Wars of the Roses*, pp. 10–15.
38. Bosworth was a much smaller and shorter battle than Towton. It was also distinguished by a large number of troops deliberately not being committed by their noble commanders until late in the battle. The loss of life, lands and position by less fortunate predecessors at previous Wars of the Roses battles was taken into account by these nobles. For information on recent archaeological work at Bosworth see www.battlefieldstrust.com.
39. *Archaeologia Aeliana*, 29 (1824): pp. 343–7.
40. Candlemas—forty days after Christmas.
41. For a clear, concise statement of the argument of the importance of economic slump and financial Dislocation, see Professor Michael Hicks's new book, *The Wars of the Roses*, espec. pp. 49–55.
42. J. Fortescue, *De laudibus legum Angliae* (1917), trans. F. Grigor, p. 60; also quoted in Goodman, *The Wars of the Roses: Military Activity*, p. 153. For the lasting constitutional importance of Sir John Fortescue see Starkey, *Monarchy: From the Middle Ages to Modernity* (2007), pp. 10–13 and p. 22.
43. Waurin, *Recueil Des Croniques*, ed. Hardy, Vol. 6 (1891), Book 3, Chap. 46, p. 335.
44. Ross, *Edward IV*, p. 35.
45. Gairdner (ed.), *Paston Letters* (1910), Vol. II, No. 384, p. 3.
46. Goodman, *The Wars of the Roses: Military Activity*, p. 50.
47. *Gregory's Chronicle*, 1461–1469, pp. 210–39.

48. Prestwich, *Armies and Warfare in the Middle Ages*, p. 190.
49. For discussion of numbers, see Introduction (incl. note 4) and Chapter 10, p. 171 (and note 24) of this work.
50. Ross, *Wars of the Roses*, p. 144.
51. Tim Sutherland, the battlefield archaeologist and Project Director of the Towton Battlefield Archaeological Survey Project, has a compelling new theory to explain why Lancastrian troops were not defending Castleford. See Tim Sutherland, 'Killing Time: Challenging the Common Perceptions of Three Medieval Conflicts—Ferrybridge, Dintingdale and Towton', *Journal of Conflict Archaeology*, 5 (2009), pp. 1–25.
52. Waurin, *Recueil Des Croniques*, Vol. VI, Book 3, p. 325.
53. See also Gravett, *Towton* (2003), pp. 31–9 for discussion of the Battle of Ferrybridge.
54. Sutherland, 'Killing Time', *Journal of Conflict Archaeology*, pp. 1–25.
55. *Gregory's Chronicle, 1461–1469*, pp. 210–39.

10. TOWTON—PALM SUNDAY 1461

1. See Gravett, *Towton*, p. 38, for discussion of this point.
2. Boardman, *Towton*, p. 96.
3. Waurin, *Recueil Des Croniques*, Vol. VI, Book 3, Chap. 47, p. 325.
4. As with the previous chapter, the author wishes to express his thanks to Stuart Ivinson of the Royal Armouries for his assistance.
5. Waller, 'Combat Techniques', in Fiorato et al., *Blood Red Roses*, p. 150.
6. Rimer, 'Weapons', in ibid., p. 126.
7. Waller, 'Combat Techniques', in ibid., pp. 150–1.
8. Barker, *Agincourt*, p. 89.
9. Rimer, 'Weapons', in op. cit., pp. 128–9.
10. Gillingham, *Wars of the Roses*, p. 20.
11. Waurin, *Recueil Des Croniques*, eds. W. E. Hardy and E. Hardy, Vol. V, Book 4, p. 158.
12. De Pisan, *The Book of Fayttes of Arms and of Chivalry*, ed. Byles, p. 64.
13. Goodman, *The Wars of the Roses: The Soldiers' Experience*, p. 138.
14. Hall, *Chronicle* (1809), p. 255.
15. Vergil, *Three Books of Polydore Vergil's English History* (1844), ed. Ellis, Book II, p. 110.
16. Information courtesy of Church House. It also remains the custom that clergymen should be buried the opposite way—from the intention that they should face their congregations at the Resurrection.
17. This is an important part of the work of the Towton Battlefield Archaeological Survey Project, www.towtonbattle.com.
18. The printing of indulgences was to be a major factor of Caxton's commercial success, www.bl.uk/treasures/caxton/pardoners.html.
19. Those who were armigerous, i.e. entitled to bear heraldic arms.
20. With thanks to Roger Protz, the world's leading writer on beer, www.beer-pages.com/.
21. *Benet's Chronicle*, Camden Miscellany 24 (1972), p. 162 and p. 164.

22. Boardman, *Towton*, pp. 102–3.
23. The Towton Battlefield Society have an ongoing database of known participants at the battle. See also Graham Darbyshire's *The Gentry & Peerage of Towton, Vol. I* (2008), with *Vol. II* (2011).
24. See 'Introductory Chapter'. In *The Battlefields of England*, first published in 1950, Alfred H. Burne also put forward the possibility of 75,000 (pp. 104–5 of 1996 edition), but on the basis of an estimation of: i. a population of three and half million; ii. a fighting age of 15 to 40; iii. 15 per cent of the potential soldiers being at the battlefield. As per note 4 for the Introductory Chapter above, this author believes that a 75,000 figure should be based on a lower population, but also on a much wider range of fighting ages, which would thus represent 10 per cent of potential soldiers. In this he takes his lead from Professor Charles Ross, one of the greatest historians of this period. See also pp. 100–3 of Boardman's *Towton* for a discussion of combatant numbers. This author agrees with Burne's rejection of higher figures based on chronicler exaggeration and the inclusion of non-combatants: such as servants, traders, scavengers and general camp followers. Burne estimated these at 25 per cent of a 100,000 figure he attributes to Edmund Hall—the latter slightly incorrect as on pp. 254–5 of his *Chronicle*, Hall gives 60,000 for the Lancastrians and a more exact figure of 48,660 for the Yorkists (on the basis of 'they that knew it and paid the wages'). Burne's assertion, on p. 103, that those for the Yorkists were pay-roll figures seems ludicrous. But in the end, as Boardman agrees (on his p. 103) it is 'very dangerous' to get bogged down in figures and this author believes it is not just in terms of pure numbers that Towton was important. This lies in its brutality and lasting historical significance (see 'Introduction' and 'In Memoriam' of this book).
25. ODNB, Michael Hicks, 'Holland, Henry, second duke of Exeter (1430–1475)'—doi:10.1093/ref:odnb/50223.
26. Davies, *An English Chronicle*, pp. 107–8. Waurin, *Chroniques*, Vol. VI, Book 3, Chap. 45, pp. 328–9 and p. 334. Though it should be remembered that Warwick was a master of self-serving propaganda.
27. *Gregory's Chronicle, 1461–1469*, pp. 210–39.
28. ODNB, A. J. Pollard, 'Neville, William, earl of Kent (1401?–1463)—doi:10.1093/ref:odnb/19967.
29. Boardman, *Towton*, p. 63.
30. See map in Gravett, *Towton*, p. 42.
31. See Darbyshire, *The Gentry & Peerage of Towton*, insert between pp. 28–9.
32. McGill, *The Battle of Towton* (1992), p. 40.
33. Sources are divided as to whether it was snow or sleet. It is likely, given the time of the year and the severity of the conditions, that it was both. The Met Office confirms that it is perfectly possible for both to alternate during the course of a day.
32. Hall, *Chronicle* (1809), p. 255. For conditions, see also 'Hearne's Fragment' in Giles (ed.), *Chronicles of the White Rose of York* (1843), p. 9; and the *Crowland Chronicle*, p. 426.
35. The required rate for an archer to be recruited was twelve per minute. The figure of ten takes into consideration the particular difficulty of the conditions. With thanks to Stuart Ivinson of the Royal Armouries Museum for this insight.

36. The Towton Battlefield Archaeological Survey Project's recent discoveries of arrow heads give a far clearer indication of the starting point of the battle lines.

37. Waurin, *Chroniques*, Vol. VI, Book 3, Chapt. 48, pp. 339–40, speaks of a cavalry action. With this spur, Andrew Boardman presents the argument that the Lancastrian commanders, Somerset and Trollope, mounted a surprise ambush based on Castle Hill Wood to the left of the Yorkist position and that this would have assisted in the skewing of the battle lines. Skewing could also have occurred through the initial engagement of troops, as well as through Norfolk's intervention. Such a cavalry encounter at a fixed battle would have been highly singular during the 1st War of the Roses, innovative though the Lancastrian commanders undoubtedly were. Waurin was capable of being as factually inventive as Warwick the Kingmaker, whom he met personally,[*] and even he does not mention an ambush. Allowing for the fact that the wood may have been larger in 1461, it would, however, have been managed and the condition of the wood itself and general topography and distance would have made it unlikely that the Lancastrian 'cavalry' would have been undetected for sufficient time, either within the wood or charging out of it. Finally, no archaeological evidence has, as yet, been found, either by the Towton Battlefield Archaeological Survey Project or by a special archaeological investigation of the battlefield by English Heritage in 2010.

38. For these, see Santiuste, *Edward IV and the Wars of the Roses*, pp. 56–7.

39. *Gregory's Chronicle, 1461–1469*, pp. 210–39.

40. Darbyshire, *The Gentry & Peerage of Towton*, p. 30.

41. Boardman, *Towton*, p. 128.

42. It is thought with some evidence that he was buried with his horse. See Boardman, *Towton*, 87–8.

43. *Gregory's Chronicle, 1461–1469*, pp. 210–39.

44. Commynes, *Memoirs*, ed. Scoble, Vol. I, Book 3, Chapt. V, p. 192. Modern updating of translation with reference to Michael C. E. Jones trans. of 1972, p. 187; and Isabelle Cazeaux trans. of 1969.

45. Starkey, *Monarchy: From the Middle Ages to Modernity*, p. 6.

46. Brief Notes in Gairdner (ed.), *Three Fifteenth Century Chronicles*, p. 151. Also cited by Armstrong, 'Politics and the Battle of St Albans, 1455', *BIHR* 33, p. 27.

47. Hall, *Chronicle*, p. 255. Also cited in Humphrys, *Clash of Arms* (2006), p. 83.

48. Hinds, *CSP Milan*, 1461, item 78.

49. Fabyan, *Great Chronicle of London*, ed. Thomas and Thornley, p. 197.

50. Ibid.

51. ODNB, John Watts, 'Butler, James, first earl of Wiltshire and fifth earl of Ormond (1420–1461)'—doi:10.1093/ref:odnb/4188.

52. See Boardman, *Towton*, p. x.

53. Sutherland, 'Recording the Grave', in Fiorato et al., *Blood Red Roses*, p. 46. This figure includes the unattached feet of a man—thus some give the figure as thirty-seven.

54. Boardman, *Towton*, pp. 156–9.

---

[*] Livia Visser-Fuchs has brought a greater understanding of both Waurin and Warwick through her in-depth study, *Warwick and Wavrin: two case studies on the literary background and propaganda of Anglo-Burgundian relations in the Yorkist period*, London Ph.D. (2002). See also 'Select Bibliography'.

55. See *Blood Red Roses*, Fiorato et al., in its entirety.
56. Boylston, Holst and Coughlan, 'Physical Anthropology', ibid., p. 48.
57. See especially, Part II, Chapters 5–9, of ibid., pp. 45–118.
58. Gundula Müldner and Michael P. Richards, 'Fast or feast: reconstructing diet in later medieval England by stable isotope analysis', *Journal of Archaeological Science*, 32 (2005): pp. 39–48. The analysis of the bone collagen from the skeletons in the Towton mass grave broadly conforms to other examples of the Medieval period. Examination of the Towton skeletons strongly points to changes most likely brought about by physical stress through continual use of the longbow over many years, see Knüsel, 'Activity-Related Skeletal Change', in Fiorato et al., *Blood Red Roses*, p. 116.
59. Even as late as A. L. Rowse. See *Bosworth Field and the Wars of the Roses* (1966).

IN MEMORIAM

1. De Pisan, *The Book of Fayttes of Arms and of Chivalry*, ed. Byles, p. 79.
2. Hinds, *CSP Milan*, 1461, item 79.
3. Ibid., item 79.
4. Ibid., item 83.
5. Ibid., item 91.
6. Ibid., item 89.
7. Gairdner (ed.), *Paston Letters*, Vol. II, No. 385, pp. 4–6.
8. ODNB, Rosemary Horrox, 'Edward V (1470–1483)'—doi:10.1093/ ref:odnb/8521.
9. The general areas of reburial are thought to include Saxton churchyard and the Memorial Chapel. A careful archaeological examination of the pits would still reveal important evidence.
10. As a tribute to McFarlane's importance, see ODNB, G. L. Harriss, 'McFarlane, (Kenneth) Bruce (1903–1966)'—doi:10.1093/ref:odnb/41133.
11. See Starkey, presenter, *Henry VIII: Mind of a Tyrant* DVD, 2009.
12. Firth and Rait (eds.), *Acts and Ordinances of the Interregnum, 1642–1660* (1911), pp. 1253–5.

SELECT BIBLIOGRAPHY

◊ Available online through subscription to British History Online

Allmand, Christopher. 1992. *Henry V*. London: Methuen.

Anderson, Michael. 1996. *British Population History: From the Black Death to the Present Day*. Cambridge: Cambridge University Press.

Armstrong, C. A. J. 1960. 'Politics and the Battle of St Albans, 1455'. *Bulletin of the Institute of Historical Research* 33, no. 87: 1–72.

Bark, Nigel. 2002. 'Did Schizophrenia Change the Course of English History? The Mental Illness of Henry VI'. *Medical Hypotheses* 59, no. 4 (October 1): 416–21.

Barker, Juliet. 2006. *Agincourt: The King, the Campaign, the Battle*. Paperback edition. London: Abacus.

———. 2009. *Conquest: The English Kingdom of France, 1417–1450*. London: Little Brown.

Barron, C. M. 1981. 'London and the Crown, 1451–61' in *The Crown and Local Communities: In England and France in the Fifteenth Century*. Ed. J. R. L. Highfield and Robin Jeffs. Gloucester: Sutton.

Benet, John, G. L. Harriss and M. A. Harriss. 1972. *John Benet's Chronicle for the years 1400 to 1462*. Camden Miscellany 24. London: Royal Historical Society.

◊ Bird, W. H. B., and K. H. Ledward, eds. 1949. *Calendar of the Close Rolls Preserved in the Public Record Office*. Vol. 1. London: HMSO.

Blacman, John. 1919. *Henry the Sixth*. Ed. M. R. James. Cambridge: Cambridge University Press.

Boardman, A. W. 1998. *The Medieval Soldier in the Wars of the Roses*. Stroud: Sutton.

———. 2009. *Towton: The Bloodiest Battle*. New ed. Stroud, Gloucestershire: History Press.

Capgrave, John. 1858. *The Book of the Illustrious Henries*. London: Longman Brown Green Longmans & Roberts.

Carpenter, Christine, and Linda Clark, eds. 2004. *Political Culture in Late Medieval Britain*. Woodbridge, Suffolk: Boydell Press.

Castor, Helen. 2005. *Blood & Roses: The Paston Family in the Fifteenth Century*. London: Faber.

Cavell, Emma, and Richard III and Yorkist History Trust. 2009. *The Heralds' Memoir 1486–1490: Court Ceremony, Royal Progress and Rebellion*. Donington: Richard III and Yorkist History Trust in association with Shaun Tyas.

Commynes, Philippe. 1855. *The Memoirs of Philip de Commines, Lord of Argenton.* Ed. Andrew Scoble. London: H. G. Bohn.

Cornwell, Bernard. 2009. *Harlequin*. London: Harper.

Coss, Peter, and Maurice Hugh Keen, eds. 2008. *Heraldry, Pageantry and Social Display in Medieval England*. Woodbridge: Boydell Press.

Cox, Helen. 2010. *The Battle of Wakefield Revisited*. York: Herstory Writing & Interpretation.

Crawford, Anne. 1994. *The Letters of the Queens of England, 1066–1547*. Stroud, Gloucestershire: A. Sutton.

Curry, Anne. 1993. *The Hundred Years War. British History in Perspective*. Basingstoke: Macmillan.

Darbyshire, Graham A. 2008. *The Gentry & Peerage of Towton*. Vol. 1. Lincoln: Freezywater Publications.

Davies, John Silvester, ed. 1856. *An English Chronicle of the Reigns of Richard II, Henry IV, Henry V, and Henry VI Written Before the Year 1471*. Camden Society no. 64. London: Printed for the Camden Society.

De Pisan. 1932. *The Book of Fayttes of Arms and of Chivalry*. Ed. Alfred Thomas Plested Byles. Trans. William Caxton. Early English Text Society 189. London: Oxford University Press for the Early English Text Society.

Dockray, Keith. 2000. *Henry VI, Margaret of Anjou and the Wars of the Roses: A Source Book*. Sutton history paperbacks. Stroud: Sutton.

Dyer, Christopher. 1994. *Everyday Life in Medieval England*. London: Hambledon Press.

———. 2009. *Making a Living in the Middle Ages: The People of Britain 850–1520*. New Haven, Conn.: Yale University Press.

———. 1989. *Standards of Living in the Later Middle Ages: Social Change in England c. 1200–1520*. Cambridge medieval textbooks. Cambridge: Cambridge University Press.

Ellis, Henry. 1824. *Original Letters, Illustrative of English History: Including Numerous Royal Letters: From Autographs in the British Museum, and One or Two Other Collections*. London: Printed for Harding, Triphook, & Lepard.

Fabyan, Robert. 1811. *The New Chronicles of England and France: In Two Parts*. London: Printed for F. C. & J. Rivington [etc.].

Fabyan, Robert, and Guildhall Library (London, England). 1938. *The Great Chronicle of London.* Ed. A. H. Thomas and I. D. Thornley. London: Printed by G. W. Jones at the sign of the Dolphin.

Fiorato, Veronica, Anthea Boylston and Christopher Knüsel, eds. 2007. *Blood Red Roses: The Archaeology of a Mass Grave from the Battle of Towton AD 1461.* 2nd ed. Oxford: Oxbow Books.

◊ Gairdner, James, ed. 1876. 'Gregory's Chronicle' in *The Historical Collections of a Citizen of London in the Fifteenth Century.* [Westminster]: Printed for the Camden Society.

———. 1910. *The Paston Letters, 1422–1509 AD: A Reprint of the Edition of 1872–5, Which Contained Upwards of Five Hundred Letters.* Edinburgh: J. Grant.

———. 1880. *Three Fifteenth-Century Chronicles: With Historical Memoranda by John Stowe, and Contemporary Notes of Occurrences Written by Him in the Reign of Queen Elizabeth.* London: Camden Society.

Genet, Jean, ed. 1977. *Four English Political Tracts of the Later Middle Ages.* London: Offices of the Royal Historical Society, University College London.

Gillingham, John. 2001. *The Wars of the Roses: Peace and Conflict in 15th Century England.* New ed. London: Phoenix.

Given-Wilson, Chris (gen. ed.), Anne Curry (contrib. ed. 1422–53), Rosemary Horrox (contrib. ed. 1455–1504). 2005. *The Parliament Rolls of Medieval England, 1275–1504.* Woodbridge: Boydell, National Archives & The History of Parliament Trust.

Goodman, Anthony. 1981. *The Wars of the Roses: Military Activity and English Society, 1452–97.* London: Routledge & Kegan Paul.

———. 2005. *The Wars of the Roses: The Soldiers' Experience.* Stroud: Tempus.

Gravett, Christopher. 2003. *Towton 1471: England's Bloodiest Battle.* 1st ed. Oxford: Osprey.

Griffiths, Ralph Alan. 1998. *The Reign of King Henry VI.* Stroud: Sutton.

Gummer, Benedict. 2009. *The Scourging Angel: The Black Death in the British Isles.* London: Bodley Head.

Haigh, Philip. 2002. *From Wakefield to Towton: The Wars of the Roses.* Barnsley, South Yorkshire: Leo Cooper.

Hall, Edward. 1809. *Hall's Chronicle Containing the History of England During the Reign of Henry the Fourth and the Succeeding Monarchs, to the Ennd of the Reign of Henry the Eighth.* London: J. Johnson.

Hallam, Elizabeth. 1988. *The Chronicles of the Wars of the Roses.* London: Weidenfeld & Nicolson.

Hardy, Robert. 1992. *Longbow: A Social and Military History.* 3rd ed. Sparkford: P. Stephens.

Hardyment, Christina. 2005. *Malory: The Knight who Became King Arthur's Chronicler*. 1st ed. New York: HarperCollins.

Harriss, G. L. 1988. *Cardinal Beaufort: A Study of Lancastrian Ascendancy and Decline*. Oxford: Clarendon.

———. 1960. 'The Struggle for Calais: An Aspect of the Rivalry between Lancaster and York'. *The English Historical Review* 75, no. 294 (January): 30–53.

Harvey, I. M. W. 1991. *Jack Cade's Rebellion of 1450*. Oxford: Clarendon Press.

Hicks, Michael. 2004. *Edward IV*. London: Arnold.

———. 2010. *The Wars of the Roses*. New Haven, Conn., and London: Yale University Press.

———. 1998. *Warwick the Kingmaker*. Oxford: Blackwell.

Hilton, Lisa. 2008. *Queens Consort: England's Medieval Queens*. London: Weidenfeld & Nicolson.

Hinde, Andrew. 2003. *England's Population: A History Since the Domesday Survey*. London: Hodder Arnold.

Hinds, A., and Public Record Office Great Britain. 1912. *Calendar of State Papers and Manuscripts Existing in the Archives and Collections of Milan*. London: HMSO.

Humphrys, Julian. 2006. *Clash of Arms: 12 English Battles*. Swindon: English Heritage.

Hutton, Ronald. 1996. *The Rise and Fall of Merry England: The Ritual Year 1400–1700*. Oxford: Oxford University Press.

Johnson, P. A. 1988. *Duke Richard of York, 1411–1460*. Oxford: Clarendon.

Jones, Dan. 2009. *Summer of Blood: The Peasants' Revolt of 1381*. London: HarperPress.

Jones, Michael. 1989. 'Somerset, York and the Wars of the Roses'. *English Historical Review* 104, no. 411: 285.

Kaufman, Alexander L. 2009. *The Historical Literature of the Jack Cade Rebellion*. Farnham: Ashgate.

Keen, Maurice Hugh. 1984. *Chivalry*. New Haven, Conn.: Yale University Press.

———. 1990. *English Society in the Later Middle Ages, 1348–1500*. London: Penguin.

Kekewich, Margaret Lucille, ed. 1995. *The Politics of Fifteenth-Century England: John Vale's Book*. Stroud: Sutton for Richard III and Yorkist History Trust.

Kendall, Paul. 2002. *Warwick the Kingmaker*. London: Phoenix Press.

Kingsford, Charles. 1913. *English Historical Literature in the Fifteenth Century*, Oxford: Clarendon Press.

Kleineke, Hannes. 2008. *Edward IV*. Abingdon, Oxon: Routledge.

Lander, J. 1990. *Wars of the Roses.* Gloucester: Sutton.

Laynesmith, J. L. 2004. *The Last Medieval Queens: English Queenship 1445–1503.* Oxford: Oxford University Press.

Lovatt, Roger. 1984. 'A Collector of Apocryphal Anecdotes: John Blacman Revisited' in *Property and Politics: Essays in Later Medieval English History.* Ed. A. J. Pollard. Gloucester: A. Sutton.

Marks, Richard, and Paul Williamson, eds. 2003. *Gothic: Art for England 1400–1547.* London: V & A Publications.

Marquis of Ruvigny and Raineval. 1911. *The Plantagenet Roll of the Blood Royal.* London: Melville & Company.

Matthew, H. C. G., and B. Harrison, eds. 2004. *The Oxford Dictionary of National Biography.* Oxford: Oxford University Press.

Maurer, Helen. 2003. *Margaret of Anjou: Queenship and Power in Late Medieval England.* Woodbridge: Boydell Press.

McFarlane, K. 1981. *England in the Fifteenth Century: Collected Essays.* London: Hambledon Press.

McGill, Pat. 1992. *The Battle of Towton, 1461.* Lincoln: Freezywater Publications.

McGlynn, Sean. 2008. *By Sword and Fire: Cruelty and Atrocity in Medieval Warfare.* London: Weidenfeld & Nicolson.

Mortimer, Ian. 2009. *The Time Traveller's Guide to Medieval England.* London: Vintage.

Myers, A. R., ed. 1996. *English Historical Documents.* London: Routledge.

Neillands, Robin. 2006. *The Wars of the Roses.* London: Phoenix Orion.

Nicolas, Nicholas Harris, ed. 1834. *Proceedings and Ordinances of the Privy Council of England.* London: G. Eyre and A. Spottiswoode.

Oman, Charles. 1920. *The History of England from the Accession of Richard II to the Death of Richard III, 1377–1485.* London: Longman.

Pollard, A. J. 2001. *The Wars of the Roses: British History in Perspective.* 2nd ed. British History in Perspective. Houndmills, Basingstoke: Palgrave.

———, ed. 1995. *The Wars of the Roses.* London: Macmillan.

———. 2007. *Warwick the Kingmaker: Politics, Power and Fame.* London: Hambledon Continuum.

Prestwich, Michael. 1996. *Armies and Warfare in the Middle Ages: The English Experience.* New Haven, Conn.: Yale University Press.

Richmond, C. F. 1977. 'The Nobility and the Wars of the Roses, 1459–61'. *Nottingham Medieval Studies* 21.

Riley, Henry Thomas, ed. 1854. *Ingulph's Chronicle of the Abbey of Crowland: With the Continuations by Peter of Blois and Anonymous Writers.* London: H. G. Bohn.

Rolle, Richard. 1957. *The Melos Amoris*. Ed. E. J. F. Arnould. Oxford: B. Blackwell.

Ross, Charles. 1974. *Edward IV*. London: Eyre Methuen.

———. 1976. *The Wars of the Roses: A Concise History*. London: Thames and Hudson.

Rowse, A. 1968. *Bosworth Field and the Wars of the Roses*. London: Panther Books.

Santiuste, David. 2010. *Edward IV and the Wars of the Roses*. Barnsley: Pen & Sword Military.

Smurthwaite, David. 1989. *The Ordnance Survey Complete Guide to the Battlefields of Britain*. Camberley: Webb & Bower.

Starkey, David, ed. 1987. *The English Court: From the Wars of the Roses to the Civil War*. London: Longman.

———. 2009. *Henry VIII: Mind of a Tyrant* [DVD]. 2 Entertain, May 4.

———. 2007. *Monarchy: From the Middle Ages to Modernity*. London: Harper Perennial.

Stevenson, Joseph. 1861. *Letters and Papers Illustrative of the Wars of the English in France During the Reign of Henry the Sixth, King of England*. Rerum britannicarum medii ævi scriptores / Great Britain. Public Record Office 22. London: Longman.

Storey, R. 1999. *The End of the House of Lancaster*. 2nd ed. Gloucester: Sutton.

Strickland, Matthew, and Robert Hardy. 2005. *The Great Warbow: From Hastings to the Mary Rose*. 1st ed. Stroud: Sutton.

Strong, Roy. 2006. *Coronation: From the 8th to the 21st century*. London: Harper Perennial.

Sumption, Jonathan. 1990. *The Hundred Years War*. 3 vols. London: Faber & Faber.

Sutherland, Tim. 2009. 'Killing Time: Challenging the Common Perceptions of Three Medieval Conflicts—Ferrybridge, Dintingdale and Towton'. *Journal of Conflict Archaeology* 5: 1–25.

Transactions of the Devonshire Association. 1903. Volume XXXV. Sidmouth.

Turner, T. H. 1992. 'Schizophrenia as a Permanent Problem. Some Aspects of Historical Evidence in the Recency (New Disease) Hypothesis'. *History of Psychiatry* 3, no. 12: 413–29.

Vegetius Renatus, Flavius. 1993. *Epitome of Military Science*. Ed. N. P. Milner. Translated texts for historians v. 16. Liverpool: Liverpool University Press.

———. 1935. *Knyghthode and Bataile: A 15th Century Verse Paraphrase of Flavius Vegetius Renatus' Treatise 'De Re Militari'*. Ed. Roman Dyboski and Z. M. Arend. London: Published for the Early English Text Society, by H. Milford, Oxford University Press.

Vergil, Polydore. 1844. *Three Books of Polydore Vergil's English History, Comprising the Reigns of Henry VI., Edward IV., and Richard III. from an Early Translation, Preserved Among the Mss. of the Old Royal Library in the British Museum*. Camden Society no. 29. London: Printed for the Camden Society, by J. B. Nichols and Sons.

Virgoe, Roger. 1965. 'The Death of William de la Pole, Duke of Suffolk'. *Bulletin of the John Rylands Library* 47: 489–502.

Visser-Fuchs, Livia. 2001. 'Warwick, by Himself: Richard Neville, Earl of Warwick, the Kingmaker, in the Recueil des Croniques d'Engleterre of Jean de Wavrin'. *Publications du Centre Européen d'Etudes Bourguignonnes* 41: 145–56.

Warner, Philip. 2002. *British Battlefields: The Definitive Guide to Warfare in England and Scotland*. London: Cassell.

Watts, John. 1999. *Henry VI and the Politics of Kingship*. Cambridge: Cambridge University Press.

Wavrin, Jehan de. 1864. *Recueil Des Croniques Et Anchiennes Istories De La Grant Bretaigne: A Present Nomme Engleterre*. Ed. William Hardy and Edward L. C. P. Hardy. 5 vols. Rerum britannicarum medii ævi scriptores / Great Britain. Public Record Office 39. London: Longman.

Weir, Alison. 2009. *Lancaster and York: The Wars of the Roses*. London: Vintage.

Whethamstede, Johannes. 1872. *Registra quorundam abbatum monasterii S. Albani, qui saeculo XV mo. floruere*. Ed. H. T. Riley. London: Longman.

Wilkinson, B. 1969. *Essays in Medieval History Presented to Bertie Wilkinson*. Toronto: University of Toronto Press.

Wolffe, Bertram Percy. 2001. *Henry VI*. Yale English Monarchs. New Haven, Conn.: Yale University Press.

Woolgar, C. M. 2001. 'Fast and Feast: Conspicuous Consumption and the Diet of the Nobility in the Fifteenth Century' in *Revolution and Consumption in Late Medieval England*. Ed. Michael Hicks. The Fifteenth Century v. 2. Woodbridge: Boydell Press.

Woolgar, C. M., D. Serjeantson and T. Waldron, eds. 2006. *Food in Medieval England: Diet and Nutrition*. Oxford: Oxford University Press.

SELECTED PLACES TO VISIT
AND RELATED ORGANISATIONS

Information at time of going to press. Updates may be available on www
.georgegoodwin.com

IMMEDIATE TO TOWTON

The Towton Battlefield Society is the official organisation for promoting
understanding of the Battle of Towton and for research of the battlefield under
protected conditions. Run by an extremely lively and friendly group of volun-
teers, and dedicated to encouraging educational and popular interest in an
extraordinary event in English history, the TBS is one of the most go-ahead
battlefield societies in the country. You don't have to be a local to get full value
from membership of this Society, which is affiliated to the Battlefields Trust.
For full details of the TBS itself, of its visitor centre and of the Frei Compagnie
(its group of re-enactors), www.towton.org.uk

Towton Battlefield Archaeological Survey Project. Tim Sutherland is the
leading archaeological authority on the battlefield. He was a key member
of the team from Bradford University that investigated the mass grave from
1996 and has run a number of subsequent projects that have made major
discoveries. For more information, and if you are interested in funding further professionally led excavations, www.towtonbattle.com or contact tim@
sutherland6579.freeserve.co.uk

The Royal Armouries Museum—Leeds. The Royal Armouries is home
to the United Kingdom's national collection of arms and armour, and is the

country's oldest museum. In addition to personal armour and small arms, the Leeds museum houses the reserve, study and archive collections. Among their curators are some of the country's leading experts on fifteenth-century warfare, who have taken a particular interest in the Battle of Towton. As a starting point for general information, www.royal armouries.org

University of Bradford—The Biological Anthropology Research Centre (BARC). Details on the work of the specialist department responsible for the Towton Mass Grave Project, www.brad.ac.uk/archenvi/ research/Towton

York's Micklegate Bar—www.micklegatebar.com

York Minster—www.yorkminster.org

Pontefract Castle—www.wakefieldmuseums.org/our_sites_pontefract_cas.htm

NATIONAL ORGANISATIONS

The Battlefields Trust is the UK charity dedicated to the preservation and interpretation of Britain's battlefields. Information on joining, together with extensive material on Blore Heath, Northampton, Mortimer's Cross and Towton, as well as the later battles of the Wars of the Roses, is available on the Trust's website: www.battlefieldstrust.com

The Wars of the Roses Federation is an umbrella group of approximately thirty-five medieval member groups. For further information: www.et-tu.com/wotrf1/cgi-bin/index.cgi. For a good example of an individual group, see www .beaufort-companye.org.uk

ENGLAND AND WALES
In and around London

The Tower of London. Nowadays the UK's most-visited historic attraction, the Tower was repeatedly the scene of important events during the Wars of the Roses, including the murder of Henry VI (the only English crowned king to be killed there). See www.hrp.org.uk/TowerofLondon/stories.aspx. The Tower also houses the London collection of the Royal Armouries www.royalarmouries .org/visit-us/tower-of-london

Westminster Abbey—www.westminster-abbey.org

Westminster Hall—www.parliament.uk/visiting/online-tours/virtualtours/ westminster-hall-tours/westminster-hall/

Houses of Parliament—www.parliament.uk/education. Search 'Houses of History' for timeline

Windsor Castle—www.royal.gov.uk/TheRoyalResidences/WindsorCastle/ WindsorCastle.aspx

Eton College—www.etoncollege.com/visitstoeton.aspx

King's College, Cambridge—www.kings.cam.ac.uk/visit

Canterbury Cathedral –www.canterbury-cathedral.org

Saint Albans (1st and 2nd Battles of Saint Albans)—www.stalbans.gov.uk/ leisure-and-culture/tourism-and-travel/guided-walks/ and www.stalbanscathedral .org

Winchester Cathedral—www.winchester-cathedral.org.uk

THE NORTH

Raby Castle—www.rabycastle.com

Sandal Castle—www.wakefieldmuseums.org/our sites sandal.htm (and for Battle of Wakefield)

Castles at Middleham, Richmond, Barnard Castle and Warkworth—www .english-heritage.org.uk

Castles at Bamburgh—www.bamburghcastle.com; Alnwick—www.alnwick castle.com; Dunstanburgh—www.nationaltrust.org.uk/main/w-dunstan burghcastle

Mount Grace Priory (Carthusian) www.english-heritage.org.uk/daysout/ properties/mount-grace-priory

THE MIDLANDS

Beauchamp Memorial Chapel—Saint Mary, Warwick—www.saintmarys church.co.uk. Identification of the mourning figures on the facing side of the tomb of the 13th Earl—see first section of illustrations: Richard Neville, Earl of Salisbury; Edmund Beaufort, Duke of Somerset; Humphrey Stafford, Duke of Buckingham; John Talbot, Earl of Shrewsbury; Richard Neville, Earl of Warwick. Their respective fates are described in the main text and final 'Dramatis Personae' (pp. 185–87). See also 'Family Trees' (pp. 190–91).

Warwick Castle—www.warwick-castle.co.uk/plan-your-day/history.aspx?css=1

Kenilworth—www.english-heritage.org.uk/daysout/properties/kenilworth -castle/history

Tattershall Castle—www.nationaltrust.org.uk/main/w-vh/w-visits/ w-findaplace/w-tattershallcastle

Crowland Abbey—http://crowlandabbey.org.uk/index.html

WALES AND THE WEST

Ludlow—www.ludlowcastle.com

Cardiff—www.castlewales.com/cardiff.html

Croft Castle—www.nationaltrust.org.uk/main/w-croftcastle

Pembroke—www.pembroke-castle.co.uk

Castles at Harlech, Monmouth and Raglan—www.cadw.wales.gov.uk

Exeter Cathedral—www.exeter-cathedral.org.uk

SOME CONTINENTAL CONNECTIONS

France: the great cathedrals of Paris—www.notredamedeparis.fr; Reims—www.cathedrale-reims.com/notre-dame-saint-jacques-reims; Rouen—www.cathedrale-rouen.net

Italy: Milan, Sforza Castle—www.milanocastellow.it/ita/home.html; Pienza (birthplace of Pius II that was re-named after him)—www.pienza.com

ACKNOWLEDGEMENTS

My first thanks must go to David Starkey, world-leading academic and popular historian, for his introduction to *Fatal Colours*. As always, his prose glitters with insight, style and precision.

My thanks also to the great Henry VI and Wars of the Roses experts, including Michael Hicks, Ralph Griffiths, John Watts, Tony Pollard, Anne Curry and Rosemary Horrox for their kind permission to use quotations from their work. Particular thanks go to Tony Goodman, who not only allowed me to quote him extensively but who read through my proofs and crucially redirected me in places. Though very many of the judgments of the late Bertram Wolffe's *Henry VI* may now be challenged—particularly his view on John Blacman, brilliantly reappraised by Roger Lovatt—it remains a tremendous read with the addition of John Watts's new introduction. I have also been able to draw on the work of the fifteenth- and sixteenth-century chroniclers, the great Victorian transcribers and modern historians through online resources as well as books. Foremost amongst the former are British History Online (available to all through a small subscription) and the Oxford Dictionary of National Biography, which brings the lives of almost 60,000 Britons to your desk top, often accessible through subscription to your local library. Libraries which have been particularly useful to me have been the Institute of Historical Research, the Cambridge University Library, the British Library and my local library in Richmond and, through it, the London library consortium.

For my conclusions on the state of mind of Henry VI, I owe a great debt to Trevor Turner and Nigel Bark of the Royal College of Psychiatrists. Trevor in meetings and e-mails set me off in the right direction. My thanks also to Peter Jones for looking through my interpretation of his work.

Members of the Towton Battlefield Society (TBS) have gone out of their way to help me. Nothing has been too much trouble for Mark Taylor, Graham Darbyshire, Helen Cox, Peter Algar, Russell Marwood and Neil Wilson. Mark and Graham also took me around the battlefield and looked through the manuscript at an early stage and though they do not agree with all points of my interpretation, they have been extremely kind in being ready to give theirs to me. That is also true of battlefield archaeologist Tim Sutherland who definitely does not agree with me and many TBS members on the size of the battle—but is in no doubt about its extraordinary importance. My thanks also to Dave Cooke, TBS member and Yorkshire branch chairman of the Battlefields Trust, who read through my proofs kindly and enthusiastically, and to military historian Julian Humphrys, who, with the TBS's own Mark Taylor, has done so much to fight for the protection of British battlefields. I have also received repeated kind and unstinting help from Stuart Ivinson of the Royal Armouries in Leeds.

Though I believe *Fatal Colours* approaches Towton from a new perspective, it is not the first modern book on Towton and I thank Andrew Boardman, Christopher Gravett and David Santiuste in particular for their work.

Others who have given gladly of their time and expertise have been Lynn Curtis, Karen Hearn, Catherine Cullis, Timothy Duke, Kate Pocock, Tracy Borman, Tom O'Leary, David Souden and Richard Harrold (with their entrée to The Tower), Margaret Willes, Livia Visser-Fuchs, Allan Harley, Jonny Prichard, Andy Pring and Roger Protz (on beer).

Roger Keech, Chantry Westwell, Matt Mowbray and Stuart Ivinson (again) have been incredibly helpful with the illustrations.

The book owes its existence first to Malcolm Edwards thinking of me and to Alan Samson and Susan Lamb for commissioning me. Lucinda McNeile, my editor, has been my rock and Lisa Shakespeare (the Shakespeare whose word you can rely upon!) incredibly enthusiastic in promoting *Fatal Colours* and linking me into a highly proactive sales team. Tim Edwards was there at 'first thought stage' and again five years later to check my theology. My thanks to him for both, and also to Anne O'Brien for her copyediting skills and to Helen Smith for compiling the index. I am also very grateful to all those others at Orion whose work will come between now and publication and on into the future. With the future in mind, I am extremely grateful to Midas PR for setting up my website and for preparing me for talking as well as writing about history.

For the US edition of *Fatal Colours*, I am grateful for the enthusiastic support of Melody Conroy; Melody's continuing guidance has been greatly welcomed and heartily enjoyed. I should also like to thank the Norton editorial board, production manager Devon Zahn, managing editor Nancy Palmquist, proofreader Laura Starrett, project editor Tara Powers and art director Eleen Cheung. I know that at time of writing, and well before publication, sales and marketing director Bill Rusin and his sales team are already hard at work on behalf of *Fatal Colours*, as is publicist Jess Purcell; to all of them, my grateful thanks.

At this stage authors thank their family for being supportive, but mine have done much better than that. My wife Frances has read through the manuscript (more than once) and got me to improve it, with additions such as the 'Wound Man' being completely down to her. Our son Arthur has brought his language skills to bear in translating Medieval Latin and English and his practical ones to the maps; while our daughter Cecily not only listened to long explanations of the Wars of the Roses, she also took the author photograph for the jacket. For these reasons and for many more, this book is dedicated to them.

INDEX